Praise for Douglas Whynott's
A UNIT OF WATER, A UNIT OF TIME

"This is a book about the value of work, about the beauty of craftsmanship, and about a group of people whose ritual days help keep a vanishing world alive."
—*Boston Magazine*

"An affectionate, affirmative, yet lighter-than-air look at the life and work of Joel White."
—*Kirkus Reviews*

"*A UNIT OF WATER, A UNIT OF TIME* is as lovingly constructed as the boat it describes, and offers its readers the chance for a calm but vivid voyage."
—Bill McKibben, author of *Maybe One*

"With understated grace, the author evokes a sense of maritime community as well as a fierce devotion to boats and a love of the sea, which emerges as an almost mystical form of communion with nature and the cosmos. . . . E.B. White would have approved of this quietly profound book; it's a real beauty."
—*Publishers Weekly*

"This is a charming and moving depiction of a contemporary genius at work, one who happens to be engaged in the ancient art of making boats. It is a necessary book for anyone afflicted with the passion for messing around with boats."
—Tracy Kidder, author of *Home Town*

"Whynott skillfully weaves a story that speaks both of the love of his craft and the art of writing."
—*Library Journal*

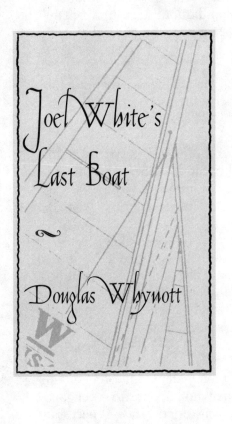

Joel White's
Last Boat

~

Douglas Whynott

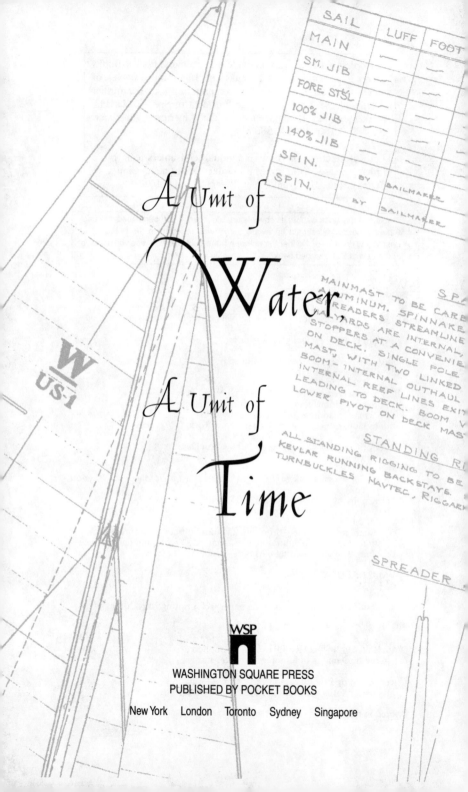

A Unit of

Water,

A Unit of

Time

WSP

WASHINGTON SQUARE PRESS
PUBLISHED BY POCKET BOOKS

New York   London   Toronto   Sydney   Singapore

WSP

A Washington Square Press Publication of
POCKET BOOKS, a division of Simon & Schuster Inc.
1230 Avenue of the Americas, New York, NY 10020

Copyright © 1999 by Douglas Whynott

Published by arrangement with Doubleday,
a division of Random House, Inc.

Library of Congress Cataloging-in-Publication Data

Whynott, Douglas, 1950–
    A unit of water, a unit of time : Joel White's last boat / Douglas Whynott.
      p. cm.
    Originally published: New York : Doubleday, 1999.
    Includes bibliographical references.
    ISBN 0-671-78526-5
    1. Boatyards—Maine—Brooklin. 2. Brooklin Boat Yard (Brooklin, Me.) 3. White, Joel. 4. Whynnot, Douglas, 1950– 5. Yacht building—Maine—Brooklin. 6. Yacht building—Maine—Brooklin. I. Title.

    VM321.52.U6 W48 2000
    623.8'380974145—dc21   00-022751

First Washington Square Press trade paperback printing May 2000

10 9 8 7 6 5 4 3 2 1

WASHINGTON SQUARE PRESS and colophon are registered trademarks of Simon & Schuster Inc.

Cover design by Brigid Pearson
Front cover photos © Benjamin Mendlowitz

Printed in the U.S.A.

For Kathy Olsen

Sailing is a wonderful and unique thing, and the sensation of being noiselessly and smoothly propelled without cost of fuel is one of the most satisfactory pleasures known, but when you add to this the fact that the sailboat itself is one of the most interesting things which God has let man make—well, then you get a combination which is almost sacred.

L. Francis Herreshoff

A small sailing craft is not only beautiful, it is seductive and full of strange promise and the hint of trouble. If it happens to be an auxiliary cruising boat, it is without question the most compact and ingenious arrangement for living ever devised by the restless mind of man.

E. B. White

Perhaps the first Wanderer will slip into Center Harbor at sunset. The owners, friendly folk, will invite me aboard, and sitting below at the cabin table, I will look around and it will all be just as I imagine it—the feeling of space and comfort, soft highlights glinting off the varnished trim, the combination of aromas that emanate from the interior of a choice wooden vessel—cedar, teak, and tar, supper and rum, and the accumulated wind and sunshine of a good day's run.

Joel White

Acknowledgments

I'd like to thank the people of Brooklin, those who spoke with me, the many who gave information and advice, good times and conversation. A special note of thanks to Maynard Bray for reading parts of this manuscript and offering technical and historical suggestions. I'd like to thank the boatbuilders and workmen at Brooklin Boat Yard, many who talked with me at length, who talked with me during those times when I'd sidle up and say, "So, what are you doing?" I'd like to thank the White family for their help, and especially Steve White for letting me wander freely around the yard. I must say thanks to Dorothy Jordan and her six cats for their kind hospitality. And finally, my heartfelt thanks to Kathy Olsen, who gave loving friendship and encouragement, all the way through.

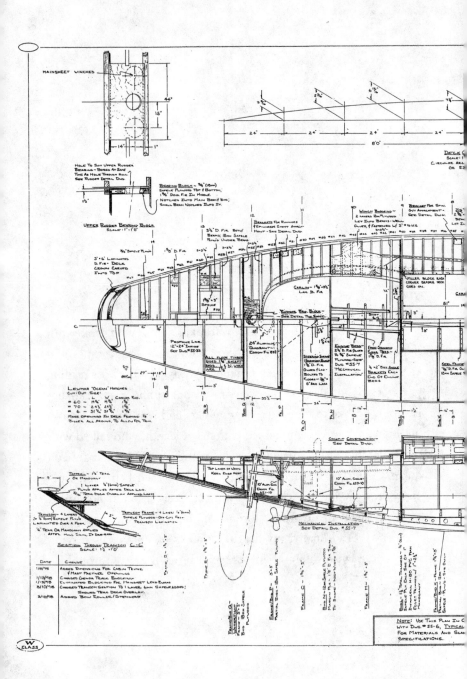

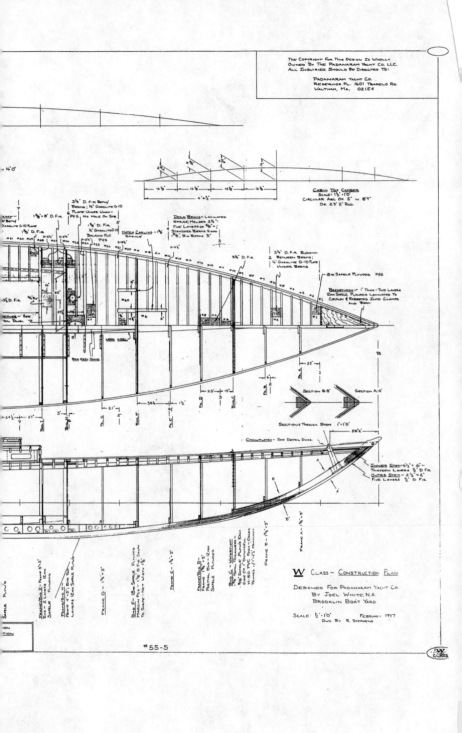

CABIN TOP CAMBER
SCALE 1 1/2" = 1'-0"
CIRCULAR ARC OR 5" IN 8'-4"
OR 23' 2" RAD.

SECTION B-B   SECTION A-A

SECTIONS THROUGH STEM 1" = 1'-0"

W CLASS ~ CONSTRUCTION PLAN

DESIGNED FOR PADANARAM YACHT CO.
BY JOEL WHITE, N.A.
BROOKLIN BOAT YARD

SCALE 1/2" = 1'-0"   FEBRUARY 1997
DWG BY R. STEPHENS

#55-5

Chapter 1

Launchings

June 1996

It's a good day for sailing, at Center Harbor in Brooklin, Maine. The sky is clear and the temperature has risen through the fifties, and there's just enough of a breeze, gentle on the land and slightly stiff over the water. At Brooklin Boat Yard it's a launching day, and among those gathered at the yard—the boatbuilders, those coming to watch the launch, those here to sail the new boats—there are many shades of anticipation, concern, and excitement. Launching days are big events, after all, a time when the work of the year is revealed and the dreams of the owners hopefully come true.

Two boats are sitting in the yard, up on jackstands, one behind the other. They seem suspended in motion, like stilled thoughts, some element of gravity missing just now (water) and some aspect of time (forward movement). The boatbuilders hurry about, climbing up and down ladders, moving to and from the shop, rigging lines and bending on sails, thirty feet from the dock. There's a huge mechanical contraption standing nearby, the Travel-lift, soon to pick the boats up in slings and set them into the water, once the high tide has come.

The boats are of a new design called the Center Harbor 31.

They are beautiful to look at. The curved lines that run along the surface and toward the bow are instinctively pleasing, comfortable to rest the eye upon. At the bows of both boats are wreaths—dressed in ribbons and flowers, wearing lustrous white, with the lovely lines, these two Center Harbor 31s, called *Grace* and *Linda,* could seem like two beautiful schoolgirls off to the prom.

They are the product of the design work of Joel White, who began his career as a boatbuilder forty years before, constructing wooden lobster boats with an older boatbuilder. He bought the yard, built many more boats, and as of late has been creating a style of design that has become his own, one that he's become famous for—boats simple of line yet sound in engineering, traditional above water and modern below.

Steve White, Joel's son, runs the yard now, and through the morning organizes the work on *Grace* and *Linda*. He also spends some time rigging, the work he enjoys most. Suspended on a bosun's chair from a hoist on the Travel-lift, he goes about attaching the roller furling jib unit to the mast. Nearby is Bob Stephens, project foreman for the two boats, helping to get the sails on.

The owner of *Grace,* whose name is Frank Henry, was by early this morning to check on the progress. He and his wife have a summer home in Brooklin. Frank Henry had come up to the yard from New Hampshire several times over the winter to see the progress of the construction and to talk to the boatbuilders—he'd been surprised that the crew had been willing to take time out to talk to him, even though the pressure was on to finish by the launch date. In the fall when they were still in the planning stages, Henry had been in Brooklin to confer with Joel White on the design. He had built *Grace* in fact, in order to have the experience of participating in the development of a new boat.

Grace is the result of that effort and for Frank Henry this is a satisfying day. His children and grandchildren will be at the launching, and his wife, Grace Henry.

Previously the Henrys had owned a 42-foot racing yawl, with eight berths, a charcoal stove, and a supply of hot water. They had raced to Bermuda, cruised the Great Lakes, and sailed to New Brunswick, and the boat was the vehicle of many family memories, but after the Henrys' children grew up and got their own families and boats, the 42-foot racing yawl seemed much too big. One afternoon when they were sailing in Eggemoggin Reach the Henrys came upon a red-colored daysailer with beautiful lines—Joel White's personal boat, *Ellisha,* a fiberglass model called the Bridges Point 24 that Joel designed for a local boatbuilder. When Grace Henry saw *Ellisha* she said, "Now that's more like it."

Frank Henry sailed a Bridges Point 24, and he considered buying one. But Henry wanted something more in a boat, and he wanted an experience in designing it. After talking with Joel White he looked through books about boats and yachting. In *Sensible Cruising Designs,* by L. Francis Herreshoff, he came across a 29′ 6″ daysailer called *Quiet Tune,* one of Herreshoff's "lifestyle boats," based on a simple approach to sailing. *Quiet Tune,* built in Maine in 1945, was designed for short cruises for two people. It was set up with a ketch rig—with two masts, a mainmast ahead of the cabin and a smaller mizzen mast stepped just forward of the tiller. *Quiet Tune* appealed to Frank Henry. He liked the simplicity of the boat, and its size, and he liked the ketch rig because of the many sail combinations. They would allow him to make a lot of adjustments, to pull a lot of strings, as it's said, yet the boat would also be small enough for him to sail alone.

Joel White drew a preliminary sail plan based on the lines of *Quiet Tune.* He tried to convince Frank Henry to build the boat as a sloop, but Henry wanted a ketch rig, and so Joel eventually devised a way of incorporating a mizzen and its rigging without too much awkwardness. Henry liked the looks of the sail plan and lines drawing, so they moved on to more detailed ones. They faxed comments and ideas to each other. As the two interacted, a new boat grew out of *Quiet Tune,* and eventually the names on the drawings changed to the Center Harbor 31 and *Grace.* Henry, who had studied engineering in college before going to law school, enjoyed both the technical exchanges and the creative part of the process, the dreaming up of a boat that met both his and his wife's needs.

But before he signed a construction contract he made a condition that the yard must find a second client, since building two boats would substantially cut the costs. That second client was Alan Stern. He had arrived in Brooklin the night before with his son, Brian. They'd just come from Brian's college graduation, and planned to sail their boat back to Connecticut. Stern had built several boats, sailing them primarily on Long Island Sound. When he called Joel in the fall and heard about the Center Harbor 31 project, he soon signed on. But Stern didn't want a ketch rig. He wanted a sloop, with its bigger mainsail, so as to better utilize the light airs of Long Island Sound. Stern also wanted an enclosed head and a self-bailing cockpit, and he wanted to be able to fly a big spinnaker. So Joel drew a boat with a deeper ballast keel, and slightly more freeboard, and a bow with more forward overhang. Stern named it *Linda,* after his wife.

Stern was pleased with the looks of *Linda.* He liked the big cockpit with the eight-foot seats of sculpted teak, and he liked the way that the above-water appearance of a boat of forty to fifty years ago matched with the modern below-water appearance. Stern felt that with *Linda,* he had contributed to the development of the Center Harbor 31 in its sloop version.

The people from the General Store arrive at the yard, and set up a buffet table. Others come from the town. There's Doug Hylan, who runs a boatyard down the road, Benjamin River Marine, and who used to work for Joel White. There's Maynard Bray, who has also worked here, over the years, who is an old friend of Joel's, and who like Joel has written technical pieces and reviews of boat designs for *WoodenBoat* magazine. And Jon Wilson, the founding editor of *WoodenBoat*. There are the families of the boatbuilders. The cars are parked in the lot by the shop, and along the road up the hill from the harbor.

Amid the preparations and the gathering of the crowd, Joel White arrives. He's walking with crutches, and his wife, Allene, is with him. This is Joel's first time at the yard since undergoing an operation to have a section of his lung removed in Boston a few weeks ago. He's been dealing with lung cancer for the past six months, and he's been using crutches since undergoing a bone graft in his leg, also the result of cancer. He's bald from chemotherapy, wearing a visor cap, and moving gingerly, but Joel is cheerful. There's warmth and curiosity in his eyes. He's a handsome man, grown from the handsome boatbuilder of twenty years ago, and the handsome boy who moved here with his parents, E. B. White and Katharine S. White, sixty years ago.

They take a seat on some planking ahead of *Grace,* and soon people start coming up to say hello. One friend, named Bill Mayher, stands a few feet away and asks, with a deep look, "So, how are you doing?"

"Pretty good," Joel says.

Then another friend comes up, looking concerned, even a bit afraid.

"How are you?"

"Good," Joel says. He smiles, says he'd been to "Thoracic Park," that he'd asked the doctor if he knew the difference between a "lobeotomy" and a "lobotomy," and that the doctor had said it was just a matter of a different spelling. He laughs a bit shyly.

Of course there's a deep affection for Joel among these people, his friends, those he's sailed with, people he's employed and taught about boatbuilding or boat design. Many feel they've been touched by him in some way. Joel is described as brother, father, friend by them. He's someone who creates beautiful boats in a place where people appreciate beautiful boats.

"How are you feeling?" someone else asks.

"Pretty good," Joel says, smiling, glancing away.

I've known Joel White since January, when I toured the coast of Maine looking for a boatyard where I could watch the construction of a wooden boat. When we met, Joel had just found out that he had cancer, but he didn't say anything about it. He showed me some of the projects at the yard. The hulls of *Grace* and *Linda* were being planked then, and so was a Buzzards Bay 25, another of Joel's traditional but modern renditions, in this case a Nathanael Herreshoff boat. We looked in on *Easterner,* a 12-Meter racing sloop built in the late 1950s and once a candidate for the America's Cup, undergoing a thorough rebuilding of the hull. Joel drove me to other boatyards in Brooklin, to Eric Dow's shop, where they were building an *Araminta,* an L. Francis Herreshoff design from the era of *Quiet Tune,* and to Doug Hylan's shop, where he and his crew were putting new frames, or ribs, in an old sardine carrier being restored and converted into a yacht. He took me to Junior Day's shop, where that seventy-five-year-old boatbuilder was shaping out the keel for a 24-foot lobster boat. Joel and I got sandwiches at the General Store and stopped to have lunch in the parking lot of his yard, where it was snowing lightly, and we talked about nature—I told him about when I'd trained dolphins, and when I let a giant sea turtle go in Nantucket Sound, and Joel told me about how on another snowy day, the kind of storm with big flakes, he'd seen an eagle soar down near the windows of his design studio.

And we also talked about writing, and about his dad. I'd been teaching journalism and writing for several years as a college lecturer, and I said that I'd used E. B. White's *Elements of Style* in courses. When I quoted from it, or rather misquoted, saying one of the rules as "Cut unnecessary words," Joel corrected me, saying, "*Omit* unnecessary words." He told me his dad said that Professor Strunk omitted so many words he was left to repeat himself: "Omit unnecessary words, omit unnecessary words, omit unnecessary words!" Joel said with a little laugh. It was such a pleasure to talk about both boats and writing. At the end of this visit, while I stood in Joel's office, a third-floor studio with a spectacular view of the harbor, I asked him if he was the boy in E. B. White's essay "Once More to the Lake," as tender a look of a father to a son as I'd ever read. Joel said he was, and then looked down so that the visor of his hat covered his eyes.

After that day, I was also someone who'd been given something by Joel, through the mere pleasant experience of talking about boats and writing. For a good day can be an aesthetic experience in itself.

Now at the launching, in between the greetings, Joel and I talk again. The yard has come a long way from the time he'd taken it over, thirty-five years ago. Since Steve had begun running the yard during the 1980s, business had increased by three or four times.

Steve had added on, and bought the Travel-lift, for $80,000—
"Something I would have had a lot of trouble doing," Joel says.

Steve had taken over at the right time. "I've been very lucky in
my life," Joel says, "that things have come along at the right time."

This seems a bit peculiar, for someone to say how lucky he's
been, just after having a section of his lung removed. But the remark struck a chord too. I had read that E. B. White also thought
of himself as lucky and believed in his luck, even pointing to the
date of his birthday, July 11, 7/11, as a symbol for it. Once when
asked what a writer needed to be successful he had said, "Be
lucky."

Grace is in the slings of the Travel-lift, her stern toward the
water, her bow pointed at the crowd, the ribbons streaming. Frank
and Grace Henry walk over and stand under the bow, and their
family gathers nearby. Frank Henry thanks the crew, and points
out Bob Stephens, whom he'd known at another yard in southern
Maine. Bob had made the project all the more enjoyable, Henry
says. He thanks Joel for the design and for the experience of working with him. "*Grace* will be staying right here in Center Harbor,"
Henry says, "where everyone can see her."

Then Grace Henry speaks. She tells about being on their yawl
and coming upon *Ellisha*. She says she saw the Center Harbor 31
when they were building it, "when it was on its belly." It had
looked awfully big then, she says, and they told her it would look
smaller in the water, but still she's not sure. Grace Henry takes a
slip of paper from her pocket and reads it:

> "May she bring pleasure to her captain and crew,
>   May she be well found and fast,
>   May she be the envy of all,
>   I name her *Grace*."

She swings a bottle of champagne at the stem, and swings again. Cheers go up, hands are raised in applause. Cameras are held high. The Travel-lift starts up with a cloud of smoke, and beeps its way down the tracks of the dock. *Grace* is then lowered gently into the water, like a nurse setting a baby into a bed. The slings go slack, the boat is floating, and there are more cheers. *Grace* turns and motors off into the harbor, and soon the sails are rising up the mast.

Linda is next. More people come up to see Joel. Allene is next to him. They met when Joel was in college, at MIT, she says. She'd been studying journalism, and now writes food columns for newspapers in Bangor and Portland. Allene had in the early years worked at the yard, keeping the books. She says that when they first put a phone in, she spent a lot of time looking for him—"It's really easy to get lost in a boatyard." But Allene says she doesn't know much about boats, that she stays away from them. Her boys are into boats, with Steve running the yard and John working as a fisherman. Allene is more interested in literary things, as is her daughter Martha, a writer—though Martha is also married to a man who owns a boatyard.

"It must have been nice to see Joel's career develop," I say.

"He was good from the beginning," she says.

When the Travel-lift positions *Linda* by the dock, Alan Stern and Brian Stern stand under the bow. They're a small group, after the Henrys. And Alan Stern's day is tempered with frustration because the jib roller isn't working, and they won't be sailing the boat very far. Stern says he hadn't known there would be this kind of celebration at the launching. But he too thanks the crew, and Joel, and finally says, "This is the most beautiful boat I've ever seen in my life."

There's no bottle breaking this time, only the sound of the Travel-lift starting up again. *Linda* swings down the dock and into the water. They motor over to the main dock and continue loading the sails. Eventually *Linda* heads out, but only under a mainsail, and it's a haphazard ride.

Grace slides through the harbor on repeated runs. The Henrys sail it, and the Henry's children sail it, and so do various crew members, deftly turning and pulling up to the dock. There are cameras going off, shouts of praise.

At the shop, people line up for the buffet and then sit out by the seawall to watch. Joel makes his way down the dock and the ramp. Leaning on his crutches, he looks at *Grace* sail by. One of those who'd been sailing on *Grace* goes up to him and says, "Those are beautiful boats!"

"Not too bad," Joel says. A few moments later someone else turns to him and says, "That's an incredible boat!"

"It's a nice boat," Joel says.

You had to wonder about this response too, so muted. We live in an age of fist pumping and self-glorification, of unselfconscious self-promotion. A nice boat?

But then again, this is the son of the man who wrote the story about the spider that wrote "humble" in the web.

⟨∾⟩

Tracing the lineages of boats is like tracing the lineages of songs. It's a matter of influences. A sheer line or bow profile is transposed, and transformed, personalized and made original. In the case of *Grace,* and before her, *Quiet Tune,* you could trace a line back to a 14-foot Bermuda racing dinghy called *Contest.* A fast boat, *Contest* was also beautiful to look at because of its shape, particularly because of the hollow or reverse curves of the waterlines.

Nathanael Herreshoff, the greatest of boat designers, creator of many America's Cup winners at the Herreshoff Mfg. Co. in Bristol, Rhode Island, may have seen *Contest* when he spent a winter in Bermuda in 1911. Herreshoff was in his sixties then, and for many years had been designing racing boats with long overhangs (projecting ends) and waterlines with simple outward curves. He took such a boat to Bermuda in 1911, 23 feet long, with low freeboard (hull area above water) and long overhangs, but found he needed something that could fare better in the strong winds and waves.

Herreshoff returned to Bermuda in 1913 with *Alerion III,* a centerboard boat with lines that may have been a refinement of the shape of *Contest.* Twenty-six feet long, *Alerion* had moderate overhangs, higher freeboard, and hollow curves at the bow, lines that are said to be of a transcendent beauty. The design of *Alerion* was a turning point for Nathanael Herreshoff, who in 1914 created the Buzzards Bay 12½, and in 1916 its enlargement, the 20-foot Fish Class sailboats. Enlarging *Alerion,* Herreshoff in 1914 designed the Newport 29, though it was a full-keeled hull and not a centerboarder. Five Buzzards Bay 25s were launched in 1914. A longer and sleeker version of *Alerion,* the Buzzards Bay 25 is said to be Nathanael Herreshoff's favorite design, and is in the opinion of some, including Joel White, the most beautiful hull shape ever created. Maynard Bray, writing in *WoodenBoat* of the Buzzards Bay 25s and of the hollow-bowed boats of Herreshoff, recommends visiting the Herreshoff Marine Museum in Bristol to look at the Buzzards Bay 25 *Aria,* suggesting that it will be an "almost religious experience . . . I guarantee she'll take your breath away." *Alerion* can be seen in the Watercraft collection at Mystic Seaport Museum.

One of Herreshoff's sons, Sidney, used the half-model for *Alerion* to create the Fishers Island 31. Twelve of those 44-feet-long boats were built between 1927 and 1930. One of them, *Cirrus*, was still sailing in Center Harbor in the 1990s, and stored at Brooklin Boat Yard.

Another of Herreshoff's sons, L. Francis, worked for the designer W. Starling Burgess during the early 1920s and opened his own design firm in Marblehead, Massachusetts, around 1926. It's been said that while Nathanael Herreshoff was the consummate engineer (studying at MIT, developing steam engines, developing America's Cup yachts), L. Francis was more the artist, and that because he was so concerned with aesthetics he lacked the competitive instinct to build winning racers. As a boy he watched his father drawing and making models—his bedroom was next door to his father's design room—and as an adult L. Francis Herreshoff showed both the influence of his father and an originality in his own work. Over a period of forty years he created about 107 designs, ranging from decked canoes to schooners to power cruisers. He is said to have designed some of the most beautiful boats ever created—the 57-foot ketch *Bounty*, designed in 1934; the 72-foot ketch *Ticonderoga*, 1936; the canoe yawl *Rozinante*, 1956. The younger Herreshoff's trademark was the ketch.

Quiet Tune was 29′ 6″ long, with hollow waterlines and a transom with a wineglass shape. Designed for Ed Hill, a marine hardware representative from Newcastle, Maine, it was built at Hodgdon Brothers in East Boothbay in 1945. Hill usually sailed it in the late afternoon. (The first *Araminta*, known as the successor to *Quiet Tune*, was also built for Ed Hill, by Norman Hodgdon in 1954; also a ketch, and a daysailer, *Araminta* was three feet longer and had a clipper bow rather than a spoon-shaped bow.) *Quiet Tune* had several owners, including one in Newport Beach, California, before she was donated to Mystic Seaport Museum in 1993. *Araminta* also visits there occasionally, and the two boats often lie side by side.

L. Francis's *Quiet Tune* is said to be a narrower, deeper version of his father's Buzzards Bay 25 design, though with a ketch rig—and so *Alerion* is a presence in the boat. But *Quiet Tune* is also within a family of 20- to 30-foot daysailers built in New England beginning in the mid-1930s. The 20-footers *Popeye* and *Mink* were designed by Charles Hodgdon and built at Hodgdon Brothers around 1935. They were followed by the Boothbay 20, designed by Geerd Hendel and built by Hodgdon Brothers and other builders from 1935 until about 1960 (two of these, *India* and *Blue Witch*, are housed at Brooklin Boat Yard). In 1936 Starling Burgess designed the Christmas Cove daysailer, also built by Hodgdon Brothers. In 1937 the Yankee One Design appeared, built by Quincy Adams and various other New England yards. In 1938 L. Francis Herreshoff designed the *Ben Ma Cree*, built by Britt Brothers in West Lynn, Massachusetts. Sonny Hodgdon built *Quiet Tune* in 1945, in East Boothbay; then, in 1954 he came out with his own design for a daysailer with lines similar to *Quiet Tune*'s and said to be just as beautiful, the Hodgdon 21—one of them, *Nasket*, has been kept at Brooklin Boat Yard for many years.

When Frank Henry chose *Quiet Tune* as the basis for his own boat, Joel White made an analysis of the design. He found that for her size *Quiet Tune* had weak sailpower, that she was underrigged. He knew that if he improved the stability of the boat, by changing its underwater configuration, he could increase sail area, and thus the power and speed—and also perhaps improve looks.

Quiet Tune was built by traditional plank on frame construction, and had a long keel with a rudder attached to the aft end. In cross section, the hull was shaped like a wineglass, and even tending toward the Y shape. This was a design that made for a high center of gravity. It also had a rather low "form stability," because of the "slack bilges," the flatness of the sides of the hull just below the waterline—which meant that when the boat heeled from the vertical, less volume was being put into the water and stability was decreasing.

Joel White designed an improved hull that was more cup-shaped and that had a few inches more beam than *Quiet Tune*. Instead a long keel faired into the bottom of the hull, made of heavy timbers and lead, Joel White designed a hull with a fin keel—an appendage that looks like a shark's fin, narrow yet deep, and which had a cigar-shaped bulb of lead at the bottom. His design would not be built of oak frames and cedar planks, but instead of light strips of cedar covered with glued layers of thin mahogany veneers running diagonally—a relatively new construction method called cold molding. Because the hull of the Center Harbor 31 would be lighter than the original *Quiet Tune* hull, more lead could be added to the bottom of the fin keel, lowering the center of gravity and increasing the stability. Yet the Center Harbor 31 has about the same displacement—7,916 pounds—as *Quiet Tune*. The changes, and increased stability, enabled him to increase sail area, from 352 to 441 square feet for a gain of 20 percent with *Grace*. The gain on *Linda* was even greater. A spade rudder was at the aft end of the waterline on both boats, a device that improved maneuverability.

The lowered vertical center of gravity, to 1.5 feet below the waterline, allowed Joel to make improvements in another area where he found shortcomings, the cockpit. Sailors and passengers in *Quiet Tune* sat on the floor of a shallow, self-bailing cockpit, in a somewhat awkward position due to the placement of backrests, and it tended to be an uncomfortable ride after a while. But on the Center Harbor 31 the cockpit was made deeper and non-self-bailing, and there were teak seats with a molded shape, and backrests, canted at a comfortable angle, that also served as the coamings, or outer walls, of the cockpit.

Quiet Tune was an austere boat, in keeping with the designer's belief that sailing should be a simple pursuit, a diversion from the trappings and trials of modern life, a way to observe and interact with the weather. The Center Harbor 31 was not quite so austere. In the cabin was a galley with a stove and sink, seats with cushions, a chemical toilet on *Grace* and an enclosed head on *Linda*.

Below water *Grace* and *Linda* were modern, with their altered shapes and increased stability. The cabin interiors tended toward the modern too, but above water *Grace* in particular looked very reminiscent of *Quiet Tune,* with its ketch rig, its lovely sheerline, and the scoop of its hollow bow.

1938

E. B. White loved boats from the time he was a boy. His father, Samuel Tilly White, gave him an Old Town canoe for an eleventh birthday present, and it was used during vacations at the Belgrade Lakes in Maine. His older brothers built a 16-foot launch from blueprints and precut frames, and Samuel White hired a boatbuilder from Long Island to help them trim the deck, fit the coamings, and caulk the seams. They named the boat *Jessie,* after their mother, and moved it to Maine by train and to the Belgrade

Lakes by wagon. In the introduction to his *Letters,* White wrote of how "we would all crowd into her, nestling together in the tiny cockpit like barn swallows in their nest, and cross the pond in all kinds of weather."

After he left a job at an advertising agency and during the summer before he began writing at *The New Yorker,* E. B. White bought a 20-foot catboat, naming it *Pequod.* It had "accommodations for one, a simple gaff rig, a marvelous compactness," he wrote in a "Notes and Comment" section of *The New Yorker.* He used it to make trips along the Long Island shore, "a remote and lotus-scented land," usually going alone. He preferred sailing alone.

He married Katharine Sergeant Angell, the fiction editor at *The New Yorker,* in 1929. Divorced, with two children from a previous marriage, she gave birth to a third child, Joel McCoun White, on December 21, 1930. E. B. White was born on a lucky day—his son was born on the solstice, the day that symbolizes the beginning of life. The birth was a difficult cesarean, and at one point, when it was thought that Katharine might die, a nurse whispered in her ear, "Do you want to say a little prayer, dearie?" "Certainly not," she answered.

On New Year's Eve, Katharine and Joel White were still in the hospital. Speaking through the persona of his dog, E.B. wrote in a letter:

> *Dear Joe:*
>
> *Am taking this opportunity to say Happy New Year, although I must say you saw very little of the old year and presumably are in no position to judge whether things are getting better or worse. . . . I walked around the block with White just before he went to the hospital with Mrs.*

White so you could be born, and we saw your star being
hoisted into place on the Christmas tree in front of the
Washington Arch—an electric star to be sure, but that's
what you're up against these days, and it is not a bad star,
Joe, as stars go.

He also began writing poems to his son, some of which would
appear in the collection *The Fox of Peapack*, published in 1938.
"Apostrophe to a Pram Rider," a song of advice, included the lines:

Some day when I'm out of sight,
Travel far but travel light!
Stalk the turtle on the log,
Watch the heron spear the frog,
Find the things you only find,
When you leave your bag behind;
Raise the sail your old man furled,
Hang your hat upon the world! . . .
Thank the God you've always doubted,
For the gifts you've never flouted;
. . . Joe, my tangible creation,
Happy in perambulation,
Work no harder than you have to.
    Do you get me?

In "The Cornfield" the author takes a walk, and speaks of the
inspiration his son gives him:

. . . My son, too young and wise to speak,
Clung with one hand to my cheek,
While in his head were slowly born,

Important mysteries of the corn.
And being present at the birth
Of my child's wonderment at earth,
I felt my own life stir again
By the still graveyard of the grain.

In "Complicated Thoughts About a Small Son," another of
the *Fox of Peapack* poems, he again speaks of inspiration and wonder, but also of death, and another theme he would continue to
explore, the transposition of generations, the presence of the father
in the son.

In you, in you I see myself,
　Or what I like to think is me:
You are the man, the little man
　I've never had the time to be.

In you I read the crystal line
　I'll never get around to writing;
In you I taste the only wine
　That makes the world at all exciting;

And that, to give you breath and blood
　Was trick beyond my simple scope,
Is everything I know of good
　And everything I see of hope.

And since, to write in blood and breath
　Was fairer than my fairest dream,
The manuscript I leave for death
　Is you, who supplied its theme.

In 1935 when Joel was four, E. B. White bought a 30-foot cutter named *Astrid*. One of Joel's earliest memories was of seeing the boat near a dock at City Island, New York. White sailed *Astrid* to Maine, where he and Katharine had bought a house and barn on Blue Hill Bay in North Brooklin. There in the summers on *Astrid* they took short sails and went mackerel fishing.

In 1938 they took up year-round residence in Maine. E. B. White would later call the move "impulsive and irresponsible" because he wasn't sure how he'd make money, or how it would be for his son to leave a private school in Manhattan and go to a two-room schoolhouse in Maine (though he did think it would expose him to a wider range of people and be a good experience for him), or how his wife would be affected by giving up her job at *The New Yorker* (according to one writer she had the best job held by any woman in America). But he felt he had to make the move. Though White had found success at *The New Yorker,* writing "Notes and Comments" and occasional essays, he felt constricted by the short length and the weekly deadline, and the "editorial we" he was required to write in. Feeling that there was much more in him as a writer, E.B. uprooted his family and left New York "in search of the first person singular," as he would later describe it, in order "to write as straight as possible, with no fuzziness."

Some luck came his way when a few days before leaving New York he was offered an assignment from *Harper's* magazine to write a monthly column. He accepted, and soon after arriving in Brooklin began writing the essays that would later be collected in *One Man's Meat.* Though largely an account of life in rural Maine, the book would be distributed to servicemen during World War II and would eventually become a Harper's Modern Classic—"establishing me officially as an American Author," White would write.

One Man's Meat is in the lineage of books that came of Thoreau's *Walden,* a contemplation of nature, and other matters of life, in a setting of retreat. (And *Walden* was White's favorite book.) Written in the first person, *One Man's Meat* is an exploration of style—an open letter one month, a story the next, a journal entry in another. It was written in his characteristically simple style, one that seemed to speak for the common person, and which had a humor that was warm and detached at the same time.

Month to month, over a five-year period, Brooklin is evoked, and animals are certainly brought to life—the family dog, the chickens, the sheep, the geese, and the barn that would become the setting for *Charlotte's Web.* And appearing here and there, as incidental character, as point of departure and vehicle of contemplation, is Joel White, seven to twelve years old.

"To my son the American Indian is a living presence, more vivid than Popeye," E. B. White writes in "Children's Books," a November 1938 essay. "To my boy next month isn't December—it is the Month of the Long Night Moon." ("Close physical contact with the field of literature leads me to the conclusion that it must be a lot of fun to write for children—reasonably easy work, perhaps even important work.")

In "Sabbath Morn" (February 1939), a look at religion and the radio, the boy enters the living room carrying a police whistle, while the writer listens to a church service. The police whistle blasts, the writer picks up a folder with the rules for a poetry contest, the boy bangs a hammer and then picks up an astronomy book. He asks if they can build a telescope; the writer says not today. The boy forms a bridge with his body and swings a jackknife from his belt. Prayers form in the writer's mind: "Oh God, save the children—the little boy with the knife, so safe, so safely swinging the knife, with nothing overhead but the wild birds and the planet Mars, safely swinging," while a line from the radio also intrudes upon the writer's mind: "He hath redeemed me and I am his child."

The boy reflects sunlight with the knife blade and asks his father why the radio is on, if it has anything to do with his work. "No," the writer answers. "Well, maybe it has, in a way." The writer says that the boy went through a period when he begged to go to church, and they "felt cheap, withholding God," so they took him twice and he never asked to go again. The church seems unimaginative, "gutted by so many fires." Religion has fallen off, the writer says, but the Lord still lingers. Part of the problem is the radio itself, its "godlike presence." The church "merely holds out the remote promise of salvation: the radio tells you if it's going to rain tomorrow."

In "Education" (March 1939) the boy goes off to the country school, where one teacher instructs the first three grades. He "already regards his teacher as his great friend, and I think tells her a great deal more than he tells us." Previously he'd been to a private school in New York, modern and progressive; during the Christmas pageant, when the angel fainted, the boy had imitated it for weeks ("Some Christmas!" he had said at the time). Now he walks the road into town and spends the day in a two-room building heated with a stove. All had been nervous about the change, but when mother and father picked him up on the road after school, carrying his lunch pail, "and got his laconic report 'All right' in answer to our inquiry about how the day had gone, our relief was vast." The school day seems to go by quicker in the country, the boy says— "Just like lightning."

In "Walden," a playful and reverent letter to Henry, the writer visits Concord, "doing fifty on Route 62." He wants to see Walden Pond. Henry's account of the place, White writes, is "a document of increasing pertinence; each year it seems to gain a little headway as the world loses ground." As he approaches Concord, the sky "had that same everlasting great look which you will find on Page 144 of the Oxford pocket edition. I could feel the road entering me, through tire, wheel, spring, and cushion; shall I not have intelligence with the earth too?" He checks into an inn, has supper, and then goes to make sure the car is locked: "It's what we all do, Henry. It is called locking the car." The next morning he sets out for the pond, walking down Thoreau Street to Route 126, and then along the edge of the cove where he hears the wonderful sound of "your frog, a full clear *troonk,* guiding me, still hoarse and solemn, bridging the years," but the frog "soon quit, and I came on a couple of young boys throwing stones at him." He sits and listens, takes note, and walks back to town along the railroad tracks. He ends with a list of expenses—hotel and meals, canvas shoes, baseball hat and fielder's glove to take back to a boy, an amount ($7.70) that Henry spent on food for eight months. The writer apologizes: "You must remember that the house where you practiced the sort of economy which I respect was haunted only by mice and squirrels. You never had to cope with a shortstop."

In "Second World War" (September 1939) the writer drives the boy to school, sees a cat hunting in a field, and thinks of "how long is the preparation before the son of man can go out and get his dinner. Even when a scholar has the multiplication table at his tongue's end, it is a long way to the first field mouse." In "The Flocks We Watch By Night" (November 1939) father and son walk home after tending to a neighbor's ewe, and the boy asks about the war, whether people have to fight whether they want to or not. " 'Some of them,' " the father says. And then, a simple but beautiful descriptive sentence: "When we got near our house we could look down and see the sheep in the pasture below us, grazing spread out, under the stars." The last line follows: " 'I can hardly wait to see the lambs,' said the boy."

In "Farm Paper" (February 1940), at daybreak on a Sunday: "The little boy burst into the bedroom and cried: 'Wake up, you got a lamb!' " Out they go to the barn, to see a lamb that lives only through the morning: "one of the briefest and most popular visitors we ever had. . . . There is something about a lamb you don't get over in a hurry."

In "The Wave of the Future" (December 1940), an essay on the war, White begins with an account of building a small boat named *Flounder,* which would be Joel's first boat. The writer buys cotton wicking, borrows caulking tools, and asks a neighbor how to build a boat. He planes cedar in the shop, with the stove going, and says that he is "perfectly happy doing anything of this sort and would rather construct something than do any other sort of work." In "A Winter Diary" (January 1941) White spends the day after a snowstorm "planking the scow I am building. Am working from *The American Boys Handy Book,* after a pardonable delay of thirty years."

In "Songbirds" (April 1942) White tends to a sick lamb and also tries to "help a scholar with his grammar." When he can't think of a pronoun used with conjunctive force or an adjectival complement the scholar becomes annoyed. "You really don't know anything about grammar, do you?" he says. "No, I don't," the writer says, "with only a trace of regret."

If Joel White is an incidental presence in some of the essays, he is the subject, in conjunction with his father, in "Once More to the Lake." And if sometimes treated with casual humor in other places, here the son is regarded with seriousness and tenderness.

White returns to the Belgrade Lakes, the place of his boyhood vacations, taking along Joel, "who had seen lily pads only from train windows." White wonders how time has changed the place. He remembers the early mornings when he got up to slip away in the canoe, and realizes things are nearly the same when on the first morning he hears the boy "sneak quietly out and go off along the shore in a boat." White begins to see himself in the boy, and to even feel the illusion he is the boy, "and therefore, by simple transposition, that I was my father." The sensation persists. He finds himself saying his father's words. "The years were a mirage and there had been no years." When they take a boat on the lake to go fishing, he looks at the boy watching the water, and sees his own hands holding the pole. It makes him feel dizzy, and unsure which pole he's holding.

But these are happy memories too. Father and son swim, eat lunch at the farmhouse, and White looks back. "It seemed to me, as I kept remembering all this, that those times and those summers had been infinitely precious and worth saving." The only objectionable thing is the noisy outboard motor, though Joel loves it—"his great desire was to achieve single-handed mastery over it, and authority, and he soon learned the trick of choking it a little (but not too much), and the adjustment of the needle valve." The writer remembers the old one-cylinder Palmer engine, the old motorboat that his brothers built.

The week goes well, but in the old setting the feeling of collapsed time continues: "Everywhere we went I had trouble making out which was I, the one walking at my side, the one walking in my pants." One afternoon a thunderstorm comes, and that too is familiar. The rain falls, campers run into the lake to swim, and the boy says he's going in too. The writer has no thought of going in, but he watches his son, "his hard little body, skinny and bare," and "saw him wince slightly as he pulled up around his vitals the small, soggy, icy garment." The next and final line of the essay is: "As he buckled the swollen belt suddenly my groin felt the chill of death."

In that line time races apart, with mortality left in its wake. It's a familiar concern, found in the poems from *The Fox of Peapack* but rendered more fully in this essay—which also might be considered the fulfillment of the attempt of the writer to find his voice. One can look at "Once More to the Lake," and at "Complicated Thoughts About a Small Son," and find a kind of literary beauty in the oldest of themes, love and death combined. This, and a confirmation of the place of the son in the heart of the writer.

"Once More to the Lake" appeared in August 1941. Thirteen years later, in 1954, the year of the 100th anniversary of E. B. White's father's birth as well as the year of his grandson Joel Steven White's birth, E. B. White wrote a letter to his brother. He had broken a toe and was using a cane, which gave him the sensation again that "I not only looked like Father, I felt like Father." He wrote that he often wondered "not only about what I received from Father but about what I handed along to Joe. Pop was not only conservative (in a rather sensible and large-spirited way) but he was tidy in large and small ways, and I think those are the traits that found their way into the second generation. I can see it in my work. I don't always like it, but I can usually see it. I don't know whether a passionate love of the natural world can be transmitted or not, but like the love of beauty it is a thing one likes to associate with the scheme of inheritance."

The year 1954 was also the 100th anniversary of the publication of *Walden,* and E. B. White wrote an essay called "A Slight

Sound at Evening." He wrote that the book should be given as a diploma to graduating seniors: "Even if some senior were to take it literally and start felling trees, there could be worse mishaps: the ax is older than the dictaphone, and it is just as well to see what kind of chips he leaves before listening to the sound of his own voice." *Walden* is a "collection of certified sentences," some "as indestructible as they are errant," and he quoted one of the most certified sentences of all: "I learned this at least by my experiment: that if one advances confidently in the direction of his dreams, and endeavors to live the life he has imagined, he will meet with a success unexpected in common hours." That was a sentence, E. B. White would say, that had "the power to resuscitate the youth drowning in the sea of doubt." *Walden,* he would say, was Thoreau's "acknowledgment of the gift of life." The same could be said of *One Man's Meat.*

Nearly thirty years later E. B. White wrote a letter to Jon Wilson, who had written an article about Joel and wooden boats. The little scow *Flounder,* White told Wilson, had provided Joel with his first solo experience on the water. "When she glided into the frog pond with thole pins ready and Joe dancing around, it was my finest hour." The "boat that launched a thousand ships" was still down at his shore, though rotting now. He wrote that it was a great satisfaction to have watched Joel "work his way into the big time—which is excellence, no matter what the product is," and that he'd forgotten he told Joel that "the big thing was to enjoy what you do. It never seemed to me that he paid much attention to anything I told him, but if he listened to that one, I feel good about it."

August 1996

Deep into summer, the pace of the work at the boatyard is much slower than at the launching. The jobs are spread throughout the yard, on the dock, in the harbor. Two of the men are building some wooden guardrails for a boat, to cut down on the abrasion of the hull when it's docked. Three others are building the framework for a windshield of a boat called *Lucayo,* now tied up at the dock; *Lucayo* was built at this yard during the winter of 1993. Inside the shop, one boat carpenter is building a hatch cover, and three more are constructing the hull of a 22-foot powerboat designed by Joel for a client. The hull is made of mahogany plywood, and the stem at the bow of the boat is wide and rounded. Steve White is moving from job to job, looking things over. Though no building project is scheduled for the fall, Steve has gotten a call from someone in Boothbay who had seen *Linda* when Alan Stern was sailing south, and he's now considering having a Center Harbor 31 built. Steve's not sure he wants to take on the project because he's going to be spending the winter in the Caribbean on his own boat, but he figures if there's interest, he won't turn it aside.

Joel's drawing studio is on the top floor of a towerlike structure built on the corner of the boatbuilding shop, the corner closest to the dock and the water. It seems a wonderful place to work, with the many windows, the views of Center Harbor, Deer Isle to the south, the Torrey Islands and Eggemoggin Reach. The harbor is packed with boats, and the studio is a great place to look down upon them. There's a stereo system in the office, and a classical music program is playing this morning, while Joel works on a drawing, a sail plan for a 63-foot sailboat.

Lunchtime at the yard is eleven-thirty, and though the boatbuilding crew eat at the shop, Joel almost always leaves for a little restaurant at the center of town, a place called the Morning Moon. We leave Joel's studio, and then the business office on the floor below, and then go down the stairway to the parking lot, where I point to a motorcycle I've ridden from Massachusetts. It's big, and purple. "You want to go on this?" I say. Joel looks at it, smiles, and says, "I haven't ridden on a motorcycle in a while, why not?"

"That's what I say." I get on and start it up, and Joel climbs on the back, holding his crutches across his lap. We glide up the hill and along the road to the center, by the post office, the old school-house—now a marine supply store—the inn, the library, and the General Store to the Morning Moon.

The waitress brings iced tea. I tell Joel that I've been reading *One Man's Meat,* in Brooklin—"the scene of the crime," he says. I say I've found it a very good book, for its range of style, for the power of some of the writing, for its humor. Joel says he likes the book because it reminds him so strongly of his childhood. "You're throughout the book," I say. "Even when I'm not in it, the memories are strong to me," he answers.

"You'll be able to hear some of the pieces on tape," he says, "read with a Maine accent." On the urging of a music producer from Blue Hill, Joel has made a recording of readings of his dad's work. It's something he has a feeling for. "When my dad was about eighty-five he fell and hit his head, after canoeing on Walkers Pond. After that, he just wasn't right, he lost something. My mother had been dead several years, and he had been disconsolate about it, but he'd handled it okay, until then. He lived for another year. For that year, for three hundred and sixty-five days," Joel says, "I stopped by his house every day after work and on weekends to read to him. He liked to be read aloud to, and as it turned out, like any writer, he liked having his own work read aloud. So I managed to get through all of it, his entire opus. I read some pieces three or four times." Joel smiles. "At the end of an essay he'd say, 'That's not too bad,' sometimes, or 'That's pretty good.'"

The boatbuilder Eric Dow comes in the restaurant and says hello. Joel asks him how the launching has gone, of the *Araminta* Eric and his crew built last winter, and Eric shakes his head. The owner didn't come to the launching—Eric had never even met him. Instead he dealt with the owner's representative, who would appear occasionally in Brooklin to inspect the work and rarely had anything positive to say about the boat. The owner was also building a bigger and grander boat in Europe, and his attention was elsewhere. "They stood around drinking their own champagne," Joel says, of Eric's crew. "One of the good things about this business is the friendships you make. You build someone a boat, and the people who own it become your friends, and they often remain your friends for years. You take that away and boatbuilding can be kind of a joyless thing."

We return to the yard on the purple motorcycle—Joel will be teased about this for days—and later that afternoon, he takes me for a ride, in *Ellisha.* The owner of *Lucayo,* Pip Wick, comes along too. The three of us get in a dinghy at the dock. Joel rows out to the boat, tosses his crutches in, and gets aboard, and we follow. We hoist the sails, cast off the mooring, and Joel heads out through the harbor. On the western end near the Center Harbor Yacht Club, he passes by *Shadow,* a Herreshoff 12½ he's owned for fifty years, since he was sixteen. He says he's leased it to his half brother Roger Angell for the month.

It's said around here that Joel is an effortless sailor, and it does seem so, as he pulls and tightens lines, as he leans out over the coaming and looks up to check the trim of the sails. There's a look of ease about him then, the pleasure of engagement. It's said he knows the Reach as well as anyone, and he does seem to know just where to tack, each time, as we round Chatto Island and make a course southeast following the Naskeag shore, going by the Torrey Islands.

Off one of the Torreys, a schooner is anchored, and a former sardine carrier, a fishing boat converted to a tour boat—Joel helped redesign her, he says. Onshore, groups from both boats are having picnics. East of the Babson Islands in Great Cove, the WoodenBoat School is in full swing, with students from a sailing class tacking around in Herreshoff 12½s and a centerboard version of that boat, designed by Joel, the Haven 12½. They're pretty much indistinguishable above water. Beyond Great Cove we tack to the southwest, just short of Hog Island. E. B. White once owned the island, Joel says, and sold it. A few years ago Joel bought it back and set up an easement for it to remain in a natural state. "Just how I like my islands," Joel says. "Without the easements it would look like Coney Island around here." In this part of Penobscot Bay there are dozens of islands. There are some three thousand islands on the Maine coast, about a hundred inhabited year-round.

We turn to the northwest, and with the wind behind us ride a straight course up the Eggemoggin Reach toward the Deer Isle Bridge. For a while I take the tiller and steer. It's a pleasant sensation to feel the resistance of it in the hand, its energy, the pressure of air and water transposed through a string of wood. The wind fills the sails, and the water crackles behind us.

Ellisha is a Bridges Point 24. Joel had designed this fiberglass sailboat in 1984 for Wade Dow, Eric Dow's brother, a lobsterman and boatbuilder. When he came to Joel and asked him to create a daysailer that he could build, Joel said they should come up with something relatively small so that Wade Dow could be competitive in the market, and he said that it should be something beautiful, which would also make it easier to sell. Joel designed a 24-foot boat with a full keel, a graceful sheerline, and a bow with hollow waterlines.

After it appeared, the Bridges Point 24 was compared to *Alerion* in at least two design reviews. One reviewer, Mike O'Brien, writing in *Boat Design Quarterly*, stated that the two boats had kindred spirits but that there were crucial differences. The Bridges Point 24 had more spring to her sheer, firmer bilges, and a bit more hollow in the bow. O'Brien also thought that the stem had a more interesting curve than *Alerion*, that it had a changing radius more appealing to the eye (L. Francis Herreshoff once wrote that any curve, to be interesting, must have a changing radius), and that it went through the water in a more efficient way. O'Brien thought that the Bridges Point 24 stem line, that Joel White's stem lines in general, "knew the difference between large and small waves."

That's an eye and hand more practiced than mine. Holding *Ellisha*'s tiller as we rode down the Reach, I can't tell what the stem line knows, though I do feel a balance in the smooth translation of energy. The idea is interesting, though, that so much could be imbued in a boat line.

Pip Wick takes a turn at the tiller too. Pip is living the sailor's dream, or one of them, migrating to the Caribbean in the winter on *Lucayo* and spending summers in Brooklin. He grew up sailing on his parents' boat, cruising in Long Island Sound and along the coast of New England. They had wintered in the Caribbean, and for two years Pip rowed to the boat of a friend of his mother's to go to school. He had worked on Wall Street, and brought his kids up sailing, and after they left home Pip and his wife, Judy, decided to get a boat more capable of making ocean cruises and confronting the Gulf Stream. Pip considered building the boat himself but figured it would take five years. He drove to Maine, the first time he'd gone there by land, and made a deal with Steve White, including a condition that he could work with the crew (and Steve put in the proviso that he could fire Pip if necessary). In the fall of 1992 they started building a Roger Marshall design, very modern, something that could ride the ocean "like a duck." Pip went to work every day, and the boatbuilders enjoyed having him around, since he did all the jobs, including sweeping floors. And they liked that he bought beer on Friday afternoons. Some thought they were taking part in a hands-on therapy for the retired stockbroker. Pip and Judy came to Brooklin braced for a long winter, but found they liked being there. After the launch of *Lucayo* they spent a winter in the Caribbean, and they've been migrating to and from Brooklin since then.

Because of the forecast for fog, Pip has brought along a small GPS Instrument, but Joel doesn't think we'll need it.

Moving up the Reach, passing the Torrey Islands again, this time on the west side, we see yet another Joel White design. This boat is magnificent—a 74-foot ketch named *Dragonera*. Earlier this morning in Joel's office he's said that *Dragonera* is his favorite of his own designs. *Dragonera* was built the year after *Lucayo,* and launched in 1994. It too spends the winter in the Caribbean and summers in Brooklin, attended to by a professional captain. Now the sails are furled, and she's motoring toward Center Harbor. After we spot her to the west we try to get closer, but she quickly slips away.

Joel takes the helm when it's time to tack back to the east and head into Center Harbor. The first boat we pass going in is *Dragonera,* already settled in at the mooring. The owner, Bruce Stevens, is sitting in a lounge chair on the afterdeck, reading a newspaper. He waves, and Joel waves back.

"All's right with the world," Joel says. "Bruce is on the deck."

"That's a beautiful boat," I say.

"She's a nice boat."

1943

After six years of living in Maine year-round, Joel left Brooklin for Exeter Academy in the fall of 1943 and the Whites returned to New York to work full-time for *The New Yorker*. Because of the war many of the staff were in the service, and so the Whites had agreed to help out. Though he had come into his own with *One Man's Meat*, E. B. White felt that he'd done enough with the monthly column and that it was time to do something else. Yet leaving Maine and returning to the city was hard on White. He thought he was having a nervous breakdown, and was saying that "his head didn't feel right." Yet he began to work on a manuscript that had been in development for about fifteen years—the children's novel *Stuart Little*—and managed to finish it in eight weeks.

Stuart Little was Joel's favorite of his dad's three children's books, partly because it reminded him of his childhood. E. B. White had created the Stuart character—a mouse who appeared to him, nattily dressed, in a dream—before Joel was born. White had created the first Stuart stories to entertain his nieces and nephews, writing them down because he didn't feel confident about making them up extemporaneously. When Joel was a boy, his dad tried some of the stories out on him.

One can imagine the delight of the little boy who was crazy about boats listening to his father tell the story of two-inch Stuart, wearing a sailor's suit and venturing out into the street, where he hitches on to a pant cuff and takes a bus ride to Central Park. There he finds a pond where people are racing model sailboats. Stuart sees a smart-looking schooner, finds the owner, and asks for a berth aboard her. The owner, impressed with the sailor suit, interviews the mouse and decides to let him race the boat against another owned by a lazy little boy who doesn't know "a squall from a squid." "Or a jib from a jibe!" cries Stuart. The race is very dramatic—Stuart falls overboard but manages to climb on deck again, and then he plows the boat into a paper bag, but manages to win. There's great applause, because when people in Central Park hear that a mouse has captained a boat they come running. Later that day when Stuart returns home his human brother George asks him what he'd been doing, and Stuart replies that he was "just knocking around town."

In another episode Stuart hides from a dog and ends up in the garbage, then on a garbage scow floating out on the ocean. He's saved by Margalo, a little bird who has come to stay with the family for a while. That night they tell Mr. Little about the adventure, "about the ocean and the gray waves curling with white crests, and the gulls in the sky." Mr. Little sighs and says he hopes he can get away from business someday "to see all those fine things."

When Margalo flies away to escape a cat that's plotting to eat her, Stuart sets out to find her. Driving a fine little car, the mouse stops in a small New England town and is introduced to a two-inch New England girl, Harriet Ames. He invites her for a canoe ride, and, "proud of his ability with boats," buys a souvenir birchbark canoe with *Summer Memories* written on the side. "Does she leak?" Stuart asks the storekeeper. "It's a nice canoe," comes the reply.

Stuart dreams of his date while he repairs the canoe, "adjusting ballast, filling seams, and getting everything shipshape for the morrow." But the next day when Harriet shows up the canoe has been vandalized and the little mouse is heartbroken. He says "gee whiz" and buries his head in his hands, and though Harriet wants to make the best of it and go dancing she doesn't realize that "some people are fussy about boats." Stuart spends the night sleeping under the canoe and heads north to find Margalo.

During summers when the Whites returned to Brooklin, Joel sailed every day he could. At first he sailed on a catboat, a model called "Brutal Beast" and named *Faint Endeavor,* a boat that Joel's older half brother and sister had used too. In 1946 with the help of his dad, Joel bought a Herreshoff 12½, changing her name from *Playboy* to *Shadow*. It was the first boat that Joel felt was his own, and in *Shadow* he explored Eggemoggin Reach and made his first solo circumnavigation of Deer Isle, a tricky passage. At the helm of *Shadow* he would watch other, bigger boats. One of them was the Herreshoff Fishers Island 31 called *Cirrus,* owned by a summer resident of Brooklin. He would look on in wonder as she rushed by.

Joel tended a few lobster traps from a rowboat in the cove by his dad's farm, and at night he took the Plymouth convertible off to visit friends. At the end of the summer of 1946 the family went to the Blue Hill Fair, and Joel took a thirteen-year-old girl for a ride on the Ferris wheel. It was an experience that would appear in *Charlotte's Web,* when Fern, growing into adolescence, becomes less interested in farm animals and more interested in a boy—Henry Fussy—who joins her for a ride on the Ferris wheel at the fair (where a spider is about to write in the web).

During his teenage years Joel was reading boating magazines, *The Rudder* and *Yachting,* which were publishing boat plans with lots of detail, sometimes even including construction plans. In *The Rudder* Joel found the drawings, plans, and writing of L. Francis Herreshoff, who had been asked to devise designs during the war

years to make people dream about boats again. In his dad's library
Joel found a book called *Sailing, Seamanship, and Yacht Construction,* by Uffa Fox, which he "kind of devoured." Fox was a British
naval architect and boatbuilder, and his books were collections of
essays about boats that were particularly successful or that he
found interesting. Fox's boat portraits were a combination of design reviews and sailing stories, as the boat was often the subject of
a voyage too, and he wrote romantically of the sea. There were
photographs of the boat and sometimes of the trip, and there were
line drawings that were inspiring to look at. After Joel graduated
from Exeter and decided to take a year off before college, he lived
with his parents in New York and got a job as an office boy with a
construction firm remodeling the New York Times building. That
winter he spent many hours at the New York Public Library reading other books by Uffa Fox.

Joel enrolled at Cornell University because his dad had gone
there. Officially he majored in liberal arts, but unofficially, as he
remembered it, he majored in having a good time. He was interested in boat design, but it seemed unlikely that he could make a
career of designing small boats, and he didn't think he wanted to
design ships. But he talked it over with his parents, and decided to
do the thing that he enjoyed most. He applied to the MIT program
in naval architecture, and to his surprise, got in. There he was a
hardworking student. In the summers he taught sailing at a camp
on Deer Isle, and was part of a crew that sailed a schooner from
Rhode Island to Maine.

Joel also began to send some of his designs to boating magazines.

· In June 1950, "Sloop by White" appeared in *The Rudder*.
A 20-foot whaleboat hull with a gaff-rig sail plan, it received com-

ments such as "Departures from conventionality are always interesting" and "Mr. White states that he has endeavored to 'provide
the most boat for the least money,' a common goal of designers
these days."

· The January 1951 issue of *The Rudder* included "Cuddy
Cabin Day Sailer by White," 23 feet long, gaff-rigged, with large
cockpit and small cuddy, "designed for the man who does not require a racing machine, but desires a practical seaworthy small
boat."

· In the December 1951 issue of *The Rudder,* "Sailing Dinghy by White," beginning with "Joel M. White of Boston, Mass.,
designed this 12-foot dinghy for his father, who required a stiff
roomy boat for fishing and sailing."

E. B. White told of the dinghy in a letter written in 1951 just
after the design appeared. Harold Ross, the founding editor of *The
New Yorker,* had died, and the Whites were feeling low; they were
hoping to get to Maine in January, during Joel's midterm vacation.
"He designs dinghies for *The Rudder* readers with one hand, and
studies the midsection of the Europa with the other. He is also deep
in the middle of love, love, love, and is going to bust out of college
if he doesn't come up for air. He has also bought a lobster boat and
built a lot of traps in order to make his fortune next summer so he
can marry the girl. He also appears in December in *The Rudder*
with a design he did for his old man, who was about to go to a
watery grave in a 12½ foot Dyer dhow and had the presence of
mind to get into something a bit quieter. I had the little boat built
by an old guy in SW Harbor last spring, and it worked out fine for
me—steady as a church, and with a lug rig that goes up and down
like an old umbrella. Another one of Joe's designs is being built by a
dry cleaner named Krushwitz, but Joe hasn't seen the boat as he

fears Krushwitz thinks the designer is a much older man, and doesn't dare go near him."

· In *Yachting,* early fifties, "15' Flat Bottom Skiff by Joel White," "a small sailboat which could be built for a minimum amount of money and in which youngsters could race and knock-about with pleasure and safety."

· In *Yachting,* August 1952, "Cruising Conversion of a Drag-ger," with sail plan, accommodations plan, and lines plan: "a 37' double-ended dragger designed by Joel M. White, of No. Brooklin, Me., looked so promising that we suggested he draw up the sketches shown here for making a cruiser of her."

· *Yachting,* 1953, "An Able 26-Foot Power Cruiser": "De-signed by Joel M. White, 58 Anderson St., Boston, Mass., this small cruiser promises to be long on seaworthiness and economy. This hull, with its springy sheer, wide decks, some inside ballast, and good flare should make her a fine seaboat."

· *Yachting,* 1953, "A Picturesque 24-Foot Clipper-Bowed Sloop," a husky "character boat" that "many sailors will admire but only a few of the saltiest will covet."

· And in 1954 when Joel was a senior at MIT, *Homeward,* a 34-foot sport fisherman with a Maine-type hull, "round-bilged and easily driven," designed to go 15 knots with a 120-horsepower engine. *Homeward* was designed for a client from Connecticut and built in Thomaston, Maine. When Joel put his official design list together, years later, this would be Design No. 01, marking the beginning of his professional career.

Joel married Allene Messer while at MIT. For two summers he lobstered commercially, setting about seventy-five traps. He out-fitted the boat himself, buying a hull from Nova Scotia for $600, then installing the engine and building the cabin. Steve White was born in 1954, and when he was a week old his grandfather went to Boston to visit him. From the Ritz-Carlton Hotel (which would become the fictional setting where a trumpet-playing swan would spend a night, dining on watercress sandwiches) E. B. White wrote Katharine: "I've just come from dinner at 81 Charles, and it was a very fine occasion. Steve is a charmer—quite big for his age, very friendly and responsive, contented with life, and obviously well cared for by Allene, who looked pretty and happy. The baby is full of smiles and good humor, and seems to love people. Joe is very proud of him and produced a weight chart showing his progress carefully recorded on graph paper. All in all a grandchild that should make you happy."

For a few months before he got drafted into the Army, Joel worked at Newport News Shipbuilding in Virginia, doing model tests for the development of nuclear carriers. He found the work interesting but hated the heat and humidity, and longed for Maine. After basic training Joel and his family—Allene, Steve, and the new baby, Martha—went to Germany. Because he could type, he was assigned as the company clerk. They traveled, and because they had young children they met people. Steve went to a nursery school, and Joel was often amused when he'd come home at night to find Steve speaking German words.

They returned to the United States by boat in 1956, and docked at Brooklyn, New York, on July 11, E. B. White's fifty-seventh birthday. The scene of 1,200 soldiers coming down the gangplank, the sight of his grandchildren on deck, was so exciting for White that "I had to be led away to a stable bench by my stable wife to set for a few minutes." Soon he traveled to Maine to see Joel and his family, who were staying at the house in North Brooklin. In the fall they moved into a house in the western part of town near the Benjamin River. E. B. White also made a trip to Boston to see the launching of his new boat, *Fern,* an 18-foot sloop built in Denmark. *Charlotte's Web* was four years into publication, on its way to becoming the best-selling children's novel of the twentieth century.

Returning to Brooklin, Joel thought about what to do for a living. He considered lobstering, but figured that since he had children he'd better get a job. Arno Day was running a small boatyard and building boats at Center Harbor, and so in 1956 Joel began working there.

Arno Day had helped Joel outfit his Nova Scotia hull for lobstering, and in Joel he found another person fascinated with boat design. It was one of the reasons he hired Joel, so that the two could talk about design. Joel knew about such things as form stability and righting moment, while Arno knew how to build lobster and fishing boats.

Arno had also spent many days in his youth sailing, on a catboat on the Benjamin River. His was a family of boatbuilders. His great-grandfather Moses Day had built tenders for schooners. His grandfather Eugene Day built working sailboats, and the first versions of Maine lobster boats when gasoline engines came into play. His father, Frank Day, began working as an auto mechanic, but when the Depression came he turned to boatbuilding too, making 12-foot rowing skiffs and selling them for $35 each. Arno spent a lot of time in his grandfather's shop, and would sometimes carve out boats for his grandfather's assessment—carving a model from wood, then building the boat in the mind, was the traditional way of design. Arno Day also worked in his father's shop, and when he was a teenager he built his first boat, a lapstrake skiff, with his father's help.

After high school he went to Boston to find work, but when World War II began Arno returned to Maine to help build cargo vessels for the Army. At the yard in Stonington one day he watched an older craftsman "loft" a boat, using a long ruler to lay out drawings full-size on the floor. As Arno put it, he became "hopelessly lost" to this way of laying out the shape of a boat. This mathematical approach to boatbuilding went against the old tradition of carving a model, of shaping it by hand. Traditional boatbuilders would call the newer-style lofted boats "line boats." But the idea of drawing a boat on paper and then expanding it to full size by lofting techniques was an exercise that Arno Day found both practical and irresistible.

When the war ended Arno joined his father and his brother, Frank Day Jr., and formed a boatyard called Frank Day and Sons. At a site on the Benjamin River they did repairs, stored boats for the winter, and built new boats. E. B. White stored both *Astrid* and *Fern* there. The Fishers Island 31 *Cirrus* was kept there. But the partnership became strained for two reasons. Arno Day wanted to loft boats, while Frank and Junior Day wanted to build them from half-models, the traditional way. And Arno also had difficulty with the issue of money. According to some who knew him, because Arno found so much personal satisfaction in boatbuilding, and had an almost religious feeling about it, he was resistant to accepting money. When the three men did a large repair job and Arno charged only about half of what it was worth, his brother and father took it hard. Arno tended to go completely silent when things went wrong, sometimes for days at a time. After a few years the partnership broke up and Arno moved on.

He was working for a man by the name of Cy Cousins at

Webbers Cove Boat Yard in East Blue Hill when in 1952 a fisherman asked Arno to build a boat for him. He found a location at Center Harbor, at the site of an abandoned sardine canning factory. His father and a partner had built boats there in 1938, until Frank Day went to work in Stonington. A century before that, schooners had been built there—the *Monitor* by Abraham Fly in 1827, the *Sailor's Delight* and *Hannah* by John Fly, *Amanda Powers* and *Louise* by Nathan Powers. Arno cleared a spot, put up a shed, and during the winter built a Maine lobster boat of his own design, and launched it in the spring. The next fall he got another order—it seemed to Arno that when you built a boat, orders for more came along. When repair work and requests for storage came in, Arno hired men to work with him. By the time Joel White arrived in 1956 there were a half dozen men working there, though the number varied with the season.

For Joel, working with Arno Day gave him a chance to learn about the practical side of boatbuilding, and he found that exciting. Each winter they built a powerboat of the traditional kind, either for fishing or for pleasure cruising. They shared the design work, making lines drawings, construction plans, doing the lofting. And there were repairs, the replacement of planks, frames, keels, and other jobs that were so instructive to the developing boatbuilder. After three years, Arno asked Joel to be his partner.

They worked six days a week, eight hours a day, and the pay for those forty-eight hours was $50. But it was a hand-to-mouth operation, and they didn't always get paid, and they never knew if they would get paid until the last moment, when Arno might or might not say, "Well, boys, there's nothing in the barrel this week." The pressure didn't settle easily on Arno, who would agonize over building a boat while also agonizing over asking for money from the client. It was said that it was great to have Arno work for you, but not great to be getting paid by him. For days at a time at the shop, Arno would go silent. The first time Joel experienced one of Arno's silent periods he told Allene, and Allene called Arno's wife, who said not to worry, he'd get over it. At the shop the crew would say, "There are days and there are days, and sometimes the days have moods." In 1961 Arno told Joel he'd become a slave to the business, and said that if Joel bought his share he'd be taking a great load off his shoulders. Joel thought it over, went to a bank to see about buying the sardine factory and property as well as the business, and he asked one of the workers, Henry Lawson, if he'd stay on and be the yard foreman—Lawson said he would as long as the work didn't come between him and his family.

Arno went back to Stonington, where for a time he built big fishing boats known as draggers. Then he formed a partnership with a fellow worker, and for about twelve years they built Arno Day designs, about eighteen or twenty of them, primarily at a yard on Deer Isle. After a heart attack, in 1974, he took some time to think about what to do next, and decided he'd like to teach young people about boatbuilding, to dedicate the rest of his life to it. First he helped a young fisherman build a boat, working alongside him and giving instructions. Later he helped a young man, a summer resident of Brooklin, to build a 30-foot sailboat. The young man had tried college, but college wasn't right, and so used money earmarked for education to pay Arno Day to work with him, to guide him in the construction, which took three years. He sailed his boat away, and eventually started his own yard. Arno then began to teach at the WoodenBoat School, at the Penobscot Marine Museum in Searsport, and at the Maine Maritime Museum at Bath. Some of the students in those classes thought of him as the inspiration for important changes in their lives.

He would sometimes say, "My work is done here." And "My

job, all through the years, was to respond to the needs of fishermen and lobstermen and come up with appropriate designs." When he was well into his seventies a man who had worked in boatyards but had never built a boat himself asked Arno for a design, and a day later Arno gave him new drawings for a 21-foot powerboat. The boatbuilder didn't know that Arno came with the deal. Arno kept coming by the shop to check on the progress of the boat, and when there was a problem the boatbuilder would sometimes find new drawings on the seat of his truck the next day.

And he said, "I grew up around here in the thirties. Then we worked for and with our neighbors. It was how we survived. I'm glad I was a part of that time, that I had that experience. Things aren't like that much anymore. There's a great pleasure in helping people."

Frank L. Day and Junior Day worked together until Frank Day died in 1978. Then Junior Day worked on his own, building Down East boats for fishing and pleasure. He was building one, lofted by his brother Arno, in 1996.

Joel looked back upon the early years when things were uncertain as the most exciting time in his boatbuilding career. In the fall of 1961 a lobsterman from Deer Isle came to Brooklin Boat Yard with a half-model under his arm, one he'd made himself, and asked if Joel could build the boat, a 34-footer. Joel said he'd love to try. He ordered a load of lumber, including some big pieces of oak for a keel, and piled it outside the shop. At that time the shop was just a shed with a dirt floor. The wind blew through the walls, and sometimes the tide flooded in. The shed was too small to build the lobsterman's boat, so they set up a lean-to and worked outdoors. A few weeks after they'd gotten started a storm blew in and left a pile of snow on the lumber, and it took several days to dig out. The temperature plunged and the harbor froze over, and then a full-moon tide rose and carried big ice cakes into the yard, leaving them around the framed-up hull. They couldn't move them, so they worked around them, sitting on the ice to plank the boats. Fitted out, Wilbur MacDonald's *Miss Caroline* was launched in the spring of 1962.

It was time to improve the yard. They built two new storage sheds, and used the old sardine factory for storage and for office space. They built a shop building, with loft space, next to the dock.

- In 1963 they launched *Kishti,* a Down East pleasure boat of Joel's design.
- In 1964, *Mañana,* a 30-foot Cyrus Hamlin design.
- In 1965, *Daisy,* a 37-foot sloop, John Alden design.
- In 1966, the 39-foot ketch *Surfing Seal,* a Thomas Gilmer design.
- In 1967, the 30-foot sailboat *Amita,* Cyrus Hamlin design.

Joel's crew consisted of six to eight men, depending on the season. Most of them had gone to the same elementary school in Brooklin that he did, but some were older. There was Ken Tainter, an ex-Marine who'd served in China, a fisherman, son of the boatbuilder George Tainter. Ken Tainter fished through the winter, and when the scallop season ended in April he worked at the yard, where his specialty was rigging. He was known as someone who had a lot of stories and a dry wit, someone who could say a lot in a few words, someone who had a soft heart. When Henry Lawson was a boy his mother died and his father moved away, and Henry moved from house to house for a while, until Tainter and his wife took him in. When Lawson went into the Navy after graduating from Brooklin High School, he had Tainter officially adopt him.

After the Navy, Lawson worked for Arno Day at the yard and then for Joel, and he supervised the difficult task of hauling the boats the yard stored each winter, dragging them across the greased wooden skidwork and into the sheds, using pulleys and winches—sometimes it took an entire day to get a boat into her storage shed. But Henry Lawson liked the job of taking care of boats, and he looked forward to seeing the owners arrive in the spring and summer to pick them up. They were the bread and butter, as he saw it; they were like family.

Henry married the daughter of Elmer Bent, a finish carpenter and sparmaker who was part of the yard crew, also known around town for his house carpentry and his work on mantelpieces. He also made a violin, and a biplane that he flew just once, it was said. He was a small man who didn't like cold weather, and he particularly didn't like sitting on ice cakes to plank a boat. He wore four or five layers of clothing in the winter, and was always stoking the stove. He was the foreman in the shop when Joel was away.

Joel was an exacting boatbuilder—he was someone who was fussy about boats. He enjoyed planking, the process of bending and shaping a long board to fit the curve of the hull, and he also liked framing out the transom, especially curved transoms. He always did the caulking of the seams between the planks. He was very particular about lines, and none more so than the sheerline, the curve of the deck as seen from the side. Joel would look at a line from all angles, walk up the stairs and look at it, come down and look some more, for a half hour sometimes. When they laid down a batten—a long, thin strip of wood—to test the fairness of the curve of the sheer, he would have someone in the crew move it again and again, making slight adjustments each time, and then he'd look at the line, while the others waited for his approval. This tweaking of the sheerline sometimes tested their patience. Joel had been called

Henry Fussy in one context. Among the boatbuilders he was sometimes referred to as Tweakus Maximus. One time when Joel was standing on the stairway he asked Elmer Bent to move a batten, and Elmer did, but he fastened it back in the same place. When Joel said, "Look's good," Elmer just glanced around at the others. In the evenings and on weekends, Joel worked in his office in the sardine factory, doing the paperwork and, when there was time, drawing boats.

Raymond Eaton was a painter, one of those at a boatyard who scrape and paint boats all day. His instinctive humility ran so deep that whenever he was asked how a job came out he would always say, "It could be better." Some say he said the same of his wife's cooking, and that his wife, a sweet and beautiful woman, didn't complain, and it was said that Eaton was so set in his ways that when he came home to lunch at eleven-thirty, if lunch wasn't on the table, he turned around and walked back to work. He painted boats at the yard until after he got Alzheimer's disease, up until the point when they had to go out and find him at the end of the day.

Sonny Williams was a carpenter known as a hard worker. He liked planking most, attaching the spiled planks and then getting on the inside of the hull to see if light came through. He liked to talk about the time when the crew went to Naskeag and felled a tree, shaped it with a chain saw, made it into a mast, and then shellacked it every day at the yard so it wouldn't split. In August he took time off to rake blueberries in Blue Hill and at the barrens in Washington County. He loved clamming, and when the tides were right he'd clam on a low tide before coming in to work and then on the second tide after work. When during the Christmas season there was a market for spruce or fir boughs, he'd go through the woods at a run cutting them off, his family coming along behind to gather them. In the shop he was known as someone who read the tabloids, believed what they said, and made reports before work in the morning about two-headed horses, alien landings, the wilder the better. Sonny Williams worked up until the point when most of the old crew were gone, all except for Henry Lawson, and decided he couldn't work anymore at the yard once they started using glue to make boats.

Belford Gray was also good at planking. It was said that he could "get out a strake a day," a course of planks all the way around a boat, an achievement that required a sure touch with the plane. But he liked to talk too, and he was known as a humorist. At lunch, when most of the crew were sitting quietly by the woodstove, Gray, it was said, would be looking around at them, and he'd have the word or phrase to set them off. He cared about his work—one day, building the interior for a boat named *Alisande,* he saw a cabinet that would be just the right place for a piece of bird's-eye maple, and then went home to get it. Sometimes at the yard he made scallop stew in a rusty pot, and they washed it down with bourbon. When the WoodenBoat School opened, he became a very popular teacher there. On the day Belford died he was building a hatch for a sailboat, and he lost consciousness just after sitting down for a coffee break. It was so traumatic for some of the crew that they couldn't talk about it or about Belford even after ten years. When the WoodenBoat School launched a Friendship sloop, the largest boat built there, which took several years to finish, they named it *Belford Gray.*

Allene came to the yard every day to bring Joel his lunch and she came in on Fridays to manage the books and write the paychecks. She worked in the office in the sardine factory, in a room heated with a single space heater. In the winter, ice formed on the stairs, so Allene kept a hatchet to cut her way up the steps. Sometimes she'd have to get after Elmer Bent to cash his checks—he was tight with money and he'd keep the checks in his wallet. She liked to look out at the harbor in May, when the barn swallows returned and nested in the sardine factory and the sheds, and she liked looking out at Ken Tainter in the summer, when he stripped down and jumped into the water to cool off. Sometimes in those days when Joel wanted a letter typed, he wrote it on a board and gave it to Allene. Joel resisted getting a phone put in as long as he could, and when he did, Allene spent a lot of time hunting around for him, finding him in the bottom of a boat or out in the harbor somewhere.

When Joel started working as a boatbuilder some people said there must be something wrong—someone with a degree from MIT? But Allene thought it was fine that Joel had become a boatbuilder, and though she was considered to be a person "from away," since she was from New Hampshire and Boston, she enjoyed living out in the country. When they moved to a house near the Benjamin River in 1956 they were neighbors of Frank Day and his wife, Myrtle, and Allene found an ally in Myrtle Day. There were many mornings when Allene took her children over to Myrtle's house and watched her cook, making doughnuts or chicken pie. Myrtle explained the social life of Brooklin to Allene, and made it easier for her to fit in. And there were those standing Saturday-night dinner parties, with baked beans, brown bread and biscuits coming from the woodstove, and raspberry Jell-O, pickled beets, biscuits with honey, and apple pie. Arno and Dot Day would come, and Junior Day, and their sister Mary Day with her husband Havilah Hawkins (who built the schooner *Mary Day*), and the Whites. Later, when Allene began to write food columns, she sometimes featured one of Myrtle Day's recipes.

A boat a year, sometimes two. In the winter of 1967 the crew built *Amita,* the 30-foot Cyrus Hamlin sailboat. Underneath the bow of that boat they fit in a smaller project, a sailboat for E. B. White. He named it *Martha,* after his granddaughter. At the launching he gave a dedicatory speech:

"This sloop was designed by the late S. S. Crocker. She is about twenty feet over all, about seventeen feet on the water, has a beam of seven feet seven inches, and draws two feet with the board up. There is a single-cylinder Palmer engine under the self-draining cockpit. That's there so I can pick up my mooring without creating a sensation in the harbor. Except for two full-length berths down below, the boat is as bare as a baby. No sink, no icebox, no water tank, no head, no telephone, no depth finder. I plan to find my depth by listening to the sound the centerboard makes as it glides over the ledges."

&

From 1962 until *Martha* was launched in 1967, Brooklin Boat Yard built seven boats, all made of wood. But that fall a lobsterman by the name of Clifford Heanssler contracted the yard to finish off a fiberglass hull, a Webbers Cove 34. He was a high-liner, a top producer, and people tended to watch him. Soon fishermen in Penobscot Bay and elsewhere began to think that if they had a fiberglass boat there wouldn't be as much maintenance, and a lot of wooden lobster boats went up for sale.

In 1970 the yard launched *Cachalot,* a scaled-up version of *Martha,* built strong and sturdy for a summer resident of Brooklin who hadn't done much sailing before. And in 1971 they launched *Nasket II,* a 35-foot ketch that was also an adaptation of an S. S. Crocker design. Then in 1972 the yard finished off and launched the 36-foot fiberglass pleasure boat *Nannook,* in 1973 two fiber-

glass commercial fishing boats, another in 1974, three in 1975—
fifteen fiberglass boats in all, finished off at Brooklin Boat Yard, in
the decade of the 1970s. Only two wooden boats were built during
that time, *Dovekie,* a 42-foot ocean-cruising ketch, and *High Time,*
a 34-foot Down East power cruiser designed by Joel White. The
orders just weren't coming in.

The crew was good at finishing off fiberglass boats, and the
yard had all the work they wanted, but they hated it for the most
part. There was all that grinding, and the noxious smells. A
boatbuilder working in wood went home smelling of cedar; a fiberglass finisher smelled like ether. So in 1980, a year when the yard
simultaneously finished off a 32-foot fiberglass lobster boat and
built the 42-foot wooden power cruiser *Lady Jeanne,* designed by
Joel, they talked about the predicament at lunch one day. Joel asked
them, "Should we not do that anymore?" and some of the crew
said, "Yeah, let's not do that anymore." So Joel stopped taking
orders for finishing fiberglass boats, and oddly enough orders for
wooden boats began coming in again.

Fortunately a wooden boat revival was underway, and Brooklin was the center of it, because *WoodenBoat* magazine was there
and the WoodenBoat School was about to open. *WoodenBoat* was
the creation of Jonathan Wilson, who had taught boatbuilding in
the Outward Bound program, and been inspired by the writing of
Howard Chapelle in *American Small Sailing Craft.* He began the
magazine in 1974 in an owner-built home tucked in the woods. He
couldn't afford to run a phone line all the way in, only partway,
and had the phone set up on a tree. Years later, when the magazine
had grown to 100,000 subscribers and was housed on an estate
overlooking Eggemoggin Reach, there was sometimes displayed in
a case by the front office a photograph of Wilson, wild-haired, thin

and angular, sitting on a log and taking notes while talking on a phone anchored to a tree.

He and the magazine staff came to Brooklin through the efforts of Joel White and Maynard Bray. The magazine had moved from Wilson's house to several offices, one of which they were burned out of, and they were in an old schoolhouse in Brooksville when Joel and Maynard Bray dropped by. Seeing the place, Joel said, "If he likes this, he'll really like what we've got." They had an old inn to offer, an elephant of a place held by a consortium of people in Brooklin. The inn had once thrived but then failed, and it had been owned by someone who tried to run a farm there and kept animals in the rooms, and then it had been a theology school which paid no taxes. When the place became available several citizens of Brooklin got together and bought it, Joel White and Maynard Bray among them, and together tried to decide what to do. *WoodenBoat* seemed a perfect solution.

Jon Wilson liked the little town of Brooksville and wanted to stay there, but he knew there were possibilities for his magazine in Brooklin. He was a creative editor with a great idea, but there were gaps in his knowledge about boats and boatbuilding, and he knew it. Wilson had gotten to know Joel White when he had covered the construction of *Dovekie* for one of the first issues. He knew that Maynard Bray, a marine engineer who had been in charge of the watercraft and shipyard at Mystic Seaport Museum and directed the refloating and restoration of the whaleship *Charles W. Morgan,* could also be a deep resource of technical expertise. Wilson also thought that perhaps the magazine might be a resource for them. When they told him the inn was his for $25,000 Wilson put up his house for collateral, got a mortgage, and in 1977 moved *WoodenBoat* to Brooklin.

By coincidence, 1977 was also the year that Steve White returned to Brooklin after a time of traveling around, and began working at the boatyard again. And it wasn't long after that when he and Joel went sailing, and he told Joel he might like to make a career at the yard.

After a time of giving technical advice to *WoodenBoat* anonymously, Maynard Bray became the technical editor in 1979, eventually giving the magazine a stamp of his own. In 1979 Joel White submitted his first article, a how-to piece called "Peapods Are for Sailing." In 1979 *WoodenBoat* also published construction plans for the Joel White Catspaw Dinghy, a design commissioned by a client of the boatyard and that was based on Nathanael Herreshoff's Columbia Dinghy. Jon Wilson thought the article about the Catspaw construction was just what his magazine should be doing—making information about wooden boats of classic sources available to anyone who wanted to build them. He found the Catspaw an ideal blend of a Herreshoff inspiration with Joel White's simple touch.

And so the collaboration continued as the wooden boat revival gathered momentum. When *WoodenBoat* opened a summer school in 1980 one of the first boats students built was a plywood skiff called *Martha*'s *Tender,* which Joel had designed in 1963. Wilson also encouraged Joel to design more boats and allow the magazine to sell their plans.

- In 1981 he designed a 20-foot sliding-seat rowing shell, the *Bangor Packet.*
- In 1982, the *Gerry Wherry,* a 23-foot rowing shell.
- In 1983, the *Nutshell Pram,* a 7′ 7″ or 9′ 6″ sailing rowboat.

There was Shearwater, a 16-foot double-ended pulling boat. And Marsh Cat, a 15-foot catboat. The Maine Coast Peapod, a 14-foot rowboat. The Haven 12½, a centerboard adaptation of the Herreshoff 12½. The 20-foot Flatfish, based on the Herreshoff Fish Class, and the 22-foot Fox Island Class Sloop. The 11-foot Shellback Dinghy, for oar and sail. And the 12′ 10″ Pooduck Skiff.

The best-selling plan was the Nutshell pram, the smallest boat and the easiest to build. It was also the design that Jon Wilson had the most enthusiasm for. To his thinking the Nutshell was an "evolutionary step in boat design," a tender that would really sail and that was so steady you could set wineglasses on the center seat and have a time of it in a summer's twilight. Arno Day and Joel White experimented with plywood as a boatbuilding material—the Nutshell used plywood as its lapstrake hull planking and had only a single frame amidships. It was easy to clean. It rowed and towed well, dragging little water behind.

When the magazine had the first Catspaw built at Brooklin Boat Yard, they couldn't afford to keep it. But as the readership grew, nationally and internationally, the offices were moved to a waterfront estate further down the Naskeag peninsula and the inn became a dormitory. Jon Wilson eventually bought the Concordia sloop *Free Spirit*. He too became friends with Joel White, sometimes sailing with him. He sometimes tried to show Joel how he felt about him, but Joel was resistant. Reticent like his father, he didn't want praise, and avoided it. But it seemed to Wilson that after Joel began to contend with cancer he had been more open to letting people express how they felt about him.

Joel's design list expanded greatly during the 1980s. On his official list, beginning with the powerboat *Homeward*, designed when he was at MIT, and moving to *Lady Jeanne*, the powerboat designed in 1979, a period of twenty-five years, Joel had eleven designs to his credit. But moving from *Alisande,* a 36-foot ketch designed in 1980, to *Sweet Olive,* a 43-foot cutter designed in 1989, he increased his output to forty designs. In the 1990s, up to *Grace* and *Linda,* he had designed fifteen more, fifty-five altogether.

WoodenBoat provided a vehicle for Joel to create more designs. But it was Steve White's presence at the yard that allowed him to spend more time at the drawing board. After E. B. White died in 1985, Joel built one more boat, a scow-schooner called *Vintage.* He then stopped working in the shop and moved permanently into the design studio.

September 1996

When Hurricane Eduardo hit hard along the mid-Atlantic and began moving up the coast, Steve White and two crew members and several volunteers hauled boats out of the harbor all of one Saturday and into the night, taking out thirty-five in all. But the hurricane withered and passed through in the form of 40-knot winds, and so they put some of the big boats back in again. September sailing is the best sailing in Penobscot Bay, it is said. The small boats, Beetle Cats, Herreshoff 12½s, Havens, a pair of Boothbay 21s, sit about the yard, as if cast there by the wind, while the cruisers sit in the thinned-out harbor, all facing into the tide flow. The soft September light falls upon them, the water, and the islands too, while in the yard there's the intermittent sound of a hammer, a saw, or a power tool breaking through the still air.

Steve is a bit weary from the boat hauling. He checks in on the repair of a big Trumpy motor yacht that's set up on blocks and jack stands in a building normally used as a paint shop, the White

House they call it. The bottom courses of planks have been re-moved, and the lower eighteen inches of the frames are being re-placed where they've rotted. A crew of about six men is working on it, crouching along near the keel. He's also waiting to meet with a man from Boston who's interested in having a 63-foot sailboat built, to the design Joel made for him a month ago. Steve is plan-ning on discouraging him from that project.

When Joel brought Steve down to the yard when he was a boy and put him to work bailing out rowboats and pumping floats, he paid him twenty-five cents an hour. In high school he earned a few dollars an hour, painting boats and occasionally rigging boats with Ken Tainter. Steve liked working with Tainter, who had a good sense of humor, and it was because of Tainter that he now thought of himself as a rigger, aside from being a manager. During summers in his teens Steve sailed a Beetle Cat, and sometimes he sailed *Shadow* in races at the yacht club. Both he and Martha went to the elementary school in Brooklin, but they didn't attend the high school, instead going to private schools in Massachusetts.

During the time that Steve worked at the yard, in high school and for a couple years in college, Joel didn't suggest to him that he think about working there someday, or about taking it over. Joel thought that it would be a good thing, and hoped that Steve might think about it, but he didn't bring the matter up. He figured it would be best if Steve thought of it himself. He told Steve that he should do what he wanted, and he said that if he needed a job in the summer one was there.

Joel didn't suggest that Steve go to college either. It was his grandfather who said he should think about college, and so Steve went to Colby and majored in environmental engineering. When he was in college he noticed that a lot of students were worrying about their future, that they were laboring over their decisions. Steve thought that he'd work with boats and around the water, and possibly at the yard, but compared to the others at school, that seemed a bit too easy. He thought that he too should struggle a little, and that he should have a few adventures away from Maine. In college he tended bar on a "booze cruise," out of Boston Harbor. After college he went to New Orleans and worked in a boatyard, framing interiors on steel boats used to ferry materials to oil rigs. He worked as a deckhand on a tugboat on the Mississippi. After a Mardi Gras he came back to Brooklin and worked at the yard for the summer, then he went to Aspen for the winter and returned to the yard again, this time to see where it led. Some thought, "How long will it be this time?" But that summer Steve went sailing with Joel and told him he'd like to stay, and Joel said, "Fine."

It was a gradual process. Steve rigged and painted, hauled and built boats. He worked alongside Henry Lawson as the yard foreman, and eventually took over. Joel formed a corporation, with himself in majority ownership, but each year the percentages shifted just a little. When E. B. White died and his financial situation changed, Joel put himself in a minority ownership.

Like his father and grandfather, Steve felt that he'd been lucky. He built a house on a promontory overlooking the yard and Center Harbor—after living with his wife, Laurie, on an Alden Malabar Jr. in the harbor for a while. But when he started running the yard, Steve also felt that he didn't want to just be the boss's son. He wanted to make changes and make the place his own. So he bought the Travel-lift and began to hire new employees, ones who saw him as the boss. Steve's employees tended not to be local Brooklin carpenters or mechanics as much as young boatbuilders who had been spurred on by the wooden boat revival. Joel's crew called the new arrivals boat nuts, and complained that all they wanted to talk about was boats. Gradually the percentages of the two kinds of workers changed, until by the time Joel moved up into the studio the majority of the crew had been hired by Steve.

When Steve returned to the yard, the crew was finishing off fiberglass boats. He looked for alternatives to fiberglass work. When they decided to build only wooden boats, three years later, Steve kept looking for alternatives. He thought that cold-molded construction might be the way.

In traditional wooden boat construction in this part of Maine, oak frames are steamed and bent and attached to a heavy oak keel, and then thick planks are spiled and bent to the frames to form the hull. A traditional boat after launching swells and becomes ever more watertight. The skill of the builders determines how tight the boat is, and so craftsmanship, traditional methods, passed from builder to builder, play an important role. There was a line, say, from Eugene Day to Arno Day to Joel White to other builders at the yard. In cold-molded construction, boat hulls draw from tradition, but they also have roots in airplane construction. Cold-molded hulls have keels, frames, and planks, but they also have bulkheads and make use of load-transfer engineering. A cold-molded hull is essentially a box frame consisting of light planks and thin veneers bonded and coated with glue, and, unlike a traditional boat, it is a sealed unit and doesn't absorb water or leak. In this sense it's like a fiberglass boat. But a cold-molded boat rides through the water like a wooden boat, goes through the waves like a wooden boat, sounds and feels like a wooden boat. If engineered correctly, the hull of a cold-molded wooden boat is lighter and has a greater potential for speed. The techniques had been developing at least since World War II, and one company, Gougeon Brothers, had been developing epoxy adhesives and coatings and publishing their applications in a book, which Steve read and absorbed.

With two other young builders, Steve built a cold-molded dinghy, using an existing dinghy as a building form. Joel designed the cold-molded rowing shell Bangor Packet, and the yard built a series of those. They built Joel's design for a 15-foot cold-molded catboat, Marsh Cat. In 1986 Steve took an order for two Hackercraft speed-boat hulls, and they came out successfully. But he also wanted to build a large cold-molded boat, a boat that was his own just as he wanted the yard to be his own. In the early 1980s he looked for a design and settled on the Swede 55, by Knud Reimers, a long and narrow hull—52 feet with only a 10-foot beam, for a ratio of five to one, and 20,000 pounds displacement, which could mean a very easily driven boat. The original design was for fiberglass, so Steve contacted Reimers and told him he wanted to build in wood. Reimers made some changes, deepening the keel and increasing the ballast.

In 1986 Steve lofted out the lines, converting metric to inches, and with Joel's help drew a sail plan and accommodations plan. In 1988 he began construction, with help from others in the crew, and since there were no construction drawings Steve "built the boat in his head," during nights at home after work. In that sense, you could say, he was following traditional methods of becoming a boatbuilder in Maine. After 7,000 hours of labor, *Vortex* was launched in 1990. Steve and Laurie cruised in the boat and entered some races. They won the Eggemoggin Reach Regatta, the New Bedford Heritage Days Race, and took first in a class of the Museum of Yachting's Classic Yacht Regatta.

For several years after Joel moved into the design studio there were no orders for large wooden boats at the yard. From 1986 when they launched *Vintage* until 1990 when they launched *Vortex* most of the boats the yard built were under 20 feet long. In 1991 the yard launched *Sweet Olive,* a traditionally built 43-foot cutter that Joel designed for the client who had built *Alisande* in 1981.

But after an article about *Vortex* appeared in *WoodenBoat,* Steve got a call from someone who wanted to build an IMA racing sailboat, 55 feet long and cold-molded with a fiberglass foam core deck. Steve and Joel drove to Newport, Rhode Island, to meet the client and the designer, Bill Tripp. It was August, and they had only a preliminary sketch, and the client wanted the boat in April. But they agreed to go ahead. By September they had the lines and had started construction. Steve hired new workers, and for the first time the number of employees went above twenty. It was a 12,000-hour project, a lot of overtime, a lot of weekends on the job, the most complex boat the yard had built by far, but they launched *Aurora* on a high tide during a cold night in April. *Aurora* was very successful on the racing circuit. Steve crewed during several races and made a transatlantic crossing.

Pip Wick came to the yard that fall. He had found *Aurora* scary to look at, too much the high-tech racer. But he was impressed with the construction and liked the yard, and the cost of construction, and so *Lucayo* was launched in 1993. After reading the article about *Vortex,* Bruce Stevens visited the yard, and though a *Vortex* was what he had in mind originally, *Dragonera* was the result, Joel White's first design of a large cold-molded boat. *Dragonera* was launched in 1994. In 1995 Brooklin Boat Yard launched two Buzzards Bay 25s, cold-molded interpretations of the 1914 Nathanael Herreshoff design taken from the original offsets in the Hart Nautical Collections at MIT, with construction drawings by Joel White. And then in 1996, *Grace* and *Linda,* cold-molded departures from *Quiet Tune.*

Steve had taken a chance on a big speculation project and succeeded. But he also took a lot of criticism for bringing "glued boats" into the yard. Some people said that Steve White was no boatbuilder. Others said he was no Joel White. Ironically, Joel

White agreed, though he found the difference an advantage. A friend of Joel's said it this way: "Steve gets a bad rap, but what he is doing is no small thing. He's running a very successful operation and keeping about thirty people employed. He's able to sell jobs, and he's able to work with people. If Joe was still running it, what would it be? Four or five guys sitting around a nail keg. Joe's genius was in handing the business over to Steve, in the way he did it. Can you show me another business transfer that went that smoothly? Steve gets a bad rap, but it's not easy to be the son of Saint Joe."

Steve has the expressive eyes of his father, and a handsome appearance, but he favors Allene with a darker coloring and a more gregarious nature. He has a thick mustache and a deep voice. Up in Joel's studio, later in the afternoon, he says that in November he'll be sailing *Vortex* from Bermuda, where it is now, to the Carribean. He and Laurie will spend the winter sailing and hanging out. "I don't know if I can do it," Steve says, of hanging out and not working. "I haven't done it in a long time."

"First chance to find out," Joel says. During the morning Joel has gone into Bangor for a chemotherapy treatment, supposedly his last, but they had to postpone it because his blood count was too low.

"I'm sure the first month or so I'll probably go nuts trying to." Steve has said he feels guilty about leaving Joel this winter. Joel, for his part, has said nothing to discourage him. "I'll probably do a little bit of racing down there in Antigua. There are lots of islands to visit. I'll spend a week here, a week there. Though Laurie and I may tear each other's heads off after the first two weeks."

He has told the client from Boston that he can't build the 63-foot sailboat this winter because he won't be around to supervise the project. But the man has asked to have a Center Harbor 31 built, and Steve has agreed to that, since they've already built two of them. "I've known him for several years, and know that he buys and builds boats. I didn't want to lose him as a customer, so I said okay, we'll build the thirty-one." Now it looked like they would be building two CH 31s this year.

After Joel leaves to go home, Steve says that the relationship between them is a good one, though they didn't know each other very well when he was growing up. "I think he was the workaholic, starting the business here. He got up very early in the morning and worked long days, and then after the day was over worked in the office. I don't have many recollections, as a child growing up, of doing things together. For the four years I was in prep school I was gone nine months of the year, and I came back even less in college. Our relationship has started since I began working here full-time. It's basically developed since then, as a man-to-man relationship.

"He never pushed me to come into this business. It was always just do what you want to do. And he has always encouraged me to do what I wanted around the yard, in terms of improvements, changes, things like that. We would work together on my ideas, and my ideas for changing things. As long as he didn't think I was doing something awful, he would say that it was probably a good idea. He'd ask if we had enough money to do it, and I'd say yes, we do. That was basically the criteria he would probably use to say absolutely not. Though he never did.

"I think the skill I've brought to this business is an ability to work with people. The rest of it I'm just trying to figure out as I go along. You know, he was perfectly happy to tell a customer to screw off, if he didn't like the way he was being treated or if the guy didn't pay his bill, something like that. But I wouldn't do that. I had only one customer who I told we were changing things around and he wasn't going to be part of the picture anymore. Whereas he wouldn't have any trouble doing that at all. There are a lot of stories about the independent boatbuilder and yard owner who tells people to screw off. Frank Day, Arno's father, at his yard on the Benjamin River, there was a scene where one year he and the owner of a boat didn't get along, they had a big row or something, and that spring he launched the boat and the guy's cradle as well, tied the cradle right up to the stern of the boat. Just left it there and that was the sign. The guy came to pick the boat up that weekend and the cradle was tied right up to the stern.

"I felt I had to change the yard to make it mine and not his. And it's not mine and not his now. I really think it's ours now. I mean, he'll be here till the day he dies. He'll never give this place up. It's his life. That's the one thing that he would never be able to do, probably the one thing that would ruin our relationship, if I was to say, I'm gonna sell the boatyard, you don't have a job anymore. When I think about it now, I realize what a leap of faith he was taking when he turned the business over to me."

❧

J tell Joel I've been invited to go for a sail on *Dragonera*. "Oh," he says, "if you've got a chance to go sailing on *Dragonera*, you should go." So I decide to spend a couple of extra days in Brooklin.

The sail is set for a Sunday afternoon. Several of the boatbuilders from the yard arrive at about noon, with their wives and a few young children. There's Brian and Sarah Stevens and their two daughters—Brian is the son of Bruce Stevens, *Dragonera*'s owner. An architect by training, he began working at the yard when *Dragonera* was built. There's Brian and Karen Larkin and their daughter. There's Keith and Allison Dibble. And Mark Littlehales.

Down on the dock, Pip Wick is working aboard *Lucayo,* and when he sees that a party is going out on *Dragonera* he stops what he's doing and decides to go for a sail.

Out on *Dragonera,* Nigel Turnbull, the captain who takes care of her and lives aboard her, gets into a rubber Zodiac and motors to the dock to ferry us out. It takes two trips. *Dragonera,* the biggest boat in the harbor, is kept at the farthest mooring. With all aboard, ten adults and three children, Nigel gets into the forward locker and throws up bags of sails. Two jibs go on, the mainsail, the mizzen. The tunes go on too, a blues tape that Nigel put together. He starts the engine, and they cast off the mooring, and the boat heads out into the Reach. After a hundred yards or so, southwest of Chatto Island, Nigel cuts the motor and the sound of the engine is replaced by the sound of winches. The sails fill, all 1,800 square feet of them, and it is magnificent, this tall boat, this tall flame, cutting eastward.

The foldup table in the cockpit is opened up, and lunch is set out. Mark Littlehales takes the wheel. It's made of wood, laminated with delicate spokes and a broad diameter, a tricky thing to make, Joel has told me, and he also said that Mark Littlehales made it. I point out what a fine piece of work it is. "It's a nice wheel," Mark says.

Brian Stevens sits on the afterdeck with his daughters, sharing sandwiches with them, keeping them from getting too close to the rails. He says that his father had the boat built, but *Dragonera* actually goes back to his grandfather. Though he was from Iowa, Brian's grandfather had an obsession with boats. He built wooden models and gave them to his children and to his grandchildren. He built a boat with Brian's father, "a terrible boat, but it was a boat. When he moved to Green Bay he built more boats, and owned many boats. The enthusiasm was passed on to my father, and to me." Brian grew up in Chicago, and raced sailboats on Lake Michigan. Because he liked designing things, he studied architecture.

Bruce Stevens wanted to build a special boat, and when his business success put him in a position to do it, he contacted Steve White. When he looked at *Vortex* it was clear he'd need a bigger boat, one with more headroom, since Stevens is six foot five. Joel said that they ought to start with a fresh piece of paper. Though Joel basically created the design, other boats entered into the discussion—William Garden's *Oceanus,* a big boat with a long waterline and light displacement, was something Stevens had admired, and there was a Philip Rhodes sheerline that seemed appealing. The drawings passed to and from Chicago and the boat design developed. When it got to the point where Joel said there would have to be a commitment before going any further, Stevens was ready, and the *Dragonera* project commenced. (The boat, incidentally, is named after an island in the Caribbean.)

Dragonera is 75 feet long overall, 59 feet on the waterline. It has a 15-foot beam, for a beam-to-length ratio of five to one, which, as with *Vortex,* meant for a very fast boat. It has a draft of seven and a half feet, a displacement of 61,000 pounds. There's a ketch rig, with a total sail area of 1,822 feet. In the forward locker is a large storage area for sails. A watertight bulkhead separates it from the quarters. These consist of a stateroom furthest forward, with a V berth and an enclosed head. Aft of that, a set of bunks on the starboard side, with another cabin and head on the port side. Aft of that, a U-shaped galley, with tall counters for a tall person. There's a refrigerator on the aft side of the U, two sinks on the forward side, and a gimbaled stove on the port outboard side. Opposite the galley is a navigation station, with desk instruments, charts and books. Aft of that is a pilothouse, and behind that, a cockpit with foldup table and seats. There's an afterdeck, and be-

low the deck, the engine room—a 170-horsepower Yanmar diesel—
that also houses an electrical generator, a hot-water heater, a fresh-
water maker, a workbench, and storage area for spare parts. In the
cabin, the trim is cherry, the deck beams are spruce, and the interior
of the cold-molded hull, exposed and left bright, is Douglas fir.

There are things that they would change about the boat, Brian
Stevens says, such as the forward placement of the master stateroom, and maybe the shape of the transom. But not the way it sails.
One of the first priorities about the boat, for the Stevenses, was that
it would sail well. "It sails beautifully in light air," Brian Stevens
says. "In heavy air it reminds me of a smaller boat, because when it
gets overpowered it just kind of slows down. It's very sea-kindly,
it's nimble, it turns quickly. I'm amazed at how fast it is. My father
sailed it from the Chesapeake to the Bahamas, and they averaged
14 knots. The hull is perfect and the rig is perfect. I think it would
probably be hard to find another boat that handles the way this
does."

Brian had first come to Brooklin to be the project manager for
Dragonera. He had discussed the plans with his father during the
development period, and knew the boat well. He liked the idea of
moving to Brooklin with his wife for a while. Though not quite
thirty, he had already had what he called a midlife crisis, sitting in a
traffic jam in Chicago one afternoon, on his way home from a job
at an architectural firm. But being the liaison between his father and
Joel White hadn't been easy either. They'd clashed over what
seemed the most minor of details, even the shapes of moldings, and
Brian had been reminded several times of the cumulative years of
experience he was confronting. He'd had to call his father in at one
point. For Brian, working with Joel White, who was dreaming out
his finest boat yet, was the most difficult professional relationship
he'd ever had.

He enjoyed working at the yard, and getting to know the boatbuilders there. To Brian, the boatbuilders didn't seem to stand out, "but once you looked at the work you saw that they made incredible things." After *Dragonera* was launched Brian sailed it to Bermuda with some of the crew from the yard. They made the trip without any previous sea trials, and they ran into a storm, pounding for days, and nothing of importance broke along the way, an incredible thing for an untried boat. It was clear that the boat was strongly built and could really sail. Brian and Sarah moved to Nashville so that Sarah could work as a singer and songwriter, but then Brian called Steve, who told him they were just getting started on two Center Harbor 31s. They moved back to Brooklin again, and Brian started working on *Grace*. When Alan Stern came to the launching, he hoped his son would talk to Brian Stevens, that he'd see that what he'd done was worth thinking about.

❧

Dragonera heads along the Reach, coasting first at four knots and then at seven as we move into more open water. While some of the other boats passing by heel hard in the wind, there's little heel on *Dragonera*. All along the way, people turn to watch, to look at her through binoculars. Perhaps Joel had this in mind too when he'd been drawing this boat in his studio.

After we move into Jericho Bay, Brian lets me take the helm. Threading along between the lobster trap lines, I hold the big wheel, the tall sails full above me. It's an easy helm, as I steer through one tack, then another. The bow, far away, is responsive to the slight touch.

My hand upon the wheel, I look ahead, and watch the sails, and feel the wind upon me. And within me there's another wind, the wind of memory, one that comes from my grandfather. This feeling, this connection to memory, is one of the reasons I'm in Brooklin looking at boats.

My grandfather, my mother's father, lived in a small town on Cape Cod, a town that was much like Brooklin when he grew up there. He was a housepainter, and his father was a carpenter who also for a time owned a general store. My grandfather's grandfather owned a general store too, after he'd retired from the sea. He'd gone to sea as a boy and become a sea captain at twenty-four, the youngest sea captain in the town, my grandfather told me. He had gone to the general store as a boy to listen to the sea captains tell stories while they waited for the mail. My grandfather had heard about some of the voyages from his father, who went to Puerto Rico for molasses and to Europe.

My grandfather's family went back to the founder of the town, a man who left England to be with the congregation in Holland that eventually became the Pilgrims, and who himself emigrated in 1635. He'd been shipwrecked in Massachusetts, losing his children, he and his wife the only survivors. I'd seen a copy of the letter he wrote after the shipwreck, which began, "I now lift my drowned pen and shaking hand to indite the saddest story ever to come from New England." I'd seen a copy of the passenger list of the ship, the *James,* in which he made the transatlantic crossing from England, and read that he listed his occupation as a tailor, though his was a clerical family, and his home as Sarum, the ancient town near Stonehenge. I knew that he called his farm on Cape Cod "The Reward," that his son had twenty-three children, that my grandfather had come along nine generations later.

I had also seen copies of the letters that the sea captain had written to his employers, during the 1870s when sailing ships were giving way to steam, when they were getting the most out of the old wooden ships. In one letter which begins, "I take pen in hand to inform you of my safe arrival in the port of San Francisco," he says he has had a "rough and unfortunate passage" that he's lost five men north of Cape Horn—"five days out, while furling jibs, strong breeze, dark cloudy weather and rough sea, the foot rope parted and two men fell into the sea and were drowned. I tried every means to save them, but it was dark and could see nothing." Another man fell from the yard while reefing the mainsail, and two men fell off the yard in a gale while furling a topsail. He writes that the ship is leaking, the mainmast is rotting, that he'll have to get a new main yard and some sails. In San Francisco he has the mainmast replaced, the ship caulked, and eventually they set out for Liverpool, but the ship still leaks, and by the time they reach the Caribbean they're pumping constantly, and so head in to the Virgin Islands to St. Thomas, "our nearest port in distress." After commanding other ships, including a barkentine in coastwise trade, he died in Yarmouth in 1901, at the age of sixty, and according to a newspaper account "was a general favorite, especially among the younger people, and the attendance at his funeral, at his home in Yarmouth, was such to testify to the general esteem and respect in which he was held."

My grandfather didn't know those details, though he did talk about his father seeing men push molasses down chutes with their feet, and he told how his father, an infant when the sea captain went on a seven-year voyage, picked him out from among the crowd at the dock on his return. I listened to my grandfather's stories when I was a boy and thought, What voyage will I take? He had never left, and I actually didn't go too far either, but I did leave Cape Cod, and I would return to tell him about things that I'd done, things that I knew he'd like to hear, such as riding around the pyramids on a camel, about hitchhiking across the country and getting picked up by a circus, about putting on dolphin shows, about being a piano tuner, while studying to be a writer. He liked to remind me about when I was a boy and had ridden my bicycle to Provincetown, forty miles each way, without telling anyone where I was going.

This was the grandfather who had taken me into a field one afternoon when I was a boy and showed me a rock with a plaque on it, which told about the ancestor who'd come from England and been shipwrecked and then settled in Yarmouth in 1639, something I knew nothing about at the time. As I looked at the plaque, and then at him, with his paint-flecked arms, no jolly smile just then, I saw my grandfather in a different way, to be sure, saw the chain of being, I thought. And whenever I thought about how I started to become a writer, a question almost every writer asks himself, or gets asked at times, it was that moment I looked to.

So there I was in Brooklin, my hand on the wheel of a 75-foot boat, and thinking of the sea captain and the grandfather—that memory, that presence, that was the wind blowing through me just then. I was in Brooklin to look at boats, but I was also there to play some of the notes of my life, some of the ones I liked to sound. I knew my grandfather would have enjoyed hearing about this boat, this place.

I was here to get to know the man who was creating beautiful boats, the man who could create a line, perhaps, that knew the difference between large and small waves. And there was the presence of his father. I knew that E. B. White's writing was an acknowledgment of the gift of life, and that he had said, "All that I hope to say in books, all that I ever hope to say, is that I love the world." That was something too. It seemed to me that if a writer communicated that, he or she had done the job. But how did you communicate a love of the world? That was no easy thing.

After we loop around Egg Rock near Swans Island, Brian Stevens takes the wheel, and *Dragonera* glides back across Jericho Bay and up Eggemoggin Reach. The blues tape plays, Brian smiles easily, and others sit on the deck in the sun. When we get near Center Harbor, Brian motors up to the mooring, and the crew takes down the sails. At the mooring, this September day, clear and warm, seems all the calmer.

"This is the nicest month we get up here," one of the crew says.

At the dock I look back at *Dragonera*. The sun is getting low and the light reflecting off the water makes the air around the boat seem luminous. *Grace* is out there, near *Dragonera,* and the Henrys are aboard. Frank Henry is standing in the cockpit, and he brings his boat up close to the bow of the other—two kindred creations, floating in the luminous air.

∞

During his seventies E. B. White wrote an essay about sailing for *Ford Times*, called "The Sea and the Wind That Blows." Waking or sleeping, he writes, he's always dreaming of boats. He's always "voyaging into unreality, driven by imaginary breezes." In one paragraph he describes the mystery of the allure of a boat.

> *If a man must be obsessed by something, I suppose a boat is as good as anything, perhaps a bit better than most. A small sailing craft is not only beautiful, it is seductive and full of strange promise and the hint of trouble. If it happens to be an auxiliary cruising boat, it is without question the most compact and ingenious arrangement for living ever devised by the restless mind of man—a home that is stable*

without being stationary, shaped less like a box than like a fish or a girl, and in which the homeowner can remove his daily affairs as far from shore as he has the nerve to take them, close hauled or running free—parlor, bedroom, and bath, suspended and alive.

White writes that he likes to sail alone, that it's like being with a girl in that you don't want anyone else along—but sailing has lately become more of a compulsion and less of a pleasure. "With me," he writes, "I cannot not sail." (Something he also said about writing.) He's lost touch with the wind, but doesn't know when to quit the sea. He's written a note to the boatyard to put the boat up for sale, but doubts he means it. He knows that when the breeze comes, the sloop will be there, and he'll get underway. He'll pass by the Torrey Islands, dodge the lobster buoys:

> *And with the tiller in my hand, I'll feel again the wind imparting life to a boat, will smell again the old menace, the one that imparts life to me: the cruel beauty of the salt world, the barnacle's tiny knives, the sharp spine of the urchin, the stinger of the sun jelly, the claw of the crab.*

It was an essay that Joel would read when making the tape recording of his dad's works in 1996. That tape recording had its beginning in the year after E. B. White had fallen after a canoe trip and struck his head, a year when he was confined to the house, and when Joel visited him daily, reading his work aloud. During that year, from 1984 until 1985, Joel not only got to know his dad's work, he got to know his dad a lot better. Though there had always been respect and love between them, Joel hadn't been close to his dad up until that time, he said. As E. B. White's gardener, Henry Allen, described their relationship, it was "close but not close."

It was also during that year that Joel came into his own as a writer. According to Martha White, when Joel wrote he felt close to his dad. Though he found the act of writing an "excruciating" process.

WoodenBoat was his primary forum, in the design reviews that began appearing in 1984. Joel had written other pieces for the magazine, going back to 1979 with "Peapods Are for Sailing." Technical writing throughout, with information such as "I use a three-inch hole saw to bore through the seat and make the mast about $2^7/8$ inches in diameter," and "The step has a round tapered hole that fits the taper at the foot of the mast. A little tallow or Vaseline at step and partners will allow . . . ," the piece ends with a characteristic flourish, a description of five people getting into the rowboat for a sail: "And that smoking run back down the river, with white caps, almost curling over the gunwales and an oar astern to help her! Try it, you'll like it!" Other technical pieces occasionally followed in *WoodenBoat,* titles such as "Other Ways: Liberated Caulking" and "On Paint Primers."

The design review "26′ Canoe Sterned Sloop" appeared in the magazine in January 1984. In this piece Joel looked at some familiar sources, a Charles Witholz interpretation of the canoe yawl *Eel,* a boat that appeared in Uffa Fox's *Sailing, Seamanship, and Yacht Construction,* the book about design he'd read in his teens after discovering it in his father's library. He praises the boat's length-displacement ratio, explaining that it will make the sloop very fast, and he gently criticizes the placement of the mast, which shouldn't be stepped on the cabin-top roof, and ends the piece with "I particularly like this design because modern ideas are so nicely mated with traditional good looks. Interestingly, it bears no resemblance whatsoever to the earlier canoe yawl *Eel,* from which it grew."

A few months later "The Feel of a Deepwater Vessel" appeared, a review of a 21-foot Nelson Zimmer sloop. Joel likes the spring of the sheer, the bold stem profile, the well-proportioned cabin trunk, the high-peaked gaff sail plan, and writes: "She certainly appeals to me. I built a boat for my dad a number of years ago that was very similar in size and type, and she has given great pleasure and good service—as would the Zimmer sloop." He ends the piece with "Below, simplicity is the theme." There's no engine, but "I would prefer to keep her a pure sailer, counting on the large rig to get me home in light airs. Were I to build one, I would be tempted to fool around with the cockpit seats—widening them and slanting them a bit, and making the cockpit coaming smooth on the inside for a more comfortable backrest. What a joy she would be!"

In "Light for Its Length," July 1984, Joel looks at an ultralight sailboat designed to be built by amateur builders, warning against using an ultralight retractable keel centerboard boat for cruising: "This is fine when the crew is alert and active and the weather is not too bad. But suddenly, when the weather is just awful, big seas are crashing aboard, the crew is seasick, exhausted, or both, and the lead ballast is slopping back and forth in the centerboard trunk instead of being securely fastened to the underside of the hull—well, that's just not my cup of tea." He ends by dispelling some of the illusion of building a boat at home: "But remember: three or four weekends of work won't finish it. A quarter an hour of labor per pound of displacement isn't a bad figure for estimating time on most wooden boats. For the Ensenada 25, that works out to nineteen 40-hour work weeks."

"Grace and Speed at Sea," appearing in November 1984, reviews *Porpoise,* a 60-foot sportfishing boat designed by Geerd Hendel. He says he's never seen the boat, just as he's never seen Sophia Loren, but that in no way diminishes his respect. "The long, continuous flow of the sheerline, starting from a relatively low freeboard at the after end of the superstructure, and rising steadily to the flaring clipper bow profile, is one element of the design that gladdens the eye." Saying that "beauty is so rare and nowadays so neglected in the design process," he criticizes a trend he's seen in modern design. "Most modern powerboats fall into two categories of appearance. The first is based on maximum interior volume on minimum overall length, and the resulting designs look like condominiums afloat—Winnebagos of the waterways. The other is based on the Buck Rogers spaceship concept. The aim here seems to be to design something that will float, but look as little as a boat as possible. Most such boats would be improved in looks with the addition of wings. The interior decor leans heavily on the use of shag carpeting, even on the overheads."

The writing in the design reviews throughout 1984 is authoritative, informative, and at times entertaining. But it can be said that the review of *Martha,* appearing in January 1985, was of a different kind. The voice of the writer has come into its own in this piece when Joel writes about the boat he built for his dad, during the time he was reading to his dad. "Simplicity, Not Extravagance" begins:

> *I have a theory, difficult to prove but intriguing to think about, that the best yacht designers are able to instill some of their character traits into their designs. Nat Herreshoff, genius designer, workaholic, a demon for speed, turned out a huge body of work, meticulously designed and crafted, fast and long-lived. His son, L. Francis, was inventive, eccentric, a lover of beauty and simplicity; he*

produced a number of beautiful and simple yachts as well as some that were more inventive than beautiful. John Alden, ardent racer and deep water sailor, took the fisherman-type schooner and modified the design into offshore yachts that were simple, strong, and economically appealing to the yachtsmen of the Depression years.

I am sorry that I never knew S. S. (Sam) Crocker, but over the years I have come to know a number of his boats. I have built two boats to his design, stored and maintained several others. If my theory is correct, Sam Crocker must have been a practical, sensible man, one who enjoyed comfort and rugged good looks, a man who preferred simplicity to extravagance. . . .

In 1967, I was privileged to build the little sloop shown here for a rather special client. I had a great deal of enjoyment with the project, and the client has enjoyed a great little boat for the past 17 years. The passage of time has diminished his use of the sloop, but his grandchildren and great-grandchildren sail her now.

It's interesting to observe that while Joel is defining the traits of the designers he most admires, he's using terms that also would come to describe him and his work: Nat Herreshoff (workaholic, meticulous), L. Francis Herreshoff (lover of beauty and simplicity), Sam Crocker (practical and sensible). In a parallel vein, some of these words also apply to E. B. White's writing. Joel writes of the boat:

Perhaps more than any other boat in Center Harbor, people stop to admire her looks and inquire about the origins of this sloop named Martha. I can see her now out of my drafting-room window, looking extremely jaunty with her dark green topsides, red bottom, white topstrake and cabin sides. Her spars and deck are painted a fisherman buff, and her trailboards have three leaping dolphins picked out in gold leaf. The only varnished item on the boat is her oak tiller.

Joel ends the piece not with a simple flourish but with his own philosophy of the practical function of beauty:

I have another theory, one which I think can be proved, that good-looking boats last longer than plain ones. The boat that gives one pleasure merely to look at it is a great joy, evoking favorable comment from others. This fills the owner with pride, causing him to take extra care with the boat's appearance. More attention is paid to a handsome craft by everyone involved in her care, whether owner or paid professional; her paint and varnish are better kept, dirt and grime are washed away, problems are dealt with as soon as they appear. Such a boat will last much longer than the homely and less-loved craft on the next mooring. I suspect Mr. Crocker knew this to be true; certainly he designed attractive boats, and many of them have aged gracefully. We look after a 40' Crocker ketch that was built in 1936, and is still in the hands of the original owner. It would be hard to improve on that longevity record.

During the same period Joel wrote the introduction to a book about Crocker's designs, called *Sam Crocker's Boats*, and again it's interesting to look at Joel's career as a designer in light of what he has to say about Crocker. Joel explains that Crocker spent most of his career designing sailing cruisers of 20 to 60 feet, both by choice and because of the clients he had. He describes the typical Crocker boat—short ends, "good sheer with considerable height at the bow," hollow waterlines, low cabin house, a big and comfortable cockpit, "all blended to give a staunch, workmanlike feeling to the vessel and a general sense of looking 'right.' " He praises Crocker's construction plans for their "clarity, completeness, and—happily—simplicity," and says that by looking at the layout of the backbone timbers it's obvious that he was a boatbuilder. Joel tells of the Crocker boat he mentioned at the end of the *Martha* review, *Lands End,* that it had spent fifty years in the same family and was presently stored in a shed at Center Harbor, and he tells of going below in another Crocker boat, *Blue Peter,* where he found "comfort, serenity, and good cheer," and as the owner mixed cocktails, "realized for the first time that cruising doesn't have to be like a camping trip." In the final paragraph he says that the Crocker boats have a timeless quality, and Joel expresses what might be a bit of envy when he writes that Crocker "was fortunate enough to have spent his working years during the heyday of American wooden yacht building, his career coming to an end before the near demise of the craft in the 1960s and 1970s."

Early in his career Joel built Crocker boats, and designs of his own, of traditional construction with sturdy backbone timbers, but then the fiberglass era came along and his career was disrupted. But writing in 1984 and 1985, he didn't know Brooklin Boat Yard would soon enter into another era, the cold-molded one, and that rather than emulating Crocker, the Herreshoffs would become the source from which he departed.

After the death of E. B. White, in the December 1985 issue of *WoodenBoat,* Joel examines an early cold-molded boat in Cyrus

Hamlin's *Wanderer*. He wrote that the boat "is a design that was ahead of its time when drawn 25 years ago, and it remains one whose time has never come, for no boat has ever been built to the plans." The light displacement was possible because of the strong construction—a backbone of laminated oak, cedar strip planking, two layers of mahogany veneers, glued and nailed. Joel writes that he's had continuous contact with Hamlin's cold-molded boats over the years, as builder and maintainer, and was convinced the system worked and required less maintenance.

In this essay, written during a time when Joel was most truly a son, and when he was about to turn the boatyard over to his own son, he ends with this paragraph of lyric beauty:

> *Perhaps the first* Wanderer *will slip into Center Harbor at sunset. The owners, friendly folk, will invite me aboard, and sitting below at the cabin table, I will look around and it will be just as I imagined it—the feeling of space and comfort, soft highlights glinting off the varnished trim, the combination of aromas that emanate from the interior of a choice wooden vessel—cedar, teak, and tar, supper and rum, and the accumulated wind and sunshine of a good day's run.*

Increasingly as the months passed Joel reviewed cold-molded boats that were traditional in concept but modern in design. In "A Contemporary Cutter," a Charles Witholz design for a 49-foot cruiser, he writes: "Witholz is one of America's most versatile naval-architects, and I find all his designs good-looking, well-engineered, and carefully conceived. This cutter, using glued strip-planking over laminated frames and backbone, shows his adaptability in the use of new construction techniques and 1980s styling."

In the March 1988 review "*Oceanus*—Old and New," he looks at the William Garden design that would figure into *Dragonera* and says: "It is an axiom of sailboat design that long waterlines and light displacements always produce speedy shapes; hence the long hull, narrow beam and light weight. . . . This is a big, simple, beautiful boat that will sail with the grace of a greyhound."

In July 1988, in the review "*Saskianna*—Bruce King Contemporary Cutter," he describes the sources of the design and writes: "So all these 'traditional' features have real reasons for being there—not just that King was trying to make the boat look like an L. Francis Herreshoff design. He can design good-looking boats on his own, without having to imitate anyone."

And in December 1988, in "St. Lawrence Yawl," a Tim Evans design, Joel writes that this boat, of cold-molded construction with a ballasted fin keel and skeg-mounted rudder, puts him in "a 19th century frame of mind" above water.

Most of the designs falling into this category try to exploit some of the so-called advantages of modern technology while retaining the basic character of the original type from which they are derived. Many owners like and want the aesthetic feel of an earlier boat while hoping to sail faster, to have a boat requiring less maintenance, and to be able to cruise in luxury rather than in cramped quarters found in the original vessels. One can hardly argue with the validity of these aspirations, but achieving them is not always easy.

While examining and debating the technical and philosophical approaches of the trend in cold molding, Joel also wrote the text for a book of boat photography by Benjamin Mendlowitz, called *Wood, Water & Light*, published in 1988. Twenty-four boats are depicted, ranging from 14-foot Maine peapod rowboats to a 96-foot power yacht that cruises in Seattle. Many of the boats, at least half of them, can be seen in the waters around Center Harbor and in Penobscot Bay, and to some degree in *Wood, Water & Light* Joel is writing a private memoir. His text has, he states in the introduction, a "thread of wistful lament for changing times," unintentional but there nevertheless. "I have been around long enough to know that there is always change, and the world of wooden boats is not immune from it. . . . The wooden boat, however, will not vanish in my lifetime, nor in yours; fine wooden boats are being built every day."

The opening essay looks at *Aida,* Anne and Maynard Bray's 34-foot Nathanael Herreshoff cruising yawl (the book is dedicated to the Brays). "*Aida* is a lucky boat. Designed by Herreshoff of Bristol, she is owned by . . . two of the most enthusiast and capable Herreshoff buffs anywhere. It is obvious that *Aida* is treated as a member of the family, and thrives in their care." He describes the care given her, the use, the accommodations, says she was built in 1926, and goes into the pedigree: "*Aida* reminds me of *Alerion,* but half again as big and somewhat stouter."

Writing of *Intermezzo II,* a 1929 runabout, a lake boat, Joel writes that he is a saltwater dweller, but "there is something that happens on a lake deep in the woods—time flows more slowly there, and contentment seems to rise from the surface of the water."

In a chapter on wooden lobster boats, he writes that although fiberglass boats have replaced the wooden ones forever, "some of the wooden boats which were the forerunners of these modern workhorses were beautiful examples of functional design and construction, executed by a variety of small boat shops along the coast. The shops were usually one- or two-man enterprises, and each master builder developed his own designs and construction methods."

The treatment of the Herreshoff 12½ features a photograph of Joel's *Shadow* at a mooring in Center Harbor and on a cradle in the boatyard. "The Herreshoff 12½ is probably the best small boat design ever drawn. . . . They seem much bigger than they are—more like a tiny ship than a small boat. . . . The magic of these boats lies not only in their good qualities but in the beauty of their shape. Handsome from all angles, the beauty of the bow is of particular interest."

Joel looks at the Maine schooners that work the tourist trade, the *Heritage,* the *Stephen Taber,* the *J. & E. Riggin,* the *Mary Day,* and he looks at the peapods built in Brooklin by Jimmy Steele, who had once worked for Arno Day. In a chapter on *Jericho,* a Bunker and Ellis powerboat built in 1956 on Mount Desert Island, Joel tells of Jericho Bay, "the lower extension of Blue Hill Bay, one of the prettiest stretches of water anywhere . . ." In a chapter on Beetle Cats, a fleet racing along reminds Joel of a flock of ducks, "splashing about with immense good cheer and an unconscious feeling of invincibility." In a section on sardine carriers, one of them, *Pauline,* is up for sale, "a victim of changing times and the mysteries of the herring schools . . ." (Joel would soon get the commission to design a conversion of *Pauline* for passenger-carrying cruises for hire.)

The climactic chapter of *Wood, Water & Light* is a treatment of *Cirrus,* the Herreshoff Fishers Island 31 that had been in Brooklin since Joel was a boy. He tells about Alan Bemis, who owned the boat for fifty years, "loved her, cared for her, enjoyed her, and perfected her," and says that when Bemis decided to give the boat up a few years ago, "all those who knew the man and the boat felt the wrench of separation." Joel says that his first commission as a naval architect in 1954 was to design a new sail plan for a yawl rig for *Cirrus*. He describes the boat:

> *Cirrus is red and beautiful. Above her "special red" topsides, a wide band of varnished teak top strake and rail stretch from bow to stern, with a gold-leaf cove strip separating the two and accentuating the sheer. Her sheer line is classic and without blemish. When the wind is right, she heels to the gold stripe, which dances just above the rushing leeside wave, her sheer exactly conforming to the water bent by her passage. Her white sails are reflected in the water below. Under sail, she is a picture; once seen, she is not soon forgotten. There is nothing quite like her.*

Joel also describes a fiftieth birthday party for *Cirrus* held in 1980 in Brooklin. Many other Fisher Island 31s arrived. *Cirrus* floated at the dock, where people admired her:

> *Looking out the picture window onto the dock scene below, it was easy to time-warp back several decades, when all the boats were wooden, and I was just a boy sailing a Herreshoff 12½, wonderstruck at the big red sloop rushing to windward in a smother of foam.*

Reading this last line, you could think it was the kind of image that Joel had been waiting to write, waiting since boyhood. And you could think that the clarity of the line went back to his father's writing, which Joel knew so well then. And you could also think back further, to the E. B. White essay "Once More to the Lake," and of the theme of the father seeing himself in the son. It was something to think of how the boy from "Once More to the Lake," the boy in *Shadow,* became a writer, of how the boy took the role of the father again, and of how it must have felt to his father in that time. Could a writer ask for anything more, at the end of life, than to have his child read his work to him? It's too bad that E. B. White couldn't have written about it.

⟡

Joel continued to write design reviews into the 1990s—though by 1996 he was thinking it was time to stop. One of his favorites was the 1992 review of his own boat, *Northern Crown,* written just after he'd sold it to his daughter Martha and her husband, Taylor Allen. Joel tells of how in 1957 he saw a photo of *Northern Crown* in a magazine, and saved it. When he saw the boat advertised for sale in Camden in 1972 he bought it. He says he's happy to write the review of a boat he knows so intimately, but "boat ownership is such a subjective thing—a love affair, in effect—that I may find it more difficult to be objective." He describes the beautifully sculpted round stern, and says that on voyages to Cape Breton and Bermuda the hull has proved seaworthy. "We have only once filled her cockpit with water, while running before a gale across the Strait of Canso." The cabin has a feeling of "beauty, comfort, and fine craftsmanship without being fussy or ornate." He speculates on what one learns from sailing a boat for twenty years. Boats have a character, felt by their crews. *Northern Crown*'s character is "one of competence, sturdiness, and unquestioned ability. Her seaworthiness is supreme. I find her beautiful, in a rugged sort of way, not delicate or dainty, but beautiful nonetheless." He says that it's a strange feeling now to look out the window and find her mooring empty.

Looking through Joel's design reviews and his other writings through the 1980s and into the 1990s, it does seem that the inspiration that blossomed in the review of *Martha* culminated in a review of a boat called *Candle in the Wind,* which appeared in *Wooden-Boat* in September 1992. In this essay Joel tells the story of the development of the boat, a 30-foot yawl built at the Gannon and Benjamin Boat Yard in Martha's Vineyard. An Englishman with a summer home in Massachusetts, hoping to keep two teenaged boys busy, specified he wanted a two-masted gaff rig without a self-tending jib and the maximum number of strings to pull. The designer Nat Benjamin, Joel writes, enjoyed the challenge of finding a blend of performance, comfort, and good looks. Here again Joel speaks of simplicity, as he'd long experienced it:

> The greatest fun in boating usually comes in the simplest boats. The main thing that so attracted me to sailing and particularly to cruising more than 50 years ago was the total change in lifestyle—no hot baths, an icebox with real ice rather than a refrigerator, oil lamps, the isolation from the daily affairs on shore, the good smell of tarred marline and manila rope mixed with the aroma of cedar and bilgewater—all combined to make even an overnight cruise an adventure. Curled up in the red Hudson Bay blanket on the kapok bunk cushion, listening to the water moving against the hull, I felt transported to a different world. And I still feel that way about cruising.
>
> Most modern boats are simply too complicated. They are so full of systems, which all too often fail to work, that the feeling of self-reliance—that wonderful ingredient in the pleasures of cruising—is now missing. The modern cruising boat makes the owner a slave to the systems and to the

chore of keeping them all working. . . . On my Dad's old
cutter Astrid, *the only "system" was the 1932 four cylinder*
Palmer, and I don't recall that it ever failed to start. We
never missed an expedition, whether for mackerel fishing, or
for a weekend cruise, due to system failure. Keep it simple
and have more fun.

And of course one could find resonance again with the work
of his father, and with his father's favorite writer, in the essay "A
Slight Sound at Evening," about Thoreau and *Walden*:

> *In our uneasy season, when all men unconsciously*
> *seek a retreat from a world that has got almost completely*
> *out of hand, his house in the Concord woods is a haven. In*
> *our culture of gadgetry and the multiplicity of convenience,*
> *his cry "Simplicity, simplicity, simplicity!" has the insistence*
> *of a fire alarm.*

Beauty, simplicity, practicality—all the way down the line,
you might say.

⁓

Henry Allen lives on the road that runs through Brooklin. He
was the gardener and caretaker for E. B. and Katharine White,
working for them for thirty-six years. Henry appears here and there
in E. B. White's writing—suggesting a remedy for a sick pig, cutting
cords of wood, passing bulbs from a bag to Katharine. In "Clear
Days," from *One Man's Meat*, Henry tells about how he killed five
foxes. "It was the first chance Henry had ever had to tell me con-
fidentially about himself, and it seemed significant that he had

plunged without preliminaries into his triumphant chapter. From his dull galaxy of days he had picked out these five bright mornings. Every man has his memory of achievement. It is something to have known where a fox was going to cross the road."

Henry and his wife have a summer home and a winter home. They're both on the Brooklin road, about a mile apart. They own one, an uncle owns the other. Sitting on the porch of the western-most place, Henry talks about his days of employment, his work in the garden:

"First day, I waited around. Mr. White came out and said, 'This is your place. You do what you want.' They made it easy. The first caretaker, he wouldn't let Mr. White work with him, but he worked with me. I told him that he had to put up with me talking to myself. We never had a squabble. We'd work together, weeding the garden and picking out flowers.

"I was on full-time. I would paint in the winter. Painted floors, chopped wood. I just did what I had to do. Gardening, I would go in over breakfast and we'd plan the day. I worked six days a week at first, then went to five. When it came to gardening, I'd be there almost seven. But when I couldn't get there I'd leave a list and tell him what to do, and he'd always do it. He'd always tell me Monday what he'd done.

"Some days he was quiet. I presumed he was thinking, that his mind was working on some book. We'd be working along and he'd say, 'I got to leave you for a minute.' Something would come to his mind and he'd go in to jot it down.

"After I started I went to help them pack. Joel was going off to school. Mr. White said, 'I bet Joe is the first student to go off to MIT with a pocketful of lobster money and a pregnant wife.' Joel was a good fisherman. Lobstering, one summer, two summers.

"Mrs. White was a brilliant woman. Mr. White said, 'She

used to cover up all my mistakes.' When I was there, Mrs. White always came whistling, so I'd know she was coming.

"I'd take him down to the train. One time we went to Bangor. We were late leaving, and when we got close to Bangor we had a flat tire. We couldn't get the jack under the car. I told him to go to a house and call a taxi. I got it fixed after he left. Mr. White sent me a nice letter, and he sent me five dollars to clean my clothes.

"Sometimes he was funny. He loved his animals, especially the sheep. He enjoyed them immensely, fussing over them.

"One Memorial Day service, he spoke at the church. He had to walk all the way down from North Brooklin, to get his mind settled and to quiet himself. He said it was hard to speak in front of a group. He'd rather talk one on one.

"When Mrs. White died, I was the only one at the service who wasn't part of the family. The flowers were from my garden. Mr. White and I put them together. Mr. White had gone to the church, but he couldn't go to the funeral. He didn't want people to see him break down. I went to see him the next morning to have coffee, and he was quite upset. He told me how terribly he felt. We talked close.

"They were thoughtful of the community. The library was their pride and joy.

"He had a small boat, *Fern,* then *Martha.* He would go sailing in August, maybe four or five times during the month. The last of it, a friend would go with him. They enjoyed each other's company.

"Mr. White was sick about a year. He went to Walker's Pond to go canoeing, stubbed his toe on a limb and fell down. After that I noticed it. He had trouble remembering.

"Joel was very faithful to him that year. He was busy before that, but he took time out. He read to him every day. The next morning Mr. White would tell me what he read. It helped him pass the time. He was worried about things, about losing his mind, about not being able to remember things. Joel was awful good to him. He didn't hurry, he'd come in and talk to him.

"Joel looks like his father. He walks like his father. Always did. Some people might not see it, but I can. He's just about Mr. White's stature. The voices are a little different, but not much."

Every man *does* have his memory of achievement. It is something to have worked in the garden. Again, with a smile, Henry says of Mr. White:

"Sometimes he'd just go. When he'd come back he'd say, 'Well, I had to get that thought down.'"

Chapter 2

Setting Up

October 1996

Early on a fall morning before sunrise the sky above Center Harbor flushes with gold and streaks with blue. The sun rises over the trees on the eastern cove, and in a moment, the mast tops in the harbor light up. As the hulls grow bright, so does the far shore on Deer Isle, the leaves growing reddish gold. The daylight moves down the tree trunks on Chatto Island, and travels along the shore, over the green rockweed and the brown granite, the barnacles and black mussels, and from the weather vane on top of the tower down to the buildings at the yard and to the dock.

Pip and Judy Wick are carrying groceries down the dock and stowing them aboard *Lucayo,* supplies for their trip to Bermuda. Pip has on a fur hat, and is red-faced in the cool morning. He looks happy and excited and worried at once.

"Nice day."

"It's supposed to get terrible in a couple of days," Pip says.

"You'll be in a different place by then."

"I hope it's different enough."

Judy Wick says they'll be back in November for Thanksgiving. Later, Pip says the same. "What a life," I say.

"Somebody's got to live it," Pip answers. "Might as well be me." The day warming, *Lucayo* casts free, passes through the harbor and into the Reach.

Boats are coming out of the water every day now, but a few remain. There's *Free Spirit,* Jon Wilson's Concordia sloop, and nearby, two Concordia yawls. The long and sleek P-Boat, *Olympian. Ellisha* and *Cirrus.* Mike O'Brien's Tancook Whaler, a fiberglass reduction of the traditional Nova Scotia fishing schooner. *Blue Witch,* a Boothbay 21. A Herreshoff 12½. Furthest out in the deepest water, *Senta,* a 56-foot Philip Rhodes cutter.

The crew begins to arrive, the pickup trucks and cars coming down the hill, and the workers go into the shop, gathering at the south end by the woodstove, by a bank of windows looking out on the harbor. At 7 A.M. there are about twenty-five men there, and the talk grows louder and louder until with a word from Steve, they get up from the benches and chairs, or break from their standing groups, and go off to their various jobs.

There's room for three full-sized boats in the shop, and last winter three had been built there, *Grace, Linda,* and *Tomahawk,* the Buzzards Bay 25. Two of the spaces face the overhead bay doors in the newer part of the building by the parking lot. The third is in the southern end, tucked in a niche amid the woodworking shop. The woodstove and gathering area is nearby, the band saw and drill press and table saw and planer, and hanging from the ceiling, a roll of tissue paper the workers use to clean themselves off and blow the dust from their noses. There are notices and memos tacked to the beams, for investment plans and vacation time, and underneath the stairway to the second floor, pads of time-and-material sheets used for the ongoing repair and new construction jobs. The woodworking shop has an elevated wood floor, and along the western side are scarred workbenches with wooden vises, and by the windows on the west wall are stacks of long drill bits, reflecting a steely light. There's a view to the west, to Deer Isle. Saw blades hang in the windows, and there are piles of wood, and various relics such as the sign that reads *Aurora,* or upstairs, a dusty framed photo of the sloop *Martha.*

The south end of the shop is built up to within a few feet of the granite-and-concrete wall that faces the water and at high tide breaks the waves. During storms, water splashes on the windows, and sometimes spills over and floods into the building.

The woodworking shop is L-shaped, and the boatbuilding space fits into the L. There's a second floor, set up so that it forms a balcony from which the boatbuilders can walk on the deck of a boat in the works. One crew can be working on the hull on the ground floor while others can come and go to the deck and interior, walking onto the boat from upstairs just as they might from a dock.

And so the shop is divided roughly into four quarters—three boatbuilding spaces and a woodworking shop with two floors. On this day, *Grace* is in a front bay and a painter, Kevin Duddy, is giving her a coat of varnish—he moves to and from the boat from the balcony. Below, a boatbuilder, Pete Chase, has taken off *Grace*'s rudder and is adjusting the rudder stock, which had been turning stiffly. (*Linda* has the same problem, and will also get this warranty work—the boat is now being sailed from Connecticut and will arrive in another day.)

Next to *Grace,* in the right forward space of the shop, is the newly built 22-foot runabout on which two boatbuilders, Norm Whyte and Bob Stephens, are installing a teak deck.

In the bay at the south end, Rick Clifton and Brian Stevens are setting up the molds for the next Center Harbor 31. This boat will be owned by Jim Geier, a retired businessman who summers in

Boothbay. He had seen *Linda* on her trip south last summer and sailed on her. Geier had long been a fan of various Herreshoff boats, and he'd been impressed with *Linda*'s handling abilities. This would be a sloop, and it would have accommodations similar to *Linda*'s, but Geier had asked Joel to stretch the boat out a little, to get the more elegant proportions of *Grace*. This Center Harbor 31 would consequently be closer to 33 feet in length. The launch date is now set for May.

The molds look like slices of bread, but with spaces between them—an incomplete loaf. The hull is being built upside down, and so each mold is a bell-shaped slice that represents the interior shape of the hull. There are eighteen in all, standing up on a platform called a "strongback." The smallest mold is at the front near where the bow will be, and is about three feet tall; over it arches the long tusk-shaped stem, made of sixteen laminated layers of ash, that reaches down to the floor. This is a curve, of course, that will form a smart bow, one that knows the difference between large and small waves.

Another mold is at the stern, supporting the frame for the transom. There are molds at the front and back of the cabin, a mold at the aft end of the cockpit. Nine-layer laminated frames are attached to the outer edges of some of the molds and conform to their shapes. Five molds are really permanent bulkheads, transverse walls like the compartment walls in airplanes. Four bulkheads support the cabin, while the fifth is at the aft end of the cockpit where the tiller will be. All bulkheads are meant to strengthen the hull against the pounding of waves (approximately one million cycles in four summers of normal weekend sailing) and the stresses of the wind upon the mast.

Now Rick and Brian are checking the positions of the molds, bracing them, fairing them, and adding small "cheekpieces" to reinforce some of the edges. Another member of the crew, Jeep Gulliver, is at a workbench sanding deck beams.

Rick Clifton is the project manager for the Geier boat—and because of that it will be called "Rick's boat" in the shop. He will be in charge while Steve is away this winter and will be responsible for the boat's outcome. It worries him a bit that Steve won't be here to make decisions. But Rick has an easygoing manner. He smiles often and laughs easily.

On the wall near the molds are two drawings, a construction plan and a strongback drawing, and Rick studies these. He moves from the molds to the drawings, back to the molds and to the drawings again. He says that these molds were used last year for *Grace* and then *Linda,* and then they were stored outdoors for the winter. They'd been uncovered, brought into the shop, and were only now settling down. "They're made of wood, and wood moves," Rick says.

"We work slowly on this part," he says. "If you're careful here, things go well later on. If a mold's out of place or uneven, you might have to take off wood to fair the hull later on."

"You're working from two-dimensional drawings to make a three-dimensional form," I say.

"And it's not square. It's curved."

Brian Stevens has been planing the notch at the top of the molds for the keelson, or inner keel piece—three layers of mahogany, one of plywood, more than twenty feet long—which they will fit in later today. But Rick calls him over to help with the placement of two mold stations, E and J, at the point 9' 7" and 17' 7" from the bow. These are the molds for the forward and aft bulkheads of the cabin. Last year they had been a sixteenth of an inch off, Rick says, and as a result the cabintop, which is built separately, didn't fit into place correctly and they had to make adjustments. Now he checks the measurement with a tape and the placement with a square.

"It's like the old adage," Rick says. "Measure three times and cut once."

With a little smile Brian says, "Measure twice and hammer to fit."

Rick laughs. They fasten a wooden brace, and he moves back to look at the drawings.

Rick is wearing coveralls and a blue corduroy shirt he says is a favorite. He's light on his feet, essential for someone who is working on staging and climbing into boats. He has blue eyes that are penetrating and sympathetic and convey happiness. He has a full-bodied sixties acid laugh, longish graying hair, a mustache, and steel-rimmed glasses that with his thick eyebrows make him look like John Lennon—playing in bands, playing Beatles music, Rick has been accused of being John Lennon. When Rick started at the yard sixteen years ago, he was one of the youngest members of the crew, the first to be hired "from away." Rick had worked with Ken Tainter, Belford Gray, Henry Lawson, and built boats with Joel. Now he was one of the older generation at the shop, and he didn't find it an easy change to accept.

He grew up on the Long Island shore, in Westhampton, and had a "nautical upbringing." There were five boys in his family, and the lesson plan was basically the same for each boy. For four weeks Rick's stepfather, a lawyer, "the Duke, we called him, a huge man, especially in a sixteen-foot dinghy," took the boy out on the water, "taught us how to tack, how to get around the buoys, how to do the right things on the water, how to tie knots," and then left him on his own. "It probably wasn't the best way to learn to sail, but we were on the water from April to October."

On a gaff-rigged sloop that needed a crew of two and "a third member to bail," Rick raced well up into his teens, quitting when he thought that competition was getting the best of his good nature. He went to a college in Maine for a while, and then with his high school girlfriend, later his wife, Jane, went to Oregon to be with a brother who was fishing for salmon. Rick went out fishing with him, a hundred miles offshore in a 35-foot wooden boat that was sixty years old. He was sick the entire time, and thought that if he ever got his own boat he'd stay at anchor. But when he was out at sea he read a copy of *WoodenBoat*. The idea of becoming a boatbuilder "struck a chord with me as it did with hundreds of other people."

They returned to Maine and toured the coast so that Rick could find a job at a boatyard. He soon realized that "it doesn't take long to get denied a job," but in Brooklin he did find one at Benjamin River Boat Yard, in one of its permutations after Frank and Junior Day sold it. The Cliftons packed a U-Haul and drove to Blue Hill, and found a farmhouse to rent, overlooking Blue Hill Bay. But working at Benjamin River was not so sweet. Rick had long hair, and he was from away, and he got ridden hard. He spent nine months scraping and painting the bottoms of hulls, and didn't learn much of anything about boatbuilding. But as he saw it, he didn't leave with a grudge because "there were dues I was overdue in paying."

Rick left Benjamin River Boat Yard to work for Arno Day "because somehow I had gotten him to agree to hire me." He had taken one of Day's boatbuilding courses on Deer Isle and then visited his shop, where Arno was building a Down East pleasure boat, one of his own designs. Arno thought he was getting a finish carpenter, but Rick wasn't at that level yet. Nor did Rick know much about Arno. He realized he'd become a disappointment to Arno after Arno stopped talking to him. After two weeks of the silent treatment Rick picked up his tools and left.

He worked at carpentry and house building and occasionally got work at one of the fiberglass yards finishing off a boat. Every spring for several years Rick went down to Brooklin Boat Yard and asked Joel for a job. During those years Rick built a skiff working from drawings in Howard Chapelle's *Boatbuilding,* and he and Jane had their first child, and "when a nesting panic set in" they bought an old house in West Brooklin. It had a single faucet in the kitchen and two electrical outlets, and a view of the Benjamin River. The house was down the road from Junior Day, and Henry Lawson lived nearby too. Rick got to know Henry, who told him to keep coming to the yard. After a fourth time of applying in the spring ("All you had to do was drive down that road to the harbor and look out there to know there was something good going on") he got a call from Joel, who told him to come down and give it a try.

At first he worked at sanding and painting and wondered if he was right back at the beginning, but he knew something was different. "The place was stable and the people were stable and I figured, If I don't do something really stupid I can make a go of it." Then he worked with Ken Tainter rigging boats, the first time he had set up deepwater sailing boats. When Joel sent Rick down to the dock to do a small carpentry job, putting a hatch cover on a boat, Rick saw it as a test, and figured that if he passed he'd be in the yard permanently.

Working with Tainter, Belford Gray, Henry Lawson, and Joel, Rick figured he learned patience, to not rush headlong into things, to stand back and look the job over and then do the best you could: "I'm not a good learner, but I'm sure I learned a lot from them." In his second winter he worked with Steve White, building three peapods. He worked with Joel building the first Bangor Packet. Rick and Steve built the mold for the second Bangor Packet, and then built about a dozen more. They built a cold-molded dinghy laid up over another dinghy to give it shape. In 1987 Rick and Steve worked on building Marsh Cat, Joel's cold-molded catboat design. And he helped put the planking on *Vortex*.

But it took Rick a while to warm up to cold-molding. He saw himself as a traditionalist, someone who "loved working with timbers, linseed oil, bedding compound, bronze screws." In cold-molding there was an obvious contrast, working with "plastics, a lot of glue, no gloves," materials "not as friendly as oak and cedar." Steve was sensitive about these feelings, Rick thought, and often put him on rebuilding projects. He rebuilt several Herreshoff 12½s.

The transition from traditional wooden construction to cold-molded construction was something that Rick saw as a transition from Joel's to Steve's management. Because he thought both of them were nice people, it made the transition easier. There was also the change from an older crew to a younger one, during which from one decade to the next Rick became a senior member. He sometimes felt like he was a postgrad in a college fraternity, though the younger people had also made the yard full of life.

But sometimes Rick wondered, How much longer? He was forty-five: could he see himself there at sixty? He figured that the reason he had been at the yard so long was because of the family. They had never questioned him when he said he had to leave to do something. They had trusted him.

Rick knew that the Whites trusted him when during his second year at the yard, Joel asked him to drive E. B. White to Maine from New York. White had been in Florida, taken his car by train to Washington, and driven to New York. But the trip from there to Brooklin was a long one, and so Rick was asked to do some driving.

He went to Long Island to visit his family, then took a bus into New York and met E.B. at the Algonquin Hotel. Rick went to the room and they had a martini, mixed from a leather case. It was very impressive. They went down to the dining room, had lunch, and then got into E.B.'s car and drove to Massachusetts.

E.B. liked to stop at the same places, and on these trips to Maine he usually stopped in Sturbridge and stayed at the Sturbridge Inn. There Rick and E.B. had two martinis and dinner. Rick was rocked. ("Was he funny?" "He was when he got a couple of martinis in him.") The next morning they drove to Portsmouth, New Hampshire, and had lunch at the Burnham Inn, where E.B. always had lunch, and then Rick drove the last leg of the journey to Maine.

Rick had seen E. B. White around the yard at times. He would come by to watch, but he never asked questions—probably because he didn't want to interrupt, Rick figured. But along the way he asked a lot of questions about the yard and Joel. He wanted to know what they had been building, what Joel had been doing. Rick had the feeling that Joel had done his own thing, and that his father was trying to learn about it, but it also seemed that E.B. may have known some of the answers and just wanted to hear them from a different voice. Rick remembered thinking it strange that such a shy man could produce such great writing. Back in Brooklin, he bought E. B. White's *Letters*.

Later Rick and Brian and Jeep Gulliver pick up the inner keel, the backbone of the boat, and set it into place on the top of the molds. It lands with a ring. The hull, the "she," the receptive shape, something to rest the eye on, is yet to come. A pencil in his ear, a hand at his chin, Rick stands in front of the drawings and looks hard, looks ahead.

❧

White on White is selling well at the General Store. The tape includes excerpts from E. B. White's letters, the poem "Song of the Queen Bee," excerpts from the essay "The Ring of Time," and all of "The Sea and the Wind That Blows" ("I inherited my dad's love of boats big time," Joel says in his introduction to the essay). It ends with the love poem "Natural History." Lorna at the General Store ordered twenty-four tapes. She sold four the first night, ten the next day, and now has only four left—"what's right there," she says, pointing to the stack by the case of baked goods on the counter. Of E. B. White, Lorna says that "he was known and admired around here." And protected too, Joel has said: those who would come to Brooklin looking for E. B. White would hear, "E.B. who?"

As for Joel, when I asked if he'd been the model for Henry Fussy, he laughed and said, "I guess these things all come around eventually."

Joel has undergone his last chemotherapy treatment, he's been told. He's walking with only a cane now and is close to letting go of that. He's in what is perhaps his most creative and productive period. There are the new CH 31s and their modifications. He's designed the 63-foot ketch. Luke Allen, the father of Joel's son-in-law, Taylor Allen, has commissioned a design for a 44-foot Down East powerboat, to be called *Boss Lady*.

And yesterday a contract has been signed for a most ambitious project. A real estate developer from Massachusetts wants to design and build a fleet of 76-foot racing sloops. The inspiration is the Herreshoff New York 50, nine of which were built in 1913, the last boats of that size to be built for a racing class. This man, Donald Tofias, has paid $5,000 for the rights to the design Joel will create. He plans to promote the boat and look for other parties interested in owning what will be called the W-Class racers. Previously Tofias had his Starling Burgess cutter *Arawak* (formerly *Christmas*) rebuilt at Taylor Allen's yard, Rockport Marine. The plan at this stage is that the W-Class boats will be built both at Rockport Marine and at Brooklin Boat Yard. Joel is just beginning the sail plan.

Steve has spent a week in Bermuda, getting *Vortex* ready for the sail to Antigua, in November. Now he's getting things in order, tending to the beginning of the Center Harbor 31, to the design contracts for the W-76 and *Boss Lady,* and to various repair jobs, such as the last of the planking of the Trumpy motor yacht, and another big job about to start, a keel replacement on a Sparkman and Stephens sloop called *Fidelio,* a job that will cost about $34,000. Eight men have been working on the Trumpy, and soon they'll be moved to *Fidelio* and to the Center Harbor 31s. The quarters of the Trumpy look like a comfortable place to be. There's a full galley, hardwood paneling, staterooms with four-poster beds. There's been a last-minute addition, after the owner called and told Steve that his wife had asked about the holly-and-teak floor in the head, that he'd forgotten about it, and that it was the only time she'd ever shown interest in the boat. So Steve took Norm Whyte and Bob Stephens off the 22-foot runabout long enough for them to put in a holly-and-teak floor.

Now Norm and Bob are back on the 22-footer, working in the space just ahead of Rick's boat. The name of the 22-footer will be written in Chinese characters, a word they're pronouncing as

Cow Lung. Norm and Bob are "nibbing" the teak deck, cutting and notching the pieces so that no ends come to a sharp point. Most of the strips are curved, and nibbing requires a sure hand. Norm Whyte has that skill. Though he's only been at Brooklin Boat Yard since April, he's been working as a boatbuilder, he says, for "twenty-nine years on October 23, whenever that was." That was a few days ago. Norm started building boats at fifteen, in Findhorn, Scotland, serving a five-year apprenticeship with his "auld man," who built boats for the salmon companies over a period of fifty years. When the shore salmon fisheries declined, Norm started his own yard, building fishing and sailing boats. Steve hired Norm Whyte figuring that if he had been able to make a living building small boats on the coast of Scotland, he had to be good. His wife, an American, had asked if they could try America for a while, and so Norm had leased his shop to an employee, and they'd moved with their son to Blue Hill. Steve has already assigned Norm as the project manager for the fourth Center Harbor 31, which they'd start after Rick's crew finished with the molds.

Norm is in his mid-forties, about five foot six. Wearing kneepads, he moves quickly over the deck, his eyes lighting up now and then with the developments of the work. He makes little jokes and observations, tossing his head back when he laughs.

Bob Stephens is about ten years younger than Norm and a bit taller. He tends more toward the serious side than Norm, and is more the intellectual kind of boatbuilder, someone who as a boy kept Howard Chapelle's *American Small Sailing Craft* on his bedside table. He's written articles for *WoodenBoat* on the Adirondack guide boat and the Whitehall rowing boat. Last year Bob was the project manager for the first two CH 31s. He's also a draftsman and a boat designer, and Bob has drawn the construction plan and strongback plan that Rick is presently consulting in the south end of the shop. When Steve goes to the Caribbean this winter, Bob will be working in the design studio with Joel. Though he's glad to be availed of Norm's experience, and though Bob likes being a boat-builder, he's very much looking forward to spending the winter with Joel upstairs.

As he nibs the deck, Bob's kneepads aren't keeping him from getting sore. He straightens up, resting the butts of his hands on his knees, and his eyes seem to go wide in some kind of recognition.

I wonder if Bob intends to build a boat of his own someday. It's a commonly held dream around here, one that is often realized. I've seen a backyard project, a beamy 39-foot ketch being built by Todd Skoog, who works at Benjamin River Marine. The boat is two or three years from launching, and Skoog intends to live aboard it.

"It's about a twelve-thousand-hour job," Bob says of Skoog's boat. "A lot of time. Todd is about halfway done." Bob owns a 31-foot sloop, built in Germany in 1959, and he is planning to build an addition on his house, a room for his young daughter, but Bob thinks he might like to build a schooner someday, maybe about 40 feet. "But half the displacement of the boat Todd is building. The displacement of a boat is a good indicator of the time and money involved."

"Displacement is also equal to the weight of the boat, right?" Meaning that the amount of water displaced by a boat is equal to its weight.

"Exactly equal," Bob says.

These seem odd equivalencies, the idea that a water's weight could be equal to the time and money spent displacing it. Didn't that make a unit of water equivalent to a unit of time, and didn't this seem right, that in the boatbuilder's realm, water could some-how equal time? And I had to wonder—was there such a thing as contemplative displacement? E. B. White did think that contemplation was work. And some writers did seem to bring on a sensation of light—William Faulkner came to mind, or Walt Whitman, or Rainer Rilke. But that's getting into the mystical realm.

The teak deck looks fascinating now, all laid out like a stained-glass window before the leading.

Outside in the yard is a fiberglass fishing boat up on jackstands, *Caleb Joel,* owned by John White, Joel's younger son. He was born in 1959, the year Joel became a partner with Arno Day. John has named his boat after his father and his son. He worked at the boatyard too when he was younger ("but he didn't like sailboats," Joel has said). John went to the high school in Blue Hill, and studied marine mechanics at Washington County Tech. He bought an old wooden lobster boat which he named after his mother and dragged for scallops with it, but the force of towing was too hard on the hull, and so Joel, who was worried, and Allene, who was worried even more, convinced John to have a new fiberglass hull finished off at the yard in 1979. John has large eyes, a full mustache, a straight, long nose. It's said that he's as independent as his father and as reserved as his grandfather, and well-spoken enough to represent lobstermen in Penobscot Bay who've formed a political action group.

John is getting *Caleb Joel* ready for scallop season, which opens on the first day of November and runs through the winter. He's setting up the winches and boom, a shucking shed, and a gallows frame for dragging. When the season opens they have to use a drag four feet wide, but they shift to seven feet later on, John says. "It's active in the beginning. I got six hundred pounds of scallops one day in the early season, with a forty-eight-inch drag." He smiles. "That was a good day. Then it tends to slack off pretty quick. Now the big boats, hundred-foot draggers from New Bedford that can't fish for cod anymore, are coming up here, and they're dragging at night when they're not supposed to. They've got nowhere else to go." John says he'll get the boat in the water tomorrow or the next day, haul out some moorings from the harbor for Steve, and then it will be time to start scalloping.

In the office a computer consultant is working with Laurie White, helping her to get familiar with the on-line system she and Steve will be using on *Vortex*. With a satellite linkup and electronic messaging, Steve will communicate with the yard manager, Frank Hull, while Laurie will do the payroll right from the boat.

From the office on the second floor comes the sound of classical music playing, loudly, on the third floor. Joel is now drawing a sheerline for the W-76. He has a plastic batten laid out on the drawing table, held to the desired curve by lead weights called "ducks." Since it's said that the W-76 will in some way be an enlarged Buzzards Bay 25, this sheerline is rising from familiar sources.

Joel's office has the feeling of a sanctuary. Perhaps it's the year, the time of his life, but it feels like there's work to be done here. Sometimes the boatbuilders come in to ask questions, but not so often. Rick Clifton said that Joel always helps, but you're always aware you're in a sanctuary. As for myself, I want to stay here and watch, but I also want not to get in the way. I say one time to Joel, "What I do is somewhere between being a pain in the ass and being a researcher," and he laughs and says, "We'll let you know if you're a pain in the ass."

It seems a wonderful place to work. There's the view of the harbor, the islands, the Reach, and Deer Isle. The room is full of natural light, some of it reflected off the water. When the sun sets, sometimes the room fills with hues of red. E. B. White had his boathouse on Allen Cove, where he wrote on a typewriter, and Joel has his design studio in a tower by the harbor. From here had come *Dragonera, Grace,* and now, perhaps, the W-76.

There are two drawing tables, and Joel can pivot from one to the other. The tables are supported by wooden file drawers, which have many sheets of drawings in them. There's a cubby cabinet with rolled-up plans inside. Along the wall, bookshelves, with a prominent row of CDs, and a long shelf of books about yacht design, including Skene's *Elements of Yacht Design,* revised 1973 edition, the most frequently used book. There are collections of designs by Rhodes, Herreshoff, Crocker, Alden, Garden, and others. Joel's five-volume Uffa Fox collection is there, and A *Rudder Treasury.* There's a complete set of *WoodenBoat.* There's even an edition of *An American Boy*'s *Handybook,* which E. B White used to build the skiff *Flounder.*

On the walls are photos of boats and of people sailing boats. There's one of the scow schooner *Vintage,* another of *Elisha* with Joel and his granddaughter in the cockpit. One of Joel sailing a Beetle Cat, *Vindicator.* Joel in the cockpit of *Northern Crown,* looking up at the sails. *Northern Crown* dominates; it is also represented in a lines drawing, a charcoal sketch, a half-model, one of Kathy Bray's profile drawings, and other photographs, including one of Joel in the cockpit wearing a foxtail cap (he has been called "the fox of Eggemoggin Reach"). There are half-models on the walls, and sail plans all about, and whole models on the shelves.

When there's a call from Taylor Allen, he and Joel discuss the powerboat, *Boss Lady.* When Joel finishes, before lunch, he sits by the window in his office and tells about the boats that are still at their moorings in the harbor, the fall lingerers.

"*Free Spirit*'s a real pretty boat," he says. "A few years back we put new decks on her and re-covered the house and redesigned the cockpit. Two or three years ago I designed a new rig to go with it, a larger rig and taller mast. We were able to cover a change in the ballast that increased stability, so the boat could stand up to the larger rig.

"And beyond her," Joel says, "that long, low, black boat, that's an old P-Boat designed by William Gardner and built in 1913, I think. We've done a great deal of rebuilding, completely reframed her over the last five or six years. New planking and a lot of work on the deck and cabin house.

"There's two Concordia yawls there, very beautiful boats and a pretty famous class of boats. Hundred and one of them built, I think, most of them by Abeking and Rasmussen in Germany. I think they're all still in existence, all still sailing. They're wonderful boats, not terribly roomy down below but great boats, extremely photogenic.

"And the last boat out, the big cutter there, is a very interesting boat called *Senta*. She's a Phil Rhodes design. *Senta* was built on the West Coast in 1937. She's a sister to a boat that won the '36 Bermuda Race. *Senta* is now owned by a couple from Castine. They use her and take people out on charters in the summertime. We'll haul her out by and by.

"That one coming in now, that's *Cirrus*. Herreshoff built and designed, Fishers Island 31 Class, 43 feet long. They're great boats. She was built back in 1930. *Cirrus* and I are exactly the same age. One of the first naval architecture jobs I ever had, when I was still at MIT, was to design a yawl rig for her. I knew the owner, who's now dead. He bought her in 1932 and owned her until a few years ago. Pretty original down below. She hasn't changed much at all.

"And there's *Alisande*. She's an old William Hand design, done in 1913, I think. A couple of them were built and seem to have been very successful. A couple of them took long voyages. I had a customer show up who wanted one. There were no plans. The old William Hand plans burned up in a fire or something. So I just had a drawing in *The Rudder* to go by. I drew up a set of lines and we made a bunch of changes to the interior. I just started with the drawing and basically designed a boat that looked as much like it as possible. We built the boat, and then another guy who wanted a boat like her for long-distance cruising, he borrowed my drawings and built one. Harry Bryan, in New Brunswick. He and his family sailed to Tasmania and back. *Patience,* built off the same plans as *Alisande.*"

When Joel and I leave the studio to go to the Morning Moon, I offer to drive, but he says no, he'll drive; it's one of the few things left he can still do. At lunch Joel says that the doctors have told him he's in the clear, and that they've asked him to speak at the opening of a new cancer clinic in Bangor. He says that he hates to speak in public, but he figures that he'll come up with a few lines. Recently Joel has read to a group of kids from the Bay School, a section from *Charlotte*'s *Web,* out at his dad's barn. "I must have missed one line, because a boy said, 'No, that's not it,' and I thought, *There's* a student."

I tell Joel I've been into the library in Brooklin, that I've read through *The Fox of Peapack,* and that there are some interesting poems in the book. "That's going way back," Joel says. It was published early in his dad's career, and he's not all that familiar with it. Joel says that when his dad was young he had written a lot of poetry, written all the time, and that he'd kept a journal. E.B. had told him to burn the journal after he died, but it had been eleven years now and still he hadn't done it. I tell him I figure that if a writer can't burn his own journals he shouldn't ask his kids to do it, and I facetiously add that Joel could photocopy the journal and then burn it. "Yeah," he says, "but I think that when I got to heaven the reception might be bad."

I've memorized a few lines of one of the poems in *The Fox of Peapack*, "Apostrophe to a Pram Rider," and though I feel a bit strange about saying them, I do.

Some day when I'm out of sight,
Travel far but travel light! . . .
Raise the sail your old man furled,
Hang your hat upon the world! . . .
Joe, my tangible creation,
Happy in perambulation,
Work no harder than you have to.
   Do you get me?

"Something like that," I say. Joel smiles. He's impressed. He says he'll have to look the poem up.

Could this be a gift? Not from me, but from his father, sixty-some years after the making. Could that be the case? If so, what beauty, to lay something like that away and let it wait.

November 1996

They fair and true the molds on Rick's boat, plane and shape the inner keel and stem, and then prepare for the planking. At this stage, the crew increases to four, with Rick and Bob Bosse on one side, Brian Stevens and Norm Whyte on the other.

They draw the sheerline along the molds, and another line, the "half-girth," running equally between the inner keel and the sheerline. They measure 24 inches from the half-girth to the sheer, and along this line lay the first strip of plank.

The planks are long pieces of cedar, an inch and a quarter wide and three-quarters of an inch thick, that have been glued together in W-shaped finger joints. With the color variations, from white to reddish amber, the strips are nice to look at. The edges have been shaped concave on one side, convex on another, so as to be somewhat self-aligning when two strips are brought together or, as they say it, "to fit well on the curve." The plank edges are drilled every two feet, and a copper nail is driven in the hole. Though this is a cold-molded boat, strip planking is traditional, going back to the nineteenth century when some Maine boatbuilders used small strips of pine or cedar to make a fishing boat, and strip-planked hulls are still seen along the coast—one example is the Pulsifer Hampton boat, now built in Brunswick.

They lay down the plank along the half-girth, screw it into the frames, to the stem and transom. They paint the edge with glue, lay another course, and then a third, on the first afternoon. These are left to cure and stabilize overnight. Even with three strips on, the line of the hull is established, a single, narrow curve that suggests the greater form.

On the second day they put the fourth strip on. Rick turns the strips into the proper curve with a wooden pry bar called a crusher, while Bob Bosse screws them into the frames. On the other side, Brian Stevens holds a strip in place while Norm Whyte drives the nails in along the edges. They're wearing rubber gloves, and in the air is the acrid scent of epoxy and denatured alcohol, which they use to clean the epoxy off. Brian is wearing a paper mask.

They manage to get a course on about every thirty minutes, and by lunchtime they've gotten eight on, eleven courses altogether. About 14 inches of the hull is now visible. There's movement, excitement in the line now—it's like looking at an observatory door opening on the night sky. The poetry is becoming apparent. In various writings about boats there are descriptions of some that are said to have soul. Watching the planking, I wonder, When does a boat have soul? What about this one—is it implicit now, a kind of promise?

Recently a friend has given me a book about writing, May Sarton's *Journal of Solitude*. Sarton says that writing poetry is soul-making. What about building a boat that has soul? Is that soul-making too?

The late morning sunlight is streaming in on the new boat. The view out the windows of the shop is very fine, frames of deep-blue water, cold-weather blue.

Fidelio has now been moved into the shop, next to the 22-foot runabout. Her stern and deck are level with the loft. Tim Horton and Paul Waring have been moved over from the Trumpy to start a job that includes replacing the entire keel and the lower parts of the frames. The keel is a mahogany laminate that has come apart and caused the boat to leak. They'll replace it with oak, and the yard is now seeking a piece 22 feet long, 9 inches wide, and 5 inches thick. "Got to call around," Tim says. "You don't just walk into a lumberyard and find a piece of wood like that."

Though Tim and Paul have both started working at the yard within the past few months, Tim has returned after a fourteen-year absence. He started in 1973, left to work in the merchant marine, and then worked at other boatyards. Tim remembers the days when they finished off fiberglass boats in an open shed outdoors, and how the shed would get moved around in storms, and would have to get moved back afterward. Tim has a loyal affinity for the old ways, and he can be a bit prickly. Though Tim was the young fella at the yard at one time, Paul is the youngest now. He's from the West

Coast, has a little goatee, long blond hair, eager eyes, and enthusiasm for what he's doing. A recent graduate of the Landing School in Kennebunkport, he's come north this summer in a VW van with his girlfriend and son, and told Steve, "I want to build wooden boats!" Now he and Tim are making templates for the laminated frames they'll put in *Fidelio*.

The Trumpy is supposed to be launched in three or four days, though with 60-mile-per-hour winds forecast there's some uncertainty. The bottom has been painted, the head floor is done, they've completed the electrical work, put on the propellers, and are now lining up the shafts. Pete Chase is the boatbuilder who's in charge of the project now, and he'll keep an eye on the Trumpy once it gets in the water and while the big, flexible hull reshapes. After that, Sue Tiller will pilot the boat from Brooklin to Boothbay, where she and her husband run a company called YWorry Marine. They take care of several yachts, and move them to harbors from Maine to Florida. Sue Tiller was the first woman to graduate from Maine Maritime Academy. She's been varnishing and overseeing the finishing of the interior, right down to the placement of the beds and the pictures on the walls.

Cirrus is up on jackstands in the yard now, where she's been getting winterized before going into a storage shed. *Cirrus* is one long flourish of red, a bold stroke with glassy coats of varnish over sunburnt teak trim, and the gold cove stripe that Joel wrote of, accenting the sheerline. I climb up the ladder and look in at the rather small cockpit, the long tiller, a string of ash wood, and the vast foredeck arching away and converging off in the distance. Inside, giving the feeling of warmth, is the spare cabin.

When I climb down the ladder, another of the boatbuilders, Brian Larkin, comes by and says, "I see you're looking at *Cirrus*. She was the hottest thing around here for years. When she raced, they'd start her a half hour late and make her go around an extra buoy, and she'd *still* win." Brian says that his great-grandfather, Captain John Allen, picked the boat up at the Herreshoff plant for the first owners—it was named *Kelpie* then. And he says that when Alan Bemis owned her, Captain John Allen sailed with Bemis in the races held for retired captains. "They'd take me along with them when I was just a kid, but I wasn't allowed to drive home with them. The language! Whoa!" Brian laughs, and heads for the shop.

Inside the sheds the boats are getting packed in tightly, the tapered bodies side by side. They sit heavily on the leaden keels, while the hulls sweep up grandly, these visible manifestations of the aspiring mind. They're like dreams, but you wonder, Who is it dreaming? Joel has told me some people say that in winter the boats in the sheds talk to each other. Rick Clifton has said that sometimes he comes to the yard on weekends to use a tool, and then walks in the sheds to look at the boats and feel their presence. This matter of soul, this overused word—but there does seem to be some element of soul, some spiritual quality here. It's a presence both calming and inspiring, as the presence of soul seems to be.

I ask Sue Tiller of YWorry Marine about soul, guessing that she might have thought about it. "Boats are live," Tiller says. "They talk. The more poorly made boats talk more. The best-made boats don't talk as much. They're quiet—quiet soldiers, they call them.

"Boats take on personalities, accumulate soul over time as they're sailed. You can adjust them. Heavy helm, light helm, how it handles in the air. Some boats are happy boats, though boats are happy in general. They're happier going into the water than coming out, happier on launching day. Launching day has a much different feel to it than hauling out. They're a little sad then."

I ask, "What about the boat when it's hauled in? What about the soul then?"

She laughs, and says, "Does it stay out there?"

Again I wonder, What does it mean to create inanimate objects that accumulate soul, that are happy, that handle well in the air? What does it mean for the people in the town, who go to the launchings, who see and use the boats?

"This is wooden boat heaven," Sue Tiller says. "There's gurus here. Joel White. Frank Day Junior. Arno Day."

～

When Joel arrives he stops to talk with Bob Stephens at *Cow Lung*. Bob says he's fitting the aft seats and getting the scuppers in. He also talks about the work soon to come, in Joel's studio. Bob will be working on the interior plans for a tugboat hull that had been built at Brooklin Boat Yard a few years ago. The hull had then been shipped to Michigan. The client was a man who owned a titanium factory. He had intended to outfit the boat as a yacht, complete with a titanium workshop, but he had died before the work was done. Now his heirs are shipping the hull back to Brooklin to have it finished. Bob says he hopes they haven't done too much to it, because "there will be that much less to undo." He's going to rent a scale, weigh the hull, "run some numbers," and begin drawing plans—in about two weeks, when Steve leaves for Bermuda.

Joel moves further into the shop, stopping briefly for a look at the planking on Rick's boat. He says that today he'll be working on the drawings for the W-76, but that he also has to get the design for *Boss Lady* finished because Taylor Allen is going to start building the boat this winter. Joel is also going to meet with a girl who's doing a school project on E. B. White. He smiles, says, "She tried to interview me last night, but froze up. Her mother got on the phone and said the girl couldn't do an interview, hold the phone, and write at the same time, and asked if she could please come down and talk to me in person."

He's heard from Bruce Stevens, who has sailed *Dragonera* to Chesapeake Bay. "A wind came up and they sailed at eleven to fifteen knots for sixty hours. They broke a lot of crockery, but it was a great sail."

As he heads up the stairs to his studio, Joel says that he did speak at the cancer clinic in Bangor, and that it went all right. He's also looked up "Apostrophe for a Pram Rider" and told Martha about it. He gives a little laugh and says, "We're trying to figure out the meaning of the line 'Drunk with life and Walker Gordon.' We're wondering what Walker Gordon is, and figure it must have been something for pacifying my gums." Joel is thinking that he'll read the poem in a second tape recording of his dad's works.

Joel begins by working on the lines drawing for the W-76. It's a set of three views—actually, of the hull from three vantage points. There's a profile plan, a body plan, and a half-breadth plan. They consist of curved lines drawn over a grid, and so give a three-dimensional effect, of an object suspended in space. The profile shows the boat from the side, the character of the hull conveyed in sheerline, bow profile, transom rake, underwater profile, and various buttock lines. The body plan is a view of the boat from the ends, half-bow and half-stern, with sectional planes that convey breadth, tumblehome, and flare. The half-breadth plan shows the boat as seen from below, with the run of the waterlines and the outward curve of the sheer. They're placed on the page so as to be equidistant from each other, grid line to grid line, a constellation formed.

"This is the fun part," Joel says. "Drawing the lines." He

could have used a computer-aided system, but Joel still drew his lines by hand. He brought out an early sail plan of the W-76, with the first sheerline. The sheerline on the W-76 as it stood now seemed to have evolved, to have gone from something bold to something elegant, a sweep gentler yet more expressive.

Details for the W-76 are on the lines drawing. The boat would have an overall length of 76′ 4″, a waterline length of 53′ 11″, and a beam of 16′ 1″. The draft would be 11 feet, with a sail area of 2,239 square feet and a displacement of 52,300 pounds. As compared with *Dragonera*, the W-76 would be about 9,000 pounds lighter but with 400 more square feet of sail.

❧

At Benjamin River Marine in West Brooklin, *Grayling*, a 65-foot sardine carrier, is being restored by Doug Hylan and his crew. *Grayling* had been built in 1915 in East Boothbay, and for many years was used to catch herring, mackerel, and sardines— during one trip in 1917 the crew on *Grayling* hauled 72,000 pounds of mackerel. A narrow boat with only a 12′ 6″ beam, it had been used as a purse seiner, and then as a transport boat carrying sardines from weirs and stop seines to the canning factories. After most of the sardine canneries closed in the 1980s the sardine carriers went out of use. In 1991 a couple bought *Grayling* and moved aboard, but the boat needed to be completely rebuilt, and required an owner who could afford to do it. A man by the name of Ted Okie became that owner, and contracted with Doug Hylan and John Dunbar of Benjamin River Marine to restore it and convert it into a yacht. Okie also arranged for Maynard Bray to do the research on the original boat. In 1995 *Grayling* was towed from North Haven to Brooklin in the fall, hauled onto a cradle, and moved into BRM's shop (an extension had been built on to accommodate the long boat). The hull was measured, and Hylan came up with a lines plan, using a computer-aided design program, so that the hull could be restored to its original form.

I had seen *Grayling* with Joel on my first trip to Brooklin. On that day Hylan and his crew were steaming oak frames and bending them into the hull. When I returned again the hull had been rebuilt and the planking was about to be caulked. They were about to install a new lead ballast shoe (10,000 pounds below the keel) and another 10,000 pounds of lead inside the boat. A wood carver had been in to cut the scrollwork at the bow. Doug Hylan said they would be restoring *Grayling*'s hull close to its original state, even using the original woods—cypress and yellow pine—inexpensive woods in 1915 but not so inexpensive now. They had made one exception in sheathing the deck with plywood and acrylic fabric, because of the strengthening effects on the hull and for durability.

Doug Hylan had worked at Brooklin Boat Yard in the mideighties. He had been a chemist and a potter before moving to Brooklin, during the "great migration to the woods," and he opened a crafts shop in a run-down building in the middle of town. Doug built a Mackinaw boat, and the hull of a good-sized cruising sloop, intending to use it for a world cruise, and he had built some Nutshell prams. At Brooklin Boat Yard he worked on the scow schooner *Vintage*, and he would have liked to work more with Joel, but Joel was moving out of the shop and into the design studio. Fortunately for Doug he worked with Maynard Bray, building the first Haven 12½, and in Maynard he found a mentor, someone, he said, "whose mission in life is to restore old boats." When Doug joined with another boatbuilder, John Dunbar, and bought a run-down Benjamin River Boat Yard, Bray helped them get some interesting jobs, such as the construction of the Barnegat Bay A-Cat

Mary Ann, launched in 1988, and *Red Head,* an L. Francis Her-reshoff Rozinante canoe yawl launched in 1994. And gradually they also settled into a niche of "ground-up restoration," with *Grayling* being the most ambitious undertaking yet.

It has become a striking boat to look at, with its long and lean hull, painted white, the graceful courses of plank lines in harmony with the sheer and waterline, the plumb stem, the gray scrollwork, the bronze fittings. On the deck now, Todd Skoog, one of Doug Hylan's crew, is building the wheelhouse. He's completed the roof, and has it suspended from a chain hoist, and now is fitting in the upright supports. They're using yellow pine for this, and the seven-foot two-by-four that Skoog puts into place at a corner is worth about $30. The wheelhouse is a tall boothlike structure, with three flat sides and a curved front with windows that will be lowered with leather straps into copper-lined recesses, as on the original boat.

The launch date is tentatively set for April, while the ground is still frozen and hard enough to move the big boat across the sandy lot to the water.

The *Grayling* project is a high-end restoration, about eighteen months of work, involving a crew of about a half dozen men, a research consultant, and an owner willing to spend several hundred thousand dollars to create an unusually well-restored yacht. Benjamin River Marine occupies several buildings—office, shop, storage sheds—on a cul-de-sac at the bottom of a steep dirt road. Nearby, in an old wood building on a little muddy cove, a place that looks like it could be a storage shed, Junior Day works alone. He's building a 24-foot lobster boat, one that will be used for recreation.

There's no owner for Junior Day's boat yet, though Joel has said that one will eventually come along. I had seen the beginning of this boat with Joel in January. At that time it consisted only of a long oak timber, sitting on sawhorses. There was a pile of oak planks on the floor, and cedar planks too, the bark still on them. Now the long timber has become a keel, to which a forefoot and stem were fastened, stern timber and a curved transom, oak frames, and cedar planks. The planked hull now sits on four oak posts, so that the waterline is level. It's not far from the bank of south-facing windows. There are cedar shavings on the floor around the boat.

When I walk into the shop, Junior Day is making a sheer clamp, an oak stringer that follows the sheerline on the inside of the hull and supports the deck beams. He's at the band saw, with a long piece of oak that has a curved line marked on it, and the oak also has a bend in it. I've been told that you never actually see Junior working, that he always manages to be sitting by the wood-stove whenever anyone comes into the shop, which has been true the other times I've been here. This is the first time I've caught Junior at work.

He steps back from the saw with his piece of oak and says, "Looks quite crooked, doesn't it?" A bit of a smile rises. "You brought this bad weather with you?"

It's a windy, gray day. "I'll be taking it back," I say. I ask what he's done since I've last been by, a few weeks ago.

"Oh, put a plank on," he says.

Most people around here call him "June Day." I asked him once what I should call him and he said, "Anything you want. Just don't call me late for dinner." He said the only person who called him Frank was a teacher in school, that he wouldn't let any of his classmates call him by that name.

He's about six foot two, and solidly built, a former first base-man, and during World War II, a bridgebuilder in General Patton's Third Army. He says that during the war he got to know some of the rivers in Europe real well, and that he has hardly any memory of the towns. He was involved in the construction of a pontoon bridge across the Rhine River, one capable of supporting tank crossings. He'd had appendicitis during the war, got moved to an infirmary for an operation, and then was put back on the construction unit again. After the war he used his savings to start Frank Day and Sons, where Benjamin River Marine is now. When they sold the yard in 1966 Junior and his father moved into this building. Frank Day died in 1978, "and I've been working alone here ever since."

This shop is a quiet place, with an appealing simplicity. The lighting is sparse. Most of the light Junior works by comes through the south windows. During the latter part of the day when the sun gets low, it strikes directly on the hull and makes the wood shine and seem like a statement on a good day's work. There's the scent of lumber about the shop, primarily of cedar. There's an old planer, a lathe, a big iron G-shaped band saw. There are two woodstoves with a long pipe connecting them and leading out a chimney. By the woodstove closest to the boat are a pair of canvas deck chairs, where Junior is usually sitting when you walk in. From the chairs, you look at the boat in profile, about eye level with the waterline.

This is Junior's first 24-footer. According to one count, he's built twenty-three 32-foot Down East boats over the years and a dozen 28-footers. When he decided to build this boat, another of his "last boats" (this is Junior's fourth last boat), he asked his brother Arno to design something smaller, and Arno came to the shop with the drawings a day later.

It's a "skeg boat," with the hull faired down to a small keel. There's a bit of "tumblehome" at the stern, an inward bend of the beam at the rails—what a delightful word that is, tumblehome. The bow has a sharp flare that contrasts nicely with the tumblehome and the curved transom. The sheerline is plainly stated for most of its length, but then hops up quickly and bends in sharply into the stem, sort of like a figure skater coming to a stop. It's a line that almost seems to suggest a lighthearted humor, and maybe contrast a note of perseverance.

Junior has set the sheer clamp down and gone over to the woodstove and stoked it up. I like running my eyes over the hull from this viewing point. "Incredible," I say. "Beautiful." Junior doesn't reply to that, but he says, "A lot of people have asked me, Why don't you take a young fella or two in there and teach them how to make a boat? I tell them, I don't have anything to teach them, that I'd just teach them a lot of wrong things. By the time they finished, they'd be teaching me.

"My grandfather was a boatbuilder," he says. "I saw him work when I was a boy. Back then, they didn't use power tools, only hand tools. To make a plank they'd cut it with a rip saw and then work it down with a plane. He'd use some wooden planes that were three feet long. You'd hear it whine, and the shavings would go right over his shoulder."

He laughs, then says, "Seemed like they finished a boat in about the same amount of time too," he said.

"Back then you carved a boat as much as anything."

"Yes," he says.

He talks about some of the other boats he's built. Brian Larkin owns one, *Blue Dolphin*. Junior and his father built it in the 1960s for two women who summered in Brooklin, and Brian's great-grandfather Captain John Allen was the caretaker for the boat for a while. Brian's grandfather Aubrey Allen took care of it next, and after the two women had passed away Brian inherited the boat. He's doing some rebuilding on *Blue Dolphin* this winter; the boat is sitting in his garage, its stem often visible between the parted garage doors. Another boat was built for the author Robert Mc-

Closkey (*Make Way for Ducklings, One Summer in Maine,* and *Time of Wonder,* a book about Maine that includes the line "At Franky Day's boat yard up Benjamin River . . . men are working with the tide, pulling up sloops and yawls, ketches and motor-boats . . ."), which he used, Junior says, to ferry around the islands and to get his mail on the mainland. And there was the 35-foot lobster boat his father built in 1938, a copy of another boat from which he'd taken lines by setting strings around the hull and measuring in from them—that boat, *Tranquil C.,* was still used for lobstering by Forrest Dow, the son of Wade Dow, builder of the Bridges Point 24.

There were many repair and rebuilding jobs, including one in which they put a piano inside a boat. Paul Coolidge (a relative of Calvin Coolidge, Junior says) had found an abandoned Friendship sloop along the shore. They covered the bottom in tar paper, floated the boat, and towed it to the yard. Over the next three years, working off and on, they completely rebuilt her. "Coolidge would disappear for a while, then come back with a bunch of money and we'd do some more work. He came in to work with us every morning when he was here. For lunch he'd usually bring a single boiled egg in a blueberry carton. He lived in a henhouse over near Harriman's Point."

Before they put the cabin roof on they lowered a piano in. E. B. White was at the yard that day—he kept his boat there—and he jumped down into the boat and played a tune. Coolidge sailed the boat to New York, Junior says, and lived on it while he went to Columbia University, supporting himself as a piano tuner. "Years later Arno saw an ad for fiberglass supplies in one of the boating magazines and sent in an order. As it turned out, Coolidge owned the company. He wrote Arno a letter, and gave him ten percent off on the supplies."

I tell Junior I'll see him another time. "The boat will still be here," he says. "Bring back some better weather." As I step out of the door he says, "Don't run too fast now."

Back at Brooklin Boat Yard, Brian Larkin says he's recently been by to see Junior Day, with his grandfather Aubrey Allen. Junior and Aubrey used to work together, years ago, at Frank Day and Sons. "But Aubrey was too aggressive, always in Junior's face. Finally Junior had enough and he said, 'You're too damn ambitious!' Aubrey left not long after that. Though they're still friends."

December 1996

Steve has gone to Bermuda and with Brian Larkin and Keith Dibble sailed *Vortex* down "Highway 74" (for the longitude line), a well-traveled route this time of year. They had winds aft of the beam all the way, and averaged about eight knots, making 150 to 200 miles a day, getting to Antigua in eight days. Because the weather was good, they were able to keep the hatches open, to keep the air moving through the cabin—which Brian Larkin was thankful for. On Thanksgiving they wrapped up a turkey and cooked it on the engine, and had mashed potatoes too. Once they were in the harbor, Keith and Brian flew back to New England, and Laurie White flew to Antigua, and she and Steve began sending e-mail to the yard.

Bob Stephens has moved into the design studio. On this day he's working alone, redrawing a sheerline on the Allen powerboat, *Boss Lady*. He'd already drawn one sheerline, representing the underside of the deck, as he'd been taught, but Joel had just told him that the sheer on this boat had to be drawn to the top of the deck. There are a lot of eraser shavings on the drafting table and on the floor, and when Jeep Gulliver comes up to ask Bob about boring the propeller shaft on Geier's CH 31, he teases Bob about them. Bob smiles good-naturedly. He's happy to be in the studio.

But he's worried about Joel, who's developed another physical problem and is in Bangor this morning to see a doctor. The bone that was transplanted into his femur earlier in the year has begun to break down. Now Joel is wearing a hip brace, and using crutches again, and he's feeling depressed. He'll be in to do some work later today, but after the weekend he'll be going into Mass. General to have a hip replacement.

In the shop, Rick's crew has finished the strip planking on his 31, and they're preparing to veneer the hull. The hull looks beautiful, with its reverse curves and long lines, the variations in the cedar planks, mated together along the backbone. The shape, so hydrodynamic, has the sleek fullness of a whale's body. But it looks a bit strange too, like a body embedded in amber. After planking, they faired the hull with power sanders, and with "long boards," worked in tandem by two men. That done, they coated the hull with epoxy, and now they're sanding it again. The epoxy dust can quickly make the nasal passages sore, and Rick's crew are all wearing paper masks.

They've also cut two sets of mahogany veneers, which will run diagonally across the hull from keel to sheer, and these veneers are stacked around the hull. And they've made a "vacuum bag," which will be sucked down over the veneers by means of vacuum pumps. The bag is a three-layer arrangement, consisting of an inner layer of perforated sheet plastic (through which glue can move), a middle layer of felt (through which glue can also spread), and an outer layer of plastic that's airtight and through which the vacuum tubes run, like sucking straws. When all is done and the pumps go on, Rick says, it will be impossible to lift even a tiny fold of the plastic.

When they stop sanding, Rick climbs under the hull to look for pinholes, light coming through, spaces through which air might escape. When he finds one, he draws a circle around it, then plugs the hole with glue.

Norm Whyte is gathering pieces for the next Center Harbor 31, the George Denney boat (which would also be called "Norm's boat"). George Denney is the man who wanted to build a 63-foot boat but settled for a Center Harbor 31. He has owned many boats. ("I've had this disease a long time," he has said.) He owns a 45-foot John Alden-designed yawl, built by Paul Luke in East Boothbay. In the mid-1980s he had a boat designed to the lines of *Quiet Tune,* and it was also built by Luke. For a while Denney owned *Red Head,* the Rozinante canoe yawl built by Doug Hylan, though he changed the name to *Pudding* (when he sold it the name was changed back to *Red Head*). Denney became interested in having a CH 31 after seeing the article Joel wrote about its modifications in *Maine Boats and Harbors.* He likes the lines of the CH 31 above water, and what Joel has done to make the boat "blisteringly fast." He also likes Joel, and "the great twinkle in his eye."

Norm has laminated the stem, and he's already bent several pieces of molding for the interior. Denney's CH 31 will be trimmed in teak. Norm is hoping that he'll have enough of it, and that they cut all their teak correctly. "You make a mistake, it's a lot of money out the window," Norm says.

When Norm started as an apprentice in the shop where his father worked, building boats for the salmon fishery, he made oars. The oars were cut on a band saw and then shaped with a plane. Using a plane in this way, Norm developed what he thought was the most important skill for a boatbuilder, which he called "working the curve" or "working with a flow." Some boatbuilders, Norm thought, especially those with a mathematical approach, had difficulty working the curve, breaking from the straight line—they weren't able to flow. One time after Norm made thirty pairs of oars the representative from the salmon fishery brought them back and said they needed to have another sixteenth of an inch taken off, and Norm spent two days shaving them down. During fourteen years working with his father Norm built forty boats, "larch planks, oak frames, lapstrake riveted," spoon-bow shore boats, shallow draft, in four sizes from 13 to 30 feet long. There were no lines drawings, just basic sketches. "Boatbuilding is sweet curves and lines," Norm says. "Things have to be eye-sweet. That's what you learn in traditional boatbuilding."

After the offshore trawlers displaced the stake-net trap fishery along the coast of Scotland, Norm started his own yard in 1982. A local yachtsman contracted with him to built an 18-foot sailing dory. In his second year he got a license to build a 14-foot Drascombe daysailer, and then got permission to build more. Into the 1990s, working with three boatbuilders and two apprentices, NWQB, Norm Whyte Quality Boats, built about ten boats a year, daysailers and salmon boats ranging from 8 to 25 feet. After a recession worked northward through Great Britain, when one of the oil operations closed down, people in Norm's region became less willing to spend money on boats. In 1995 Norm and Lynn and their twelve-year-old son Luke vacationed in the United States, and when they returned to Scotland there were no orders either for new boats or for repair work. Lynn, who had "a touch of homesickness" during the trip, asked if they could try America for a while, so Norm wrote to twenty boatyards and got several job offers. They decided to live in Maine because it was most like Scotland, and because of the quality of life there, which also seemed similar to Scotland's—you didn't have to lock your doors, and it looked like Luke would be able to fit in at the school in Blue Hill. And Norm wanted a high level of workmanship at the yard, "good boats and a good feel." He'd started in April, working on *Linda,* making toe rails. "It was a crazy time down there. For the first month I didn't see nothing of Maine but the road from Blue Hill to the shop."

Norm thought the launching of *Linda* had gone well, even though it was rushed, even though he had yelled at owner Alan Stern to get out of his light—the memory of which made Norm wince and toss his head back in laughter. But he thought Stern had loved the boat. "At a launching there's always a bit of tenderness. You've built somebody's dream. It's a tender area."

By Norm's reckoning, the Denney 31 would be his 106th boat. He too is a bit nervous about being the foreman while Steve is away and not available for consultation. But Norm figures he'll consult with his crew. "I like feedback," Norm says. "I can read my rule wrong too."

On my way out of the shop, Andy Fiveland stops me. He pulls off his paper mask, asks me how I'm doing, and then says he's been elected to talk to me.

Andy Fiveland is a boatbuilder at heart, but because he was a pipefitter and is an expert welder and mechanic, he tends not to be working with wood but with metal in the yard. For many years, in East Blue Hill, Andy has been building a steel-hulled cruising boat, which he intends to finish someday and use as a retirement home. He began building during the summers he spent in Maine when he was younger, when he had a working rock group, when he stayed in his parents' place in Maine. Because Andy was so interested in boats as a boy and said he wanted to be a boatbuilder, his father got interested too, even though he told Andy he was crazy to want to be a boatbuilder. Over a period of thirty years Andy's father built an L. Francis Herreshoff design called *Nereia,* which he launched in Ellsworth.

Andy is a friendly man, a morale booster, a raconteur who as he passes through the yard and the shop often leans in and says a few words to someone, and when he moves away, they're both usually laughing.

"I want to tell you a story," he says. "There was a photographer who came in here to take some pictures. I don't know what for, but when he came, he bought some doughnuts for the guys and brought them in. That was great, everybody liked the doughnuts, but we told him, when someone comes into the shop and hangs around, he usually buys beer. So he bought doughnuts *and* beer. The guys, they were saying today, 'The book guy is here, when's he gonna buy us beer?' I said, 'He doesn't know,' so they said, 'Andy, why don't you talk to the book guy?'"

Andy smiles, and gives a sheepish look.

"How was I supposed to know?" I say.

"That's what I'm saying. You know, you buy these guys beer and they're your friends." I had heard Pip Wick say that buying beer for the crew was an inexpensive way to make friends.

"How much?"

"When it's someone's birthday he usually buys two cases of beer. For you, I'd say a case of beer and a six-pack of soda would be great." Andy offers to contribute, reaching for his pocket, but I say I'll take care of it.

I buy beer at the General Store, and later I stop at the storage shed behind the old schoolhouse. There's a marine supply store and sailmaking shop in the schoolhouse now, and offices where marine artists work. Steve White owns the building in partnership with a yacht captain and boatbuilder by the name of Phil LaFrance, and they also operate the big storage shed. Out back, two men are wrapping up the tugboat hull for the winter, the hull that Bob Stephens will be designing an interior for. It's a very large, beamy, deep-blue hull, 59 feet long. "It's no Alden," one of them says.

Joel comes into the yard in the afternoon, swinging along on a full set of crutches. Up in his studio he says that on Monday he's going to have to go into Boston to see the "orthropods," and he gives a little wry smile. Joel sits at his computer to write a letter to a model maker who has built a half-model of *Linda,* which Alan Stern has sent in as a gift. Bob works quietly at the drafting table. The radio plays softly.

At 3:30, quitting time, the crew comes into the shop and fills out their time cards. Some have a beer, some raise a bottle, smile, and say thanks. One of them, Pete Chase, asks when I'm going to do it again. When Joel comes through the shop, he glances around and says, "Another day at Joe's Bar and Grill," and then stops to talk for a while, leaning against the workbench with the others.

Andy Fiveland and I talk for a while, and he tells about how when he was a boy on Glimmerglass Bay in New Jersey he rigged up a pram with a television antenna and a cast-off sail that he found on the beach, and how it blew apart in the wind. He says he didn't go far, and he got teased about his boats, but he kept at it— instead of chasing girls, he says, he chased the wind. And he smiles about earlier in the day when he had talked to me about buying beer. "Book guy," he says, though Andy doesn't drink any of the beer himself because it gives him a headache. And Andy talks about music, of how his father made him play the accordion, his brother the violin, and wouldn't allow guitars in the house, though when the Beatles came along Andy got a guitar and practiced in his closet.

Outside Andy gets into his old, beat-up Volkswagen Bug and putts up the hill. Others get into their cars and go too. For a while I stand outside the shop door looking at the sky. Though it's early December it's warm and clear, fifty degrees on this day as the sun goes down, and the sky is filled with orange light. When Joel comes out of the shop I say it must be wonderful to walk out into this at the end of the day.

"From November to March, when the clouds pile up, the sunsets can be spectacular. They fill up the sky." He gets into his car, swiveling himself around, leans out, and pulls the door closed. Soon I'm the last one left in the parking lot, watching the blazing sky.

⁓

The preparations for vacuum bagging begin a few minutes after seven on Monday morning. The hull has been planked down well beyond the sheerline, and to that extra space Rick and Brian attach tape and a plastic skirt—the lower part of the bag. Fred Pollard, a woodworker who's been making the cabintop for Rick's boat, sets up the glue machine—a pan of glue, a set of rollers, the veneers coming out slick with glue on one side. Bob Stephens comes down from the studio to mix the two-part epoxy.

They carry the veneers over to the glue machine—port veneers on one side, starboard on the other. They ready the staple guns, filling the cartridges with plastic staples—stiff enough to hold the veneers down, but soft enough to be planed and sanded. Crew come from all over the yard, and soon the team grows to twelve. Half of them put on white paper jumpsuits and pull on latex gloves. Rick Clifton forgoes the jumpsuit, wearing hardened coveralls, but using paper gauntlets over his forearms. Some of them put on kneepads; others put tape over their shoelaces so they won't get glued together.

It begins with four men who spread glue over the hull. "Where are the trowels?" one says.

"Trowels," Rick repeats with a tone of disbelief.

"I'm a schmearer!" one of them says.

Two of the men give the planks to Fred Pollard, who feeds them through the glue machine, and two other men—Kevin Duddy and Paul Waring—carry the planks over to the boat. Both crews, port and starboard side, start in the middle but work to opposite ends. They call out the numbers marked on the veneers.

"Twenty-six!" Jeep Gulliver shouts. Rick lays the veneer down on the appropriate space. Jeep presses it into the curve. Rick fires the staple gun, and his hair rustles with the blast of compressed air.

"Twenty-seven!"

It's like a party, with little groups forming and breaking away, and the white-paper suits seem to make them feel a little giddy. Andy Fiveland comes in to get a torch, stops to say something to Paul Waring, laughs and moves on. He's part of the party too.

"Fun, isn't it?" Kevin Duddy says.

"Thirty-three!"

Kevin Duddy brings a plank over to Jeep and says, "Next time, moo." Jeep says, "I didn't know you knew how to speak cow."

"Seven!" from one side. Then "Moo-o-o!" Jeep says, "A simple way of amusing ourselves." He said he had a few drinks one night, started mooing, and the next morning, he says, remembered how.

"Eight!"

"Moo-o-o!" Other noises begin to arise, a chicken sound.

"Nine!"

"Moo-o-o!" A turkey gobble, a dog bark.

Joel's friend Bill Mayher comes into the shop. He's driving Joel and Allene to Boston today. Bill is a teacher who took early retirement and moved with his wife to Brooklin, and they've done a lot of sailing with Joel, including trips to Cape Breton Island and Bermuda on *Northern Crown*. Bill says it's supposed to snow later on, but he figures that it will turn to rain further south. Joel is worried about the driving. It's funny, Bill says, how Joel seems to be more worried about his driving than his cancer. "He's a famous worrier, but he's always been able to let the big things go. He sweats the small stuff. Maybe that's why he's been able to beat his cancer."

Watching the veneering, Bill says, "What a shame to see all this talent doing this." And then he says, "I want to build a boat like this. Less maintenance." Then he looks at his watch and leaves to pick up Joel.

I've seen Joel over the weekend, at his house in North Brooklin, and he's shown me the list of pieces he'll be reading for the second tape recording of his dad's works. He'll read "Once More to the Lake," and a section about the dachshund Fred from *One Man's Meat*, and the poem "Apostrophe to a Pram Rider." He also showed the X-rays of his thighbone and hip, a photo of several long screws going into the ball joint and a row of smaller screws— "Sheetrock screws," Joel called them—connecting a steel plate to his own femur and the transplanted bone. Telling about the procedure of installing an artificial hip and joining it to the thigh, he said, "They'll just bore a hole at the top and socket it in," explaining it just like any other repair job.

It takes about an hour to get the first course of veneers on, and then the schmearers go to work again, troweling glue over the first layer. The second layer also goes on in a 45-degree angle but runs in the opposite direction—the idea is that the crisscrossing directions of wood grain will increase the strength of the hull.

The schmearers leave first, pulling off their gloves and stepping out of their suits and going off to other jobs. Kevin and Paul bring the last pieces of veneer. Fred Pollard begins to clean up the glue machine and then rolls it into a corner.

Then the bag goes on. Rick and Jeep, Norm and Brian, and Bob Stephens pull the perforated sheet over the boat. Then the baby blanket. Then the outer layer of plastic. Jeep feeds the hoses through the outer layer, and connects them to the air pumps. They tape the outer layer down at the bottom, fasten it to the plastic skirt, and check it over thoroughly for leaks.

When Rick switches the pumps on, the effect is nearly instantaneous. The air gauges soon register 23 pounds per square inch of vacuum, and the plastic has been sucked down so tight that the hull looks like a piece of vacuum-packed meat. Glue spots show in the felt, squeezed out by the force of the surrounding atmosphere outside the boat pushing against the vacuum that's been created under the layer of plastic sheeting. What Rick has said is true—it's impossible to lift even a little fold of the bag.

The pumps have to stay on for eight hours, the time it takes for the glue to cure. But they'll probably stay on overnight since Steve isn't around. Normally he'd come down during the night and shut them off.

"I'm glad this is over," Rick says. "I don't like high-intensity work. If I was replacing frames on *Fidelio,* nothing would bother me. But did you notice how well everyone got along? The reason is Steve, the way he's assembled the crew, the choices he's made. Steve rarely misses on his choices."

The bagging is finished at lunchtime, and the crew gathers at the south end of the shop to eat, sitting on benches and chairs only a few feet away from the bagged hull and the thrumming pumps. After lunch Bob Stephens is back working on the *Boss Lady* drawings. Brian Stevens is making the deadwood for the Geier 31, and Jeep is making the shaft log. Paul Waring and Tim Horton are at *Fidelio*. Norm is gathering veneers for the day he'll be bagging his boat, and he's concerned because he has only 450 square feet and needs 900. He's got to talk to Phil LaFrance, who supplies the yard with its materials.

Outside it's beginning to snow, the first snow of the season. The tide is turning and the water is calm, and big snowflakes are coming down, falling softly on the ground and disappearing into the dark water. In the yard, Andy Fiveland is using an electric hand plane to shape a 500-pound piece of lead, a "worm shoe" that will fit into the keel of *Free Spirit,* which is up on jackstands. Pete Chase is installing a piece of wood onto the forepart of the keel where lead has been removed, a repair meant to achieve better balance on *Free Spirit,* which has had a tendency to dive a bit when under sail. By another shed, Hans Vierthaler and Rich Wright are using a winch to move *Madrigal,* a 46-foot Sparkman and Stephens yawl, into Building No. 1. While pulling the boat along the skidwork, the wooden cradle breaks, and so they go about fixing that before hauling the big boat inside.

❧

As Christmas approaches, sales of *White on White* at the General Store pick up and reach about two hundred copies, Lorna says. After a warm period in the early part of December there's been a week of rain, and that's been followed by a cold front. On the day of the Christmas party at the yard, December 20, the temperature drops thirty degrees and the winds gust to above 50 miles per hour, rattling the buildings and tossing the shed doors. Though there are whitecaps on the water at high tide there's sunlight for the first time in more than a week, and the day has a pleasant feeling to it. Beams of light pour in the shopwindows through the dust motes.

The party is on a Friday, and precedes a two-week layoff. Joel will be at the party, the first time he's been to the yard since his operation. It will be the day before his sixty-sixth birthday. The operation has been successful, Allene says, and Joel is in good spirits. With physical therapy he'll be walking with a cane again before long. Allene says that Joel has to learn to walk again. He hasn't walked on his own since February.

After the vacuum bag was removed from Rick's boat they sanded the hull again, with power sanders and long boards, and then coated it again with epoxy, and then sanded it again. They made a cut an inch above the sheerline and attached various parts to the keel, such as the skeg, shaft log, and deadwood. Then they rolled the entire unit—strongback, molds, and hull—into the forward space where *Cow Lung* had been (that boat has moved into the paint shop). Using a chainhoist, they lifted the hull off the molds, turned it over, and lowered it back to the floor. Then Rick's crew worked inside the hull—scraping, coating, sanding, and fairing. Jeep Gulliver cut out deck beams, and Rick Clifton went about making the sheer clamps, made of spruce on this boat.

While the hull was suspended in the air, the strongback was slid back into its former position at the south end of the shop, and Norm's crew began setting up and fairing the molds again for the next boat.

Steve and Laurie White have flown back from Antigua, arriving in Brooklin on the night before the Christmas party. Steve plans to stay about a week, long enough to check on the progress of the repair jobs and to match the time sheets of the Geier 31 with those of *Linda* and *Grace*.

On the morning before the party the crew works at their various jobs—getting the sheer clamps on Rick's boat, truing molds on Norm's, fitting out a keel for *Fidelio*—up until lunchtime, before they clean up the shop. Friday is always a cleanup day, when they sweep the floors and straighten the benches and pile scrap wood by the stove, but this is a more thorough cleanup. Outside, they're bracing the doors of the storage sheds against the wind.

Bob Stephens is in the design studio, working on the plans for *Boss Lady*. He's been communicating with Joel by phone, and he consults Skene's *Elements of Yacht Design* on a daily basis, he says. Bob has also drawn a preliminary sail plan for yet another Center Harbor 31 now under consideration, a sloop close to *Linda* in specifications.

Bob felt that he couldn't have asked for a better educational experience than the one he was getting from Joel. Joel was encouraging him to think about design, to do more than drafting work. And Bob had been making decisions, about such things as scantlings, about rudder size and layout. Though he was an assistant to Joel, it seemed more like they were working together. It seemed to Bob that Joel was gently pushing him along, giving him opportunities to develop. This was partly in preparation for the day when Joel retired, and when Bob would become the one doing all the drawings at the yard. For Bob, it was a challenge to live up to Joel's expectations.

There were similarities between the two, Bob thought. They were both seat-of-the-pants designers, who plunged ahead and solved problems as they went along, much the way a boatbuilder did his work. They were both quiet by nature, pensive and intelligent, ambitious, both skilled sailors. They were both left-handed, with printing styles so similar that it was difficult to tell their work apart. Both had begun drawing boats in their early teens.

Bob was the son of a private school teacher, and his family moved several times when he was growing up, from Massachusetts to Maine to Houston. He'd learned to sail in Portland, and he'd begun reading about boats and designs, and keeping a sketchbook. When Bob applied to colleges he chose Bowdoin so he could live in Maine again, and although he wanted to design boats he majored in European history, to have the experience of a liberal arts education. During his junior year he went to a college program at Mystic Seaport and sailed on a schooner across the Gulf of Mexico. During his senior year he drove along the Maine coast looking for work at boatyards. He was hired at Brooklin Boat Yard with the understanding that he'd do a lot of grunt work, but not just grunt work. He spent six months at the yard, working on three Bangor Packets with Rick Clifton, before going back to southern Maine to be with his wife.

For a while he worked at a yard in Robinhood, Maine, and became head of the woodworking department and chief loftsman. When his wife got a job as an archivist at Penobscot Marine Museum in Searsport, Bob took some time off and put a design portfolio together, a catalogue of twenty boats ranging from an 8-foot pram to a 20-foot cold-molded camp cruiser. When Steve White called and said the yard was building *Aurora*, that they were on a tight time frame, that they needed help with the construction of a fiberglass and foam core deck, Bob agreed to work three days a week. By the time *Aurora* was launched he was working full-time. Eventually Steve told Bob that he wanted someone to be in place to draw construction plans when Joel retired, and so Bob occasionally began working with Joel in the design studio. He'd done most of the drawings for *Grace* and *Linda,* and the drawings for the Geier

31. Now it looked like he'd be doing some of the drawings on the W-76 too.

The wind gauge in the office hits 57 miles per hour, and it feels like the building is about to move. In the shop, people from the General Store are bringing in food for the party. Andy Fiveland is moving wood away from the benches for them. Brian Larkin finishes doing some planing on the setup for the Denney 31, hooks a tube to a blower and vacuums shavings and sawdust from around the molds. Then Norm, Jeep, and Brian lift up the inner keel, a 25-foot curved timber, and drop it into the notches. It drops in easily. "You call that a close fit?" Jeep asks.

"No," Norm says.

Steve has come into the shop for a while, and gotten up on the staging to look into the Geier 31. He looks tanned and fit. They're about a month ahead of last year's pace, he says, partly because they've had more men working on it. "I feel confident about being away," he says. "I just hope they don't do too well without me." But Steve doesn't stay long. He hasn't seen Joel yet, and so leaves to visit him.

Santa arrives at two o'clock. Santa is a female ("Some years she's more female than others," Rick says), and her name is Santessa, though she's really Vicki Hull, Frank Hull's wife. Last year she was Claudette Claus, and dressed in a French maid's outfit. This year she's Santa's niece and she says all the boys have been very bad. Frank Hull has been giving her information throughout the year, and now each of them comes up, sits in a chair for a lecture, and gets a gift. Andy Fiveland has been bad for taking things home from the yard, scrap wood, even though he'd asked ("I better watch out, you might take me home," Santessa tells him). Tim Horton is bad for living alone on a hill, wanting to share.

Another, Joel McGraw, is bad because his Maine accent is so strong he couldn't be understood by most of the people at the Wooden Boat Show. And Steve is bad for living out his dream. He gets a battery-operated blender.

Santessa stands by the planer and Laurie stands behind her, handing out gifts. Joel is a few feet away, sitting in a chair next to a workbench, and he hands out *WoodenBoat* calendars to each crew member as he comes up. Joel has a half-cocked smile, watching Santessa. He looks refreshed and rested, the glazed edge of chemotherapy gone, his hair growing back in.

When she finishes with the boys Santessa sits on Joel's lap, on the good leg, and tells him he's been bad, really bad that year. Joel smiles and looks up at her, and if he's feeling any pain from the weight of having Santessa on his lap he doesn't show it. She gives him a gift certificate to the Morning Moon.

The party begins, but Joel doesn't stay much longer. He says it will be a while before he walks again. His X-rays look incredible, there's so much metal in him. He also says that Harper's will no longer be publishing *One Man's Meat,* so he's gotten the rights and will assign them to a friend, a former *WoodenBoat* editor who now works at a publishing house in Maine.

The Boatyard Band, five of the guys with guitars, play songs by the Beatles and the Grateful Dead. Andy gets out his accordion and plays a couple of songs, including a blues "Merry Christmas, Baby." Eventually the party moves up to the Brooklin Inn, where people tie napkins around their heads, where Laurie White, napkin tied around her head, leans into Steve and tells him he makes her hair stand on end, and Pete Chase's wife, Sophie, a lawyer with a practice in Blue Hill, crawls under the length of the table to say that Pete gets a little wild around Christmastime, while Pete laughs and says, "It wasn't me, honey, it wasn't me." They put spoons on their noses and throw napkins at each other. Steve looks around, taking it in, smiling, enjoying.

At the shop, tacked up to the "Blades and Bolts" cabinet over a workbench, is a Christmas letter from Joel. It will stay there for months.

> *Dear Family and Friends,*
>
> *I believe that this is the first Christmas letter that I have ever written. But with Christmas upon us, a large pile of cards beside me, and Allene urging action, I am compelled to examine 1996 as a year—was it good, bad, or otherwise?*
>
> *While I did not know it at the time, I entered 1996 with cancer. It appears that I am exiting the year with the disease at least under arrest. So I can only conclude that 1996 was a spectacularly successful year, and that the least I can do is to celebrate the Christmas season with a chorus of hallelujahs. Hallelujah! and a partridge in a yew tree. Hurray for Drs. . . .*
>
> *Three major operations, six rounds of chemotherapy, and twenty-five radiations later I am back to the business of growing hair and learning to walk again—pleasant occupations when you get right down to it. Growing hair is virtually effortless, while learning to walk is not. . . .*
>
> *One does not fully realize how rich or deep he is in friends until the opportunity arises for them to show their stuff and mine are full of the right stuff. I love you all, and wish that your Christmas be as merry, and your New Year as bright as Allene's and mine.*

At the bottom of the letter, a note to the crew:

> *I want to thank you for all your love and support this past year. And all the small kindnesses to make my life a little easier. I hope you all have a wonderful Christmas and New Year.*

Chapter 3

Nite Bird

January 1997

When the crew begins work again after a two-week break, the gift wrappings are still in the barrels and on the floor, where they'll remain until the cleanup on Wednesday. Now Pete Chase is shaping the forefoot of *Fidelio*, the part of the keel that makes the bend upward into the bow. It's the second forefoot Pete has made. When he started cutting the rabbet line—a groove for plank ends—on the first forefoot he ran into the heart of the tree where the wood was weak and twisty, and so had to get another piece of oak and start over. The original mahogany forefoot is now lying on a sawhorse, eight feet long, tapered and molded, looking like a stair banister set atop a plank. It serves as a reference for Pete, who is making the forefoot with a shipcarver's adze, a "lip adze" turned up along the sides so as to better cut across the grain. Like a gardener using a hoe, Pete knocks chips away through the morning.

Tim Horton and Paul Waring are nearby, shaping the keel, a 20-foot elliptical piece of oak that looks as if it could be a boat itself. The oak for this keel has come from a 160-year-old tree in Connecticut. They have it set up on sawhorses and each man works a side, cutting to the marked rabbet line with chisels and planes. Sometimes one of them uses a power plane, a motorized hand tool with a deafening high pitch that sends everyone nearby looking for the box with the earplugs. Brian Stevens, working nearby inside the Geier 31, is wearing headphones to cut the noise.

Rick's crew has built the sheer clamps, getting them into place before the Christmas break. The long pieces of spruce running along the upper edge of the hull made it look more of a boat, and served as a satisfying stopping place, an indicator of the finish work yet to come. Now three of the four in Rick's crew—Rick, Jeep Gulliver, Ken Letterman—are fastening the sheer clamps. Jeep measures for their placement, sets them with a mallet and block, while Rick and Ken drill holes through the hull and into the spruce member, and then fasten it with bronze screws. Later they'll plug the countersunk screw holes with wooden "bungs," chisel them off and sand them smooth. Brian Stevens is making the supports for the cabin seats and galley cabinets. A painter, Doug Pio, is also inside the hull, brushing on the first coat of paint.

At the south end of the shop Norm Whyte and his crew—Brian Larkin, Joel McGraw, and Bob Bosse—are fairing up the frames on the Denney 31, the fourth time they've been through the procedure. They're using battens, thin pieces of wood that run the length of the hull, to check the lines and bevels, to make them eye-sweet, as Norm says.

Keith Dibble is at a workbench on the second floor making a shipping box for a half-model of the W-76 which he's built—the box must be solid enough so the model won't "come to grief" in transit. Fred Pollard is on the second floor too, building a jib traveler track for the cabintop of the Denney 31, fitting the curved piece to the curved cabintop roof. Andy Fiveland is at a bench making a set of chocks for the CH 31s.

And so goes the work, the movement about, interaction

with the materials—the emerging hulls, the nascent boats, the developing stems, keels, forefoots, sheers, floor timbers, faired molds, and faired lines. And the interaction with each other. There's an easy pace at the yard, productive but not relentless. Pete Chase pauses in his adze work to talk with Tim Horton. Rick Clifton talks with Jeep Gulliver about the layout of the 31. Norm Whyte and Joel McGraw talk about the lay of the planking. All through the day the interaction is going on; it looks like social interaction, it looks like work interaction, a little of both all the time, while the work progresses. Maybe there's more interaction than there might have been had Steve been here. But beautiful things emerge—the hull with eye-sweet curves; a mahogany transom knee fastened with bronze bolts, soon to be painted over; a curved transom bordered now with the butt ends of cedar planking, soon to be covered with mahogany veneer. An arched piece of spruce in the shape of a sheer line inspired by a Herreshoff. A forefoot of oak cut to the shape of the bow profile—this line, on *Fidelio,* created by Olin Stephens.

Joel comes into the shop at about ten-thirty today. He's back to hand crutches again. Though he could go along the path outside the building to get to the office, Joel prefers to go through the shop, to see the work, and say hello to the crew, a quiet greeting, usually in passing. At the south end of the shop he climbs the stairs, wincing at each step, and then goes up into the design studio. Though it's a blustery, windy day, the sun is shining in and the studio is warm—solar gain, Joel calls it.

Joel has on a hat labeled WERU, a gray canvas shirt and sweater-vest, and chinos. His hair has grown back, and his eyes look a clear blue, and rested. These days, he works until he gets tired.

He has gotten a letter from the Henrys' son, Frank Henry Jr., praising *Grace* and thanking Joel for his "unintentional and yet persistent impact upon my family." He has described *Grace* as "virtuous, forgiving, robust and responsive," a ketch that "pleases the eye and comforts the body and soul."

Often when building a boat, Joel says, the people involved become friends. Such has been the case with Frank Henry, and Alan Stern, Bruce Stevens, Kim Faulkner, Pip Wick, and others. Joel says he doesn't know why, but there seems to be a special kind of people in the boating world—or, as he also puts it, people who have "a low asshole factor." In Joel's reply to the letter, he's written that one of the most satisfying things about boatbuilding has been the development of these friendships. He says he can't take credit for the phenomenon—"I think the process of creating a new boat is so pleasurable that it is difficult for this NOT to happen." He wrote that he'd gotten pleasure every day of the summer when he'd looked out the window and seen *Grace* on her mooring.

Bob Stephens is in the studio. He's made prints of the plans for *Boss Lady,* and soon they'll be going to Rockport Marine. He's begun working on the interior plans for the tugboat, but for a while this morning he's become involved in one of Joel's projects, the design of a sailing model of the W-76. It will be six feet long, cost $14,000, and be constructed over a three-month period at Rockport Marine. Joel is drawing two keels on the plans for the model. One is to scale, and another is a longer keel, a "sailing keel" that will give the small model a greater stability. "As you make things smaller," Joel says, "you have to make the keel deeper and get the lead lower so that it will sail well." Bob is concerned with the shape of the sailing keel this morning, and is wondering how its increased wetted surface will affect the speed. He's been consulting texts on naval architecture and applying a formula he's found, called the Reynolds Number; for a while he engages Joel in a dialogue about wetted surface and viscosity, and Joel obliges, though he says he's not all that confident with the Reynolds Number. They discuss hull thickness too (the hull on the model is drawn at a half-inch now, but should be a quarter-inch) and weight (ten pounds now, which is too much) and the tubes they should use for the boom and mast (the model will have a mast six feet tall) and how the electric motor will work in tandem to move the rudder and the boom.

This flurry of mathematical and technical language subsides after a few minutes, and Bob returns the texts to the bookshelf. He turns to his tugboat drawings, but Joel doesn't get right to the drawings of the W-76 model, which are laid out on his desk. Over those sheets he lays some other paper and works on a different project for a while, an estimate for an 19-foot pulling boat for a family of four who camp on the islands. They've used a Whitehall rowing boat previously, but now they want something larger and more sturdy. Joel is basing his design on Shearwater, a 16-foot pulling boat he designed and built in 1984, the plans now sold by *WoodenBoat*. The design is for a hull of lapped plywood glued with epoxy, with three removable seats, removable floorboards, two oar-lock sets, and mahogany breasthooks on each end for lifting.

The two confer. "How many sheets of plywood?" Joel says.

"Use BBC," Bob says.

"Good idea."

"Five might do it," Joel says. He estimates the hours. He says it took him fifty hours to make the first Shearwater, so he figures that for this, with two men in the shop, 150 hours times $30 an hour—$4,500 for labor.

Joel has recently looked at some old contracts from the 1960s.

They charged $3.45 per hour for new construction. Yard work was more, $5 an hour. Now the rate per hour for new construction is about $17 per hour, while yard work is $34 an hour.

He figures that for the 19-foot pulling boat the costs will be $150 for plywood, $771 for veneers, $300 for paints and fastenings. There will be 70 to 80 square feet of sail, not included in the estimate. The total is $5,700 without the sail, oars, rudder, centerboard, or spars. Joel makes a rough sketch, itemizes the estimate, then sits down to type a letter.

Wendy Carroll, the office secretary, brings up an e-mail from Steve. It says, "Go ahead and build another Center Harbor 31, with more headroom and higher freeboard." Next winter, he means. Bob will draw the sail plan. He says the construction timing might be tricky, especially if the order for the W-76 comes through.

Base price for a Center Harbor 31 is $95,000, before the engine, sails, and accessories such as a galley, toilet, or navigation instruments. Both *Linda* and *Grace* got up over $120,000, and this year's 31s will be more.

One of the last steps in the fairing process of the molds of the CH 31 is to plane and shape the backbone. On Norm's boat, three of them work at it—Joel McGraw on the stern end, Norm in the middle, and Brian Larkin on the stem. There's the clean sound of shaving strokes, broken alternately as they lay down rulers or battens to check for high spots.

Brian Larkin stands aside the stem, which arches down to the strongback. He's got a balanced stance, Norm says, an easy way, a certainty to his stroke. He's someone who can flow. By Norm's definition, fairing is working the curve.

Brian is working the stem with a compass plane, on which the bed can be adjusted to be either concave or convex. It's a tool given to him by his grandfather Aubrey Allen, a carpenter who worked in boatyards. Brian has many of Aubrey's tools, and some owned by his great-grandfather Captain John Allen. Brian says that when he began working at the yard in the mid-1980s Belford Gray asked if he had any tools, and Brian said, "Oh, yeah"; Gray was tired of people borrowing his tools, and so he told Brian to come with him and they worked together.

With a thick beard, and curly hair, and a quick laugh, Brian is another of the crew who's light on his feet, someone who can land on a staging plank with hardly a flex in it. Though his mother is an Allen, Brian grew up and attended school in Massachusetts, including a parochial school where he was taught by nuns who forced him to write with his right hand even though he's left-handed ("If I'm screwed up it's their fault," he says). His college education was truly in liberal arts, in that he attended classes for four years, studying what interested him, and left without an official degree. Brian's roots are deep in Brooklin, genealogically, emotionally, and he likes to speak in defense of the community: "You see those guys at the General Store? They look like rednecks but most of them stop by the houses of old people every day to check in on them and make sure they're doing okay, and no one ever hears about it."

He met his wife, Karen, at Rick and Jane Clifton's ten years ago, at an anniversary party. Karen is the daughter of a lobsterman and grew up working on her dad's boat. They live in Elmer Bent's old house, which they bought from Henry Lawson, Elmer's son-in-law. It seems strange to Brian that Elmer Bent was a boatbuilder, and so is he, and also that Elmer's wife was a second-grade schoolteacher and so is Karen. In the barn attached to the house Brian has

Blue Dolphin, the Day-built powerboat. He's putting in new bunks this winter, a new galley, new flooring, a toilet, a new cabintop roof. Brian figures that with his daughter Erin, a three-year-old, five generations will have been aboard *Blue Dolphin.*

Brian is aware of his family history, and likes to joke about the bright and dark side of it. Captain John Allen worked for J. P. Morgan, taking him on his yacht from Long Island to Manhattan. Captain Allen left Brooklin in the spring, returning just before winter to go fishing. They called him Pirate John too, because he was a reckless spender. After Captain John's wife died, Brian said, he left his house and wouldn't live there again. "One day he showed up at Aubrey's"—his son-in-law's place—"with a garage on the back of a truck. They put the garage on concrete blocks and he lived in it for thirty years. He hadn't even told Aubrey he was coming."

Captain John Allen's great-grandfather was also named John Allen, and he owned *William and John,* the first schooner built in Brooklin. On the way to Boston with a load of lumber during the War of 1812, the *William and John* was pursued by the British schooner *Bream.* Captain Allen ducked into a bay and waited while a barge approached with seven British soldiers aboard. Allen told them to keep off, and when they wouldn't, he had his crew shoot at them. They killed two, wounded two, and took the rest as prisoners, and moved to a cove with the barge. Negotiations ensued, with Captain Allen eventually receiving ninety dollars, two American prisoners, and a boat from Gouldsboro with property aboard valued at seven hundred dollars, and he also got the barge with the armaments, in return for turning over the British crewmen. When he reached Boston, Captain Allen was given a sword with an inscription that said he had beaten seven men on a British barge with only four men and five muskets in Pigeon Hill Bay on May 20, 1814. Brian liked to say that Captain John Allen enjoyed the experience of taking a ship so much that he kept doing it after the war, though that's oral history.

With each stroke, each clean cutting of the wood, each push down the course of the stem, the piece grows more into something to rest the eye on, something with a sweet curve. You could wonder why the eye likes to rest on the curved line, why it is that when the line breaks into a curve it begins to become interesting.

Joel McGraw is at the other end, also removing wood from the inner keel and checking for high spots with a straightedge. McGraw is also someone who has a feeling for the sculptural nature of a boat. With him, a boat is first a sculpture, and then something that is called a boat. Though he'll express this ironically, such as when late in this fairing process, fourth time through, he says, back at the stern, "It's just a damn boat." Since it's irony it has multiple meanings, which seem to be both "Let's move ahead" and "It's good that we're careful" and possibly "It's good to be working with you guys."

And he says, "If we didn't have to stop today we'd get it done," which has a meaning similar to the last thing he said. Joel has a Down East drawl, and a dry wit that makes everything seem ironic. He has dark, straight hair, a long nose, and large eyes that may be of a kind that his Aunt Dora, in a family history called *Down to the Bay,* described in an ancestor as beautiful.

His full name is Joel Long McGraw, and he grew up in East Blue Hill, the sixth generation in his mother's family. Joel lives on the original family homestead, Longfield Farm, settled by Joel Long and his son, also Joel Long, about 1815. They built some boats, one of which was a 380-ton bark, Joel McGraw says, and they also operated a sawmill in the stream that feeds into the cove in East Blue Hill.

On the McGraw side, in *Down to the Bay* Dora McGraw

Bostwick wrote that John McGraw was born in New Brunswick in 1853 and came into Maine at the age of twelve, herding a flock of sheep with his brother. Later he worked in the lumber industry, transporting bark from the woods to a tannery with a team of horses. On the weekends he drank himself "hoary-eyed" with the other woodsmen, and was a madman when drinking, his family fleeing before him—though, significantly, one daughter would clutch a Bible and stare him down. During a winter when McGraw was driving his team across a frozen river, the ice gave way. He was able to cut the wagon loose and hold on to the horses, which dragged him to shore. There John McGraw got down on his knees and made a promise to God. First converting himself, he converted seventy-five of the woodsmen, including the one who'd been selling liquor, and later formed a Methodist church in Surry, Maine. His grandson, Joel McGraw's great-grandfather, was a sea captain who made "many long and dangerous trips to many foreign ports in Spain, Italy, and China." His wife went with him during the first five years of their married life. He had himself tied to the mast during one violent storm. Back on the farm, he built ship models, and a photo of one is on the cover of *Down to the Bay*.

Joel McGraw's uncle Cy Cousins formed Webbers Cove Boat Yard in East Blue Hill and ran it for many years. When Joel was a boy he played around the yard, patching up boats and sailing them. After high school he joined the Coast Guard—it seemed an honorable, seafaring profession. He worked on a weather cutter in the northern Pacific, and then as an electrician on a relief lightship that stood in for absent lightships that were away for repair, at Portland, Boston, Nantucket, and other places along the East Coast. Aboard ship, a three-second horn blast went off every twenty seconds. The crew learned the rhythm, talking for twenty seconds and pausing for three, and it became so ingrained they did it whether the horn was going or not.

McGraw worked on a schooner yacht, as a yacht mechanic, and on his father's dairy farm. He spent a year at an art school in Portland, taking courses that would have led to a degree in sculpture. But he concluded that boatbuilding is a form of sculpture, a legitimate art form that he wanted to learn, the medium he would use to make the shapes he wanted to make. Boatbuilding, McGraw saw that year, is a visual expression in the form of fine art. Rather than build boats and think of them as sculptures, he wanted someday to build sculptures and think of them as boats. He wanted to "draw boatness and create sculpture," something with the feeling of a boat.

Working for his uncle at Webbers Cove Boat Yard, he learned how to set up masts and rig large boats. Cy Cousins also taught him hauling, how to take a 40-foot boat out of the water and get it into a shed, no simple thing to do, Joel McGraw thought. He saw his Uncle Cy as a mentor, and thought of himself as close to him, "as close as he'd let anyone get." After Uncle Cy retired he went sailing, every afternoon, in a 12-foot skiff, crossing East Blue Hill Bay. Joel helped him get set up to sail, and kept him in a boat when others were trying to keep Uncle Cy onshore.

With a cousin he formed the Longfield Dory Company, based at the Grange Hall in East Blue Hill. Coffee hour was every day at ten o'clock, and a lot of people showed up for it, Joel says. During a ten-year period they built fifty-four boats—five lobster boats, five smaller fishing boats, several fiberglass dinghies, and the Longfield Electric Dinghy, a sailing dinghy with a two-horsepower electric motor built into the keel. They built the Longfield Dory, with a fiberglass bottom and wood topsides.

One winter when the orders were slow McGraw and his

cousin went to work for John Dunbar and Doug Hylan at Benjamin River Marine. After that McGraw returned to Blue Hill and ran the company on his own, making a batch of fiberglass hatches, doing varied repairs, and continuing to build the Longfield Dory. He also began making the Flower Dory, a fiberglass flowerpot shaped like a boat. In the fall of 1995 Steve White called and said he had a lot of work, including the rebuilding of the 12-Meter *Easterner,* a project McGraw found interesting. His wife urged him to "strongly consider" the job. He already knew some of the crew, those who had worked at Webbers Cove, such as Keith Dibble. And Joel McGraw had built sea kayaks with Pete Chase in an outfit called Caterpillar Boats, located on Caterpillar Hill—a name which to McGraw meant that they would "work slow and eat up a lot of the green stuff."

He had known Joel White from when he would come to Webbers Cove to visit with Cy Cousins. McGraw knew that Joel White had spent a lifetime pursuing what he did, that the accumulated knowledge and experience was present in the yard and being put into boats, and that was appealing. Joel McGraw liked Steve's management style, the way that he ranged through the yard and made decisions, and he suspected that Steve had continued to encourage a self-imposed high level of workmanship. McGraw was happy that Steve was the one charging the fees now and not him, though he was still making the Flower Dories and marketing them along the coast. At least for a while he had rented out his shop: "It doesn't make sense to build a thirty-foot dory in a building with a sixteen-foot ceiling." On weekends this year he's helping a group of kids restore the ship's models at the Blue Hill Public Library, "so they could come in someday with their own kids and tell them they had something to do with it."

Now he's shaping a keel. Working on the setup, when Brian

Larkin says he throws left-handed but hammers with his right hand, McGraw says, "I hammer with my right hand on the starboard side, left hand on the port side."

Rick Clifton is standing nearby, and he laughs. Rick likes listening to McGraw's patter. He's looking in a tool catalogue for screwdriver bits. The company offers both hard bits and soft bits, he says.

"Why would anyone want to buy a soft bit?" Brian Larkin asks.

"If you were a retailer you'd sell more screwdrivers," McGraw says.

At the end of the day McGraw joins Brian and Norm, and they lay down a batten for the first strip of plank, which will go on tomorrow. At three-thirty the tools get put away. Norm folds up his NWQB coveralls and sets them on a frame. Fred Pollard comes down from the loft where he's been working on the cabintop, uses an air hose to blow the sawdust off his clothes, and leaves with the others. Rick Clifton walks around and checks things over in the shop, grabs a beer left from the Christmas party, and leaves, the last one out.

It's warmed suddenly, and a storm has brought a heavy rain that's freezing when it hits the ground. Slush is piling up in the parking lot and around the buildings, and the rocks along the shore are covered with a layer of ice. The tide is coming in, and it's a moon tide, a full-course tide.

Tim Horton arrives at six-thirty. He likes to get to the yard a half hour before work begins, and he tries to always be the first one there even though he drives in from Blue Hill, which is twelve miles away—and he's first today even though it's snowing in Blue Hill and icy all along the way. He waits in the lot for someone to come and open the door.

That's Rick Clifton today. Inside the shop Tim gets a fire going in the woodstove, feeding it with scraps from the pile under the stairs. By six forty-five the fire is blazing. "It's talkin', isn't it?" Tim says.

It's three weeks after the solstice, and the sun is rising a minute earlier each day, but it's still dark at seven. By then about sixteen men are gathered near the stove. Some are sitting on the benches and chairs, while others, Tim among them, stand off to the side. They're all within hearing of Frank Hull, who is in front of the woodstove, looking down the length of the shop as the clock moves past seven. Frank is standing in—literally standing in—for Steve. Frank grew up on an island in Rhode Island, and took a ferry to school as a boy, and ran a sailboat rental business on Deer Isle before coming to the yard. His specialty is rigging. He's got a thick brown beard, and eyes that pulse into shades of concern as he moves about the yard looking over the work. Though Steve often gives a little talk in the morning, Frank is not so comfortable. Instead, he's a reminder that it's time to get to work. He says, "No news today," and they all go off to their jobs.

Tim Horton is working on the *Fidelio* keel. He knocks out some wedges from the centerboard slot that he and Paul Waring put in yesterday afternoon, after the copper sheathing was caulked and hammered into place. This is the job that culminated in a "discussion" with Paul Waring, as Tim put it, a discussion that had been building for days. Tim and Paul built the new frames for *Fidelio*, just the two of them until Pete Chase came on after launching the Trumpy. Paul is enthusiastic, but Tim, as he sees it, has experience, and in his eyes Tim has taken the initiative to make decisions too many times, including yesterday when they were building and sheathing the centerboard slot. Yesterday Tim had boiled over and told Paul that he's been working on boats as long as Paul has been alive, which caught Paul by surprise. When Paul said, "Okay, if that's how you want to do it," Tim had answered, "No, that's the way it's gonna be," which really wasn't much of a discussion after all.

Now from *Fidelio* a call goes out through the shop. A dozen of the crew come over and lift the keel, all 20 feet of it, from the barrels it's been sitting on. They walk it into place under the boat, maneuvering around the jackstands, and position it underneath the bolts protruding down from the boat. The workers then go back to their jobs, while the *Fidelio* crew—Tim Horton, Paul Waring, Pete Chase—begin to raise the keel, using hydraulic floor jacks.

"We'll levitate it now," Tim says. "Don't we need smoke for that?"

Working one end, then another, they slowly fit it into place, scrambling about, checking the fit of the bolts, leaving enough of a gap to squeeze in waterproof bedding compound.

Tim walks with a limp, the result of a motorcycle accident. He wears the same basic outfit to work every day—a khaki shirt spotted with paint and glue, blue jeans spotted with paint and glue and grime, athletic shoes, and a visor cap, often one with the logo "Duffy and Duffy," a Brooklin-based company that built fiberglass boats. Tim usually wears a jackknife holder on his belt, and a tape measure, and he keeps a Sheetrock knife in his pocket. He has brown hair, and brown eyes, and a tendency toward a determined, set-jaw expression, but Tim also has a look on his face that somehow manages to convey both happiness and sadness at the same time. He lives in a house he built himself, on top of an abandoned stone quarry in Blue Hill, land his father owned, a site with a view across Blue Hill Bay. He lives alone, but spends a lot of time with his ten-year-old son, cooking for him, taking him to sports practices, and it's a close relationship—the boy calls some nights just to see how Tim's doing. There's an older son too, from a first marriage to the daughter of one of the old crew at the yard, but they don't talk much, Tim says, though he has hope. "I'm working on that," he says.

The Hortons were among the first English-American settlers in Blue Hill, from a time in the early 1700s when sea rovers were ranging up the coast from Massachusetts. Tim grew up in an apartment above his family's restaurant on the main street in Blue Hill. His two brothers started working in the kitchen when they were eight, but Tim had to wait until he was nine, until he got tall enough to reach the griddle. He worked thirty to forty hours a week, and some weeks made more than his father did. At his high school graduation Tim got the standard words from his father: "I expected you to get this far. Now you're on your own." One brother went to Maine Maritime Academy, becoming an oil tanker captain. Tim went to Washington County Tech, graduating with the first class in the boatbuilding program, in 1972. He started working at Brooklin Boat Yard a few weeks before graduation.

Joel's core crew was at the yard back then—Belford Gray, Sonny Williams, Elmer Bent, Henry Lawson, Ken Tainter, Raymond Eaton. Most were in their forties, and they all were from Brooklin. Tim started by sanding and painting, working outdoors, but eventually moved into the shop. Though he was told that nobody could work under Elmer Bent, Tim did. With Bent he learned finish carpentry, and how to build a mast. Tim built two masts with Elmer Bent, and later two on his own.

Tim got drafted into the Army in the fall of 1972, and as far as he could tell, was the "last fella drafted out of Bangor" during the Vietnam era. On leave, the next April, Tim got into a motorcycle accident that left his leg severely fractured. He spent five months in the hospital and most of the next winter undergoing bone grafts. Discharged from the Army, he went back to work wearing a leg brace and began painting bottoms again. "Joel was real nice about that," Tim says. "He said, 'Do what you can when you can.'"

When Elmer Bent retired, he and Tim were working on the interior of *High Time,* the 34-foot powerboat that Joel had designed. Elmer told Joel that he could leave Tim to finish the work, that he didn't have to bring Belford on, which naturally made Tim feel proud. "Some said Elmer was slow," Tim says, "but when he finished a job it was done right with no mistakes. Elmer could make a board longer than it was. He wouldn't show me or Belford or Sonny how to do it. I asked him once, and he said to me, 'Tim, there's some things you have to learn on your own.' But he could do it. I figure, if I ever learn how to do that, I'll consider myself a success."

He'd learned something from everyone in the old crew. Rigging and how to make an eye splice from Ken Tainter. A little bit of this and that from Henry Lawson, "jack-of-all-trades, master of quite a few." From Joel, the principle that the lines have to be fair, that you just don't put trim on a boat without putting a batten on it first. How to cut and shape planks from Belford Gray, who could get on a strake a day, and also some of the finer points of boat carpentry. And from Sonny Williams, who was Tim's father-in-law, the example of hard work: "Hardest labor you could put him on he loved. Digging clams, cutting pulpwood, he loved it. Crazier than a shithouse rat. One day, I was married to his daughter then, I went to his house and his wife said he was clamming. I went down with a six-pack, and saw him with his clam hod across the flats. This will sound awful, but I drank that whole six-pack sitting there, and he never once stood up from digging. Another Maine person.

"They were all Down East Maine, the people who made this place what it is. Those people had to survive, working here. When I started working at Brooklin Boat Yard, I knew everybody had been working there a long time and knew their trade. I figured I was there to learn from them and put in what I knew to make myself a better boatbuilder." Tim helped build *Lady Jeanne,* a 42-foot wooden powerboat. He worked on *Alisande,* which Tim thought was the prettiest boat built while he was at the yard. He worked on *Maine Idea,* the 50-foot powerboat built for A. S. Martin. He finished off a lot of fiberglass boats, from the time he started at the yard, when fiberglass was coming on strong, up until they agreed not to do fiberglass work anymore.

During those years if the wind started to blow he'd drive over to the harbor to check on things. "My brother said it best, when we were out on *Endless,* Steve's Alden—he named it that because it was an endless amount of work. My brother said, 'We don't have to worry about anything because Tim's on board. He'll take care of it.'"

He left his job at the yard on impulse, after getting a call from his brother's former roommate at Maine Maritime, then a chief engineer on a tanker. He needed a cook, and wanted to know if Tim would fly to Texas immediately. Tim said he needed a few days to think it over. He thought about his wages—in 1972 he'd gotten $2.95 an hour, $97 after taxes, and though by 1982 he'd gotten up to $6.25, the guys working at Duffy's building fiberglass boats were getting $8.50. Tim was two years into a divorce, and here was a chance to see the world, to leave Maine for the first time. He decided to test the offer out on Joel and Steve, and they told him he should do what he wanted to. Tim flew to Texas.

"It was the best move I ever made. I got to travel. As far as my son goes, I should have stayed at home. I didn't feel bad about it then, because I didn't think I was getting paid enough for my skills." He went to Aruba, Amsterdam, Venezuela, Singapore, Bombay, Bahrain, the Philippines, Seattle, Los Angeles. In L.A., Tim went to a country-and-western bar, and it was just like being at Priscilla's Bar in Bucksport. "Lot of guys on the ship were from Maine. Maine boys got a good reputation. Hard workers."

After five years Tim got engaged, telling his fiancée to let him know when she was tired of him shipping out. After the next trip, she told him she was tired of him shipping out. They got engaged on Valentine's Day and married on Valentine's Day, "just to make it romantic and all that shit," and then Tim went to work at a lumberyard doing cabinetry. He worked at Seal Cove Boat Yard as a carpenter, and subcontracted for Duffy and Duffy, finishing off fiberglass boats, until after Duffy's was taken over by Atlantic Boat. When they started laying off the highest wage earners, Tim knew his time was coming. "I got laid off on a Tuesday, had a few drinks. Wednesday morning I got up and said, 'What am I gonna do? I'm bored already.' "

He had seen Steve at a New Year's Eve party a few months before. The day after Tim got laid off he called Steve, and was told he could start on Monday. When Tim got his first paycheck at the yard he bought beer for the crew. "As it worked out, I got my first paycheck this time twenty-four years to the day after I got my first check at Brooklin Boat Yard. I kidded Steve, said it would have taken my whole paycheck from 1972 to buy beer." Tim worked on *Grace* and *Linda,* helping to attach the deadwoods and fin keels. He did some repairs and helped rebuild the Trumpy. Before that job was done, before they started planking the Trumpy, Tim had been moved to *Fidelio.* Now, before *Fidelio* was finished, before they started replanking her, he was about to get moved on to another job, rebuilding a small boat. These peregrinations made him wonder. "I'm just getting to the cream," he said, meaning the planking. "Now I'm pulled off again."

Tim saw himself as the only guy left from the old days. He arrives at the yard in the morning and waits for someone to let him in. Tim could have a key to the shop if he wanted, but he figures that if he doesn't have a key, he won't have to give one back.

⁓

The rain is still pouring down outside. The roads are icy and treacherous. The tide is rising, close to flooding into the parking lot.

On the Denney 31, the planking has begun. They put two courses on during the morning, break for lunch, and then climb into their glueing apparel again. Getting dressed, Joel McGraw says, "I'm like Mister Rogers. I keep changing my shoes." Then to Norm he says, "You're not going to goop on me, are you? You already got some on my arm." Norm says he doesn't know what's worse, getting glue on your clothes and losing little patches of them, or getting it on your arms and losing little patches of hair.

"Best thing to get it off is whiskey," Joel says.

"Scotch whiskey," Norm says.

"Yes," Joel replies. Though McGraw is not a drinker. He was, he says, but his daughter asked him to stop, and he did.

The scent of epoxy and denatured alcohol is thick in the air, and because it's raining so hard, the air seems trapped indoors.

While the rain beats on the shop roof and against the windows, the crew on *Fidelio* squeeze bedding compound into the keel joint and then fasten it tight. The crew on Rick's boat remove interior pieces they've made during the week so that they can be sanded and painted and dry by Monday. Andy Fiveland is still grinding bronze chocks.

The full-course tide rises to peak, and because the storm is pushing water and bringing rain, this tide has a vertical flux of fifteen feet. The bridge at Blue Hill Falls floods over, and the one at the Benjamin River. The water rises up the landing ramp at the yard, and over the seawall into the parking lot, and into the shop. As it begins to rise, they shut off the electrical outlets close to the floor.

The plywood under the strongback for the Denney 31 begins to lift, and Norm becomes worried that the molds will shift and the fairing will come undone. This is his boat, a proving ground for him.

As the water rises, the crew gathers in the end of the old shop, most of them, standing on the higher ground of its elevated wooden floor. All but Joel McGraw, who stands in the water, attaching the plank he's been working on. It's said that McGraw works at his own pace.

They watch him quietly, until he slowly looks up and says, "Now I know how Noah felt."

On another morning Frank Hull puts his hands in his pockets a few minutes past seven, looks out over the shop from the woodstove, and says, "Let's go earn it." They all rise, file momentarily as one, and then disperse.

Rick Clifton is working the sheerline today. It's his favorite job, he says. It's a shaping job, of the most important line on the boat. He uses a hand plane. The shaping is complicated by the need not only to make the long sheerline fair and unblemished but also to bevel the edge, to cut the sheer with a slope or "camber" conforming to the crown of the deck. And so the curve works two ways—the long sweep of the sheer running fore and aft, and the camber running side to side.

"It's very important that the sheer be pleasing to the eye," Rick says, "that when you stand back it's very good to look at, especially at the bow."

Though Rick is a worrier, by his own admission, he is also someone who can flow with a plane, and if he's worried about the character of the sheerline it doesn't show as he works. He makes his cuts easily, as he stands on the staging running around the hull, and leans into his tool and into the line. It's a job he's done many times, formerly under the eye of Joel.

Jeep Gulliver is working with Rick, also shaping the sheerline, on the port side. He doesn't have the experience of Rick, and he's not quite so confident. His cuts with the plane are more tentative. Rick breaks away and joins him now and then, helping with the assessment. Together they check the camber with a template called a beam mold, a piece of plywood with the concave shape of the deck crown along one edge of it (the crown rises 2½ inches over the 8-foot beam of the boat). They hold it across the hull and look, make pencil marks in high spots, and take off wood. This shaping of the sheer is a job that will run the course of two days, Rick says, and that will involve repeated assessments.

Rick says that Joel used to watch over all the lines, but not so much anymore. Several times in recent years Rick has seen Joel look at the lines of a boat, nearly get involved, catch himself, and then move on. "Joel is a master at judging sheerlines," Rick says. "He would look at it from all directions, look and look. I always welcomed his eye, and trusted it, and asked for his opinion." Then Rick laughs. "I knew it would be coming anyway."

Just recently he has seen Joel stop on the stairs, look at the sheerline on the Geier boat, overcome the need to control the line, and then move on. Similarly, on his way through the shop Joel has also recently stopped at the workbench where his Christmas letter is hanging, started to reach up to take it down, changed his mind, and continued on.

Joel is now in the studio, working on one of the drawings for the W-76 model while Bob Stephens works on the cabin plan for the tugboat. Bob has been drawing the placement of a built-in seat in the wheelhouse, and Joel stops to consult with him about it.

"How much headroom?" Joel asks, of the seat's position.

"Three feet," Bob says.

Joel ducks his head. He looks at the drawing. "No dining-room table?"

"They specified no table," Bob says.

Joel smiles. "I guess they're going to eat off their laps with paper plates." He asks about the titanium-grinding lab the owners want worked into the boat, something neither of them have ever worked into a design. "I was going to put a laundry in the same spot, to make use of the space," Bob says, and he smiles, "but I decided it might not be a good idea to have a laundry in a titanium lab." There will be a head stateroom, crew quarters up forward, a lounge. Up on the cabin roof will be secured an all-terrain vehicle—many needs met in one boat.

At the front of the shop ahead of *Fidelio* and Rick's 31 is a new arrival, a 12-foot catboat that's been placed upside down on a set of sawhorses. The hull has an oak sheer strake, white topsides, and a green bottom with many layers of paint. There's a worn and twisted oak skeg aft of the centerboard slot. The boat has a lovely, full, seedlike shape, a dreamy look made more ephemeral as the catboat sits by the heavily timbered *Fidelio*. Pete Chase says it's an

Arno Day catboat. Rick Clifton says that two of them were built and that the other one is still in Brooklin too. Joel says that the boat is based on a model that Arno and June Day's grandfather made. It's named *Nite Bird*.

During the morning Frank Hull comes into the shop, goes up to Tim Horton, and then the two of them leave for the office. There they look over an estimate sheet for repairs. When Tim returns he moves some things out of the way of the overhanging doors, and then he calls out for help. Ten men come over, crowd around *Nite Bird*, and carry her outdoors. After they set her down on the pavement, Brian Larkin says, "I'm totally opposed to what they're doing to that boat. That was built by Arno Day. There's nothing wrong with it." The catboat is about to be sheathed with veneers, or cold-molded, and Brian thinks it doesn't need to be done. "Nothing needs to be cold-molded as far as I'm concerned," he says.

There is presently a controversy among boatbuilders and enthusiasts as to whether old wooden boats should be sheathed with veneers. The debate is particularly hot now because a recent issue of *WoodenBoat* has carried an editorial in favor of using cold-molded processes to preserve old boats, stating that it's possible to "squeeze another century" out of some of them. "A cold-molded skin might be considered a standard midlife refit for some boats," the editor has written.

One point in the editorial has brought some fiery responses— the idea that the craftsmen who built the boats aren't around any longer and cold molding is a way to save boats that might not otherwise get saved. One reader from Martha's Vineyard wrote: "*I fear that you are setting up a self-fulfilling prophecy, and selling us out. . . . What you wrote is defeatist, it's reprehensible.*" A reader from Cape Cod wrote: "*Better a pyre of wooden boats on the beach than the bastardizing of the spark of creativity that formed* them. . . . *A new generation appreciates the customs and quality of the past . . . they refuse to compromise the tradition, the concepts of wooden tradition to which we are all proud heirs."* Even Taylor Allen of Rockport Marine has written: *"The editorial struck me as depressing. . . . I believe the opinion is flawed. . . . From Boothbay to Brooklin I quickly count at least 21 different professional, commercial wooden boatbuilding shops or repair yards. . . . Both the beauty and practicality of wooden boats is that they are easy to maintain and repair."*

When the crew goes back inside the shop, Tim Horton says, somewhat quietly, "The owner wants to preserve the boat. Even if it was recaulked and refastened, it would probably still leak." This will be Tim's first cold-molding project, the one he'll learn on. Now, wearing a heavy canvas jacket and kneepads, he gets down on the pavement, fires up a torch, and begins to burn paint off *Nite Bird*. He spends the next two hours burning and scraping, until his face is reddened with cold and his clothes are covered with black grime. When he's done, just before lunchtime, they move *Nite Bird* back inside.

Junior Day has a fire going, and he's sitting next to it. "Well, hello," he says.

Junior has put the deck beams on his 24-footer, after cutting them to shape on his band saw. They're fastened into the sheer clamp. Some arch across the boat, those at the bow and stern, while others are short and will support the part of the deck called the "washboard."

Warming my hands over the stove, I tell Junior about *Nite Bird* and ask if it's true that his grandfather designed the catboat.

He says that he did, that his name was Eugene Day. "I have the model here," Junior says. He gets up and goes over to the other side of the shop, to the shelves by the bank of windows.

He takes down a wooden carving, a half-model, and there's *Nite Bird,* though 12 inches long. A child's toy to some eyes, it's crescent-shaped and beamy, and has a smooth, hand-worn surface. Several lines are scribed into it. Like *Nite Bird,* this shape, this sculpture, has a dreamy feel to it. I ask what tools they used to make them.

"Oh, a knife, a spokeshave or a plane, and some sandpaper," Junior says.

To hold the model, and think of Tim Horton at the yard burning paint off the catboat—it's like holding time in the hand.

I say, "It seems that someone grows up around the water, and sees boats from the time he was a kid, and then someday he creates a boat in his mind and then carves it out."

"That's just about it," Junior replies.

He takes another model off the shelf, another his grandfather made, a prototype of the modern lobster boat. "It had tumblehome, for looks," Junior says, "which lobstermen wanted straightened out so they could carry more traps. It was powered first by a Model T engine and then by a Studebaker eight, which was too heavy and slowed the boat down."

There's a runabout that Junior says his brother Arno had designed early on, a long and narrow pleasure boat. There's another runabout model by Arno, an enlarged version. Junior takes down models of some of the lobster boats he built with his father, a 27-footer represented in a 27-inch model, a 32-foot boat in a 32-inch model, a 34-footer. They're wider, without tumblehome, and have a lot of flare at the bow.

He takes down some models for skiffs—a 7½-inch model, a

10-inch model, and a 12-inch model. "These belonged to George Tainter," Junior says. "He was Ken Tainter's father, and he'd built boats on Swans Island. He'd told his stories so many times even he started believing them. I used to build a skiff every spring, fish on the ponds with it until I got tired of fishing, and then I'd sell it. One time after George Tainter saw me building a skiff he showed up the next day with these models in a box and he said, 'I'm getting kind of old and I don't think I'll be building rowboats anymore. Why don't you take these.'"

They looked like little fish, these models, like trout. Yet someone's livelihood was in them, something of the legacy of this man named George Tainter. Did they have soul? I suppose they could, in a certain moment.

Then Junior demonstrates how they enlarge the shape of the model to make a boat. He takes a little strip of lead from a box, and presses it along the side of the catboat model, bending it over the sheer and the keel. Then he sets the shaped lead on a board, and traces the outline with a pencil. He quickly draws a pair of horizontal lines through the curve, and a pair of vertical lines, making a grid, and says, "The measurements are just scaled up and the molds made from them." Of the several lines scribed into the model, one was most important, the "data waterline." All measurements were taken relative to it.

Lofting is not all that different, Junior says. He pulls out a piece of plywood with lines drawn on it by Arno. The lines are full-scale, and represent the 24-footer Junior is building. They looked like many drawings on one page, the boat collapsed onto one surface—a different kind of imagining, geometrical rather than sculptural perhaps.

As for Junior Day's position on the cold-molding debate: "Each to his own," he says.

We go back to the woodstove, and I warm my hands again, and look at the 24-footer a bit longer before leaving. Such lines, such lineage in them. I shake Junior's hand before I go, a hand surprisingly soft. His voice is a throaty, melodious burble as he says, "See you later." As I walk down the dirt road I imagine him getting up on the 24-footer again, working on the deck beams.

❧

*F*rank Hull says that they should do a good cleanup today. "We'll need the whole crew to move lead to *Fidelio*. And that's all."

The sky is reddening over the dark water. Sunrise is at about ten minutes past seven now, and the sun comes over the trees along the eastern part of the harbor at about seven-thirty. The mood of Center Harbor seems to change with each hour, as the light shifts, the tide and the wind. I'm reminded—it's something to see the tide rise and fall each day, to have this evidence of the planetary pulse.

At Norm's boat there's a morning conference. The planking is now over the turn of the bilge and moving toward the backbone. They're mating planks along the stern, "fiddlin' with it." Norm likes to listen to the others, to be open to their ideas. "We don't have to do everything like our grandfathers did," he says. "If something new comes along that's an improvement, we should do it."

The four are by the transom of the 31. "That's good if it's goona wark," Norm says, with a little laugh. Then: "That's a good idea, it's just a day late," laughing again and tossing his head.

Joel McGraw thinks the 31 has the look of a sculpture now. He can feel water flowing over it now, parting at the stem, and see the stern wake bubbling. "That's what determines the quality of a hull," he says. "How it separates the water and how the water rejoins after the stern. It's starting to be a boat now, something that can go around the world. That's what I hold it up to. A boat is meant to go around the world."

"We should put a screw in here," Brian Larkin says, of a plank at the transom.

"You ready for a screw?"

A call goes out and the crew gathers at the front of the shop. They crowd around a handcart this time and push a piece of lead that weighs 8,000 pounds under *Fidelio*. Using floor jacks again, Pete Chase and Paul Waring raise the lead ballast up to the underside of the new keel timber, moving it a bit at a time, blocking it up as they go, checking the alignment with each lift. Once the ballast keel is in place Pete begins to bore a hole through it, with an auger that's about three feet long, holding the drill motor against his belly. Paul is fitting together the wedge-shaped pieces he's cut for the deadwood aft of the keel.

At *Nite Bird*, Tim Horton is attending to the sheer strake, the top plank of the hull. It's made of oak, and it has lifted away from the others. "It's a bit proud," Tim says. With a hammer and a block of wood he hits the strake until it sinks back flush with the others, proud no more. Tim is thinking about how he'll lay in the veneers, and he's looking ahead to the rebuilding of the centerboard trunk.

The sheerline on Rick's boat has turned out smooth and eye-sweet, and the two are now notching mortises in the sheer clamp for the deck beams. They chisel the notches and plane the edges of the beams until they fit snugly. Brian Stevens is inside the hull installing supports for the two bunks.

There are other jobs going on in the shop. Fred Pollard is cutting out four teak planks for the sides of the cabintop on the Denney 31. Before beginning, he's sharpened his saw at one of the benches in the loft. Fred used to run a saw-sharpening business, and he worked for the Old Town Canoe Company. It's said that he can build anything and even make the tools to do it. Fred works in the loft, one of the choice spots in the shop, with a long view to the south over the islands. Several marine supply calendars are tacked up above the windows, photos of women without their bathing suits, but Fred isn't distracted—he enjoys the company, and says those breasts watch him all day long. Also in the loft, Keith Dibble has clamped the veneers for the head door in the Geier 31—it's a curved door that turns on a right angle, a tricky thing to make. Keith, who holds a degree in photography from an art school, went to the boatbuilding program at Washington County Tech before coming to the yard and now does much of the fine cabinetwork.

Andy Fiveland is working on the bronze chocks for the CH 31s, those pieces at the stern corners and at the bow, those smart-looking pieces through which ropes pass. The set he's making will serve as patterns for other chocks. Andy has been working on them for days now. He grinds them, sands them by hand, inspects them, and soon he'll drill holes through them. From working at the wheel, his wrists and sleeves are covered with bronze filings, which reflect light coming through the windows. He's wearing a paper mask. Andy, the former union man, is one of those most careful about wearing masks.

Earlier, before Frank Hull spoke to start the workday, Andy talked about skating last night on Billings Pond—him, his wife Leslie, and his son Daniel, at sunset gliding down the ice toward home, in the wind, he said. While describing this he was interrupted, some raunchy remark from one of the others. Andy curled his lip, raised his eyebrows high, and said, "Hey, we're talking pleasure here."

Rubbing and rubbing, smoothing and checking. Andy says that they adopted Daniel when he was a month old, that he and

Leslie had tried for a long time to adopt a child. When they got accepted they drove from New Jersey to Connecticut, and on the way home, Andy says, he kept turning and looking in the back seat and thinking, "I'm a father." It seemed to him that Daniel was looking back and thinking, Who are you? He seemed so handsome, and Andy kept thinking that his life had changed. Last night, he says, after skating, Daniel had told him he was a great father, and they'd been giving each other the thumbs-up sign. Yesterday, Andy says, he left early, punching out after seven hours rather than eight so they could get out on the pond during daylight.

Now Andy puts the mask over his mouth and he rubs one of the chocks, rubs and smooths. The metal dust collects on his hands and it seems, while he rubs, that the chocks grow in some kind of human value. Will anyone who looks at the chocks on those boats see that value in them, the life rubbed into them, smoothed and polished into them—will anyone see the quality of the day inherent in them?

At one point he takes a break and goes over to check the fit of a chock on Rick's boat. He sets it on the sheer clamp and checks the placement against the stem. Rick comes over, leaving his work on the deck beam, and they look at the placement. They talk and they laugh—these two will be getting together later to rehearse music, for a band they're forming, these two sixties guys with their graying hair and their big smiles and acid laughs. Andy gets Rick to sing a little of the tune "On Broadway" with him before he goes back to the bench.

The hour leading up to lunch is a good time to be in the shop now, a time when the sunlight pours through the upper windows and shines on the two Center Harbor 31s. For a few minutes they open the door at the south end, near the water, and fresh air comes in, dispelling the heavy scent of epoxy. The tide is nearly high now, and the water is reflecting the deep blue of the sky.

But it's not warm enough to leave the doors open for long. Soon the epoxy fumes from Norm's boat are in the air again. And at *Nite Bird*, Tim Horton and Ken Letterman are running sanding machines to fair the hull and remove the paint that hadn't come off during the burning outdoors. As they work, a cloud of cedar dust and bottom paint rises up and spreads through the shop.

Between bouts of sanding Tim smears putty into gaps between the planks. "Pound and smooth, pound and smooth," he says. Then they run the sanders again, and the dust kicks out like dirt from a tire.

"This is good dust," Ken Letterman says during a lull. "Not polyester." Letterman is another graduate of the boatbuilding school at Washington County Tech.

"Polyester?" I ask.

"Fiberglass," Tim says.

"I don't grind fiberglass," Letterman says. "You can kiss my ass all day, I don't grind fiberglass. Grind monkeys, we call them. They're about as smart as monkeys too."

Tim gives Letterman a look of disapproval. "I take exception to that remark," he says. "I did a lot of that work when I first came here. We put out a lot of fiberglass boats. Anyone comes to work at a boatyard thinks they're not gonna get a little dust on them might as well stay home."

Then Tim looks toward Pete Chase, over at *Fidelio*, and says, "He's the one who's got the job today." Pete and Paul Waring have been spreading a messy bedding compound over long bolts, and pushing them up through both the lead keel and the timber keel with a floor jack. In the process they've gotten the gooey stuff on their faces, in their hair, and all over their hands. "Pete's feeling his age today," Tim says, laughing. "He played hockey last night, the night before too. Anyone playing hockey at his age ought to have his head examined."

One time after they run a bolt up through the keel, Pete and Paul stand up and pick compound out of each other's hair—a grooming behavior.

"That's boatbuilding," Rick says, from the staging by his 31.

When they've finished getting the bolts through the lead, Pete Chase helps Paul Waring cut out some big oak pieces at the band saw, pieces for the deadwood. Paul cut them a little too large. Now Pete runs them through the saw, and picks away the scrap pieces with barely a look at the blade, on a tool that produces a scary, violent sound. And Pete is missing parts of his fingers, from an accident with a dado head. He'd been pulling a board toward him to cut a groove and taken off the upper joint of his ring finger and the ends of two other fingers. It had taken until midnight to get the fingers repaired. He'd come back to work a few days later, working with bandage on his hand. The finger with the blunt knuckle is still sensitive. Pete used to play guitar, but he can't press a string to a fret-board anymore.

He has wild hair that rides out from his head as if statically charged, thin on the top, flared out on the sides. He has blue eyes, is about six foot two, and known around the yard for his physical strength and his high level of craftsmanship. Pete likes to work with the old tools in the old ways, to use an adze to shape a forefoot, and then a slick, a two-handed chisel, to cut the rabbet line. He can do cold-molding work, and has built two cold-molded Buzzards Bay 25s, but he's another of the builders who prefer traditional boatbuilding. When he's doing cold molding, he says, he misses hanging planks.

Pete's father ran a boatyard in Mamaroneck, New York, before getting into fisheries. During summers, Pete's extended family stayed at their grandfather's place on Horseshoe Cove at Cape Rosier. Pete's grandfather was a well-to-do Bostonian who had built a crude cabin on the cove to enjoy periods of simple living, but the grandchildren weren't so interested in simplicity, so Pete's father built a house with electricity. There were many boats on the family complex, a dozen or more, including a 43-foot yawl. Sometimes in the summer, Pete's father tied a string of skiffs together, bow to stern, and the kids got aboard them, and he pulled them around with an outboard. Pete remembers his grandfather rowing along behind, his grandmother sitting at the stern, holding a parasol.

He went to a private school in Vermont, where he met his wife, Sophie Spurr. He spent a year in art school, spent some time outfitting an old lobster boat for scallop dragging but missed the season when the bay froze over, worked at getting schooners ready for the summer trade, and worked for a while at a boatyard on Cape Rosier. When Sophie went to Trinity College in Dublin, Pete went along, and got work painting in a shipyard. When they took a trip to Galway, Pete saw a lot of boats laid up along shore, of a kind called Irish Hookers, which were once the pickup trucks of the western coast.

After buying a Hooker he hired an Irish boatbuilder, Michael Willey Patchey, to help him rebuild it. Patchey worked only with hand tools. And so Pete learned how to use them, and came to think that sometimes they were better than power tools, once you accepted them. "Mike Willey had a simple collection of tools, a big adze, one big plane, a three-quarter-inch chisel, a couple of hammers, a rip saw and a crosscut saw, and several hand augers. He used a hand saw to cut a four-inch piece of oak for a masthead."

They worked together through the summer, and then Pete returned to Maine to go to Washington County Tech. The next summer he returned to Ireland and finished working on the Hooker. Others in Galway who sailed Hookers showed him how to make sails for them. "They took a rope, outlined the shape of the sail, laid canvas on the ground, and started stitching." Then he sailed the boat from Ireland to England, and had it shipped to Halifax. From there he sailed to Maine and finished the boatbuilding program.

When Sophie went to law school Pete got a job at the Chesapeake Bay Maritime Museum and helped rebuild a log-bottom bugeye—a boat with a hull made of pinned-together logs below the waterline and planked above. He worked on a tugboat, and in Maine helped his brother rebuild a Friendship sloop. He built a house on Horseshoe Cove. At Caterpillar Boat Works over a period of four years he built about two hundred sea kayaks. When Steve White told Pete that he needed someone to help build two cold-molded Hackercraft speedboat hulls, Pete spent a winter at the yard, then built more kayaks. The next winter he returned and stayed, and rebuilt the decks on *Fidelio* with Belford Gray. Pete admired Belford's sense of craftsmanship, how he was "sensitive about some things," such as when they were rebuilding a Sparkman and Stephens yawl called *Impala*, and Belford used the hood ornament from Pete's Chevy Impala as a model to carve a wooden decoration for the boat.

He did several other rebuilding jobs with Belford Gray, and they built a Haven 12½ together. And then it was Pete who a few years after Belford's death rebuilt the interior of *Alisande*, tearing out Belford's work, the cedar and butternut cabinetry, replacing it with a more modern and more spacious interior. In the decade since Belford's death Pete had worked mostly alone, or with one other person, he says. Though he liked the yard when it was smaller, he also liked Steve's management style, how he'd chosen a crew that got along, how he didn't stand over you. "Joel was looking over your back a lot. I kind of missed his worrying when he wasn't in the shop."

Pete had taken the Hooker out of the water when his daughters got interested in horses and taken up blacksmithing as a hobby. The Hooker sat near his house, and birds nested in it. But now he sometimes thought about sailing the boat again. "I can sort of feel it coming back," he says.

"When I think about the boat I'll build, for me it all comes down to the Hooker. It's so basic. Built with hand tools, and the hardware is all handmade, all from iron they forged themselves. There's wooden tholepins instead of oarlocks. A stone hearth in the cabin, with the smoke going out a vent in the hatch. No sandpaper, and saw marks still showing on the planks. Just rope, wood, iron, cloth, and a compass. When I see people in boating now, there's so much stuff, with everyone worrying about breaking down. To me it's keep it simple, that's the point."

And so the man with the grandfather who valued simplicity had come to value simplicity himself, and the man who had sought mentors in craftsmanship became a mentor in this yard, to Paul Waring just now. Back at *Fidelio,* the deadwood this time is a closer fit. Paul begins to smooth the pieces down with a power plane, though the whine is so loud that the others, working on *Nite Bird,* on the Geier 31, call out in frustration, and put in earplugs.

When Andy Fiveland finishes with the chocks he leaves them in the office on Frank Hull's desk, and then he joins Pete and Paul on *Fidelio.* He puts on a face mask, sweeps a spot clean, and soon is on his knees, reaching above his head with a socket wrench to tighten bolts. He uses a car's rearview mirror to get a look at the boltheads above the keel, a tool he's brought from home. On Rick's boat, Jeep Gulliver installs the last of the forward deck beams, while Rick begins making a fiberglass pan that he will set underneath the engine. Over on *Nite Bird,* Tim Horton and Ken Letterman putty and grind the hull. On the Denney 31, Norm's crew nears the end of the planking. Toward the end of the day, the mechanic Geoff Anthony puts in some new fluorescent light tubes in some burnt-out shop light fixtures, and when he sets a ladder against them, piles of accumulated dust falls.

They finish up, and some of them pull tissue paper from the big roll, using it to wipe off the dust and blow it from their noses, the paper a substitute for running water. No water, no blower system, other than the hood over the planer. The shop seems a toxic place then, with the dust-filled, chemical-laden air. It seems unwise to not have a set of fans throwing the dirty air out, and this seems more obvious when considering the plight of Joel White, up in the studio—even more so when he labors down the stairs at the end of the day.

❧

A heavy rain comes, with strong winds, followed by freezing. Sheets of ice hang from the dock, and the rocks are covered with ice on the sides facing to the west.

On the Denney 31, Joel McGraw and Brian Larkin are crouched on top of the planked hull, running sanders. Bob Bosse and Norm are working below them, sanding by hand. Those two are pushing a long board, and moving in tandem—it seems a dance, especially when Joel McGraw finishes with the power sander and picks up a single board. There's the rhythmic sound too, the *whoosh-whoosh, whoosh-whoosh.* They're sanding to get out the bumps so that the veneers will lie flat. After two days of this they're all sore. Norm says you get sore when you use sanding boards only sporadically. He says that when they made clinker boats at his shop in Scotland they had to sand all the lapped planks, a total estimated sanding distance, push by push, of about twenty miles.

On *Fidelio,* Paul Waring has fitted the deadwood together, applied bedding compound, and set the unit next to a humidifier under a plastic sheet to swell the wood and cure the compound. Paul is now sanding the groove for the rudder stock with a piece of pipe wrapped with sandpaper. Pete Chase is fairing the ballast and timber keels with a circular grinder. Wearing a welder's face mask, he holds the tool at shoulder level, and the oak dust is thick on his shirt, shoulders, and head. He blinks when he stops, shakes his head, and swipes the dust from his hair, smiles and laughs at the dust. Then he starts again, pulling the grinding wheel across the keel in long strokes, and gradually the new oak keel takes on a fair curve, like the other curves and lines on *Fidelio.* Many curving lines on that boat, all finding a terminus in some node at stem and stern, like a set of parabolas, a collection of sound waves, a sound in harmony: sheerline, keel line, water line, cabin line, and all the implied lines suggested by them.

Rick has begun to fit the cockpit seats, which are made of shaped pieces of teak eight feet long, each piece worth about $2,000. Brian Stevens is laying a teak floor in the head. Jeep Gulliver is shaping the deck beams.

No one in the shop has a more challenging job right now than Jeep. No one is working more curves. The deckbeams are crowned—2½ inches over an 8-foot span. There are ten of them, all made by hand, and they must all be even. Not only does the crown go across the deck, beam to beam, but there's a sheer curve that extends forward from the cabin to the stem. And so the shape that

Jeep is controlling is something of a rounded wedge. To make it more complicated, the deck crown has to increase, or rise, as it reaches the stem to prevent the "powder-horn effect," a dip in the deckline as in the toe of a boot.

This is Jeep's first time shaping the deckbeams. He's using a plane and a strip of wood that he bends over the various curves to check their fairness. When Jeep presses down the batten and finds a high spot, he makes a pencil mark and then shaves with the plane. He's found the job daunting, as anyone might, approaching it the first time. But Rick is keeping an eye on him, and he's checking in with him, lending his eye. Rick says that it's good for Jeep to go through a job like this one. He compares this to when his father taught him to row, towing him along from another boat, his father's motto being "Give him some rope but not enough to hang himself." Normally talkative and gregarious, Jeep had become quiet lately.

Jeep went to the boatbuilding school at Washington County Tech almost twenty years ago and worked at boatyards for a few years, but then he got into house carpentry. He ran a bicycle shop and sold insurance and then returned to carpentry again. Occasionally he came down to Brooklin Boat Yard to look in on things, and he'd been to the launching of *Aurora*. When he heard from his neighbor Joel McGraw that Steve was building three boats in 1995, a Buzzards Bay 25 and two Center Harbor 31s, he asked Steve for a job. "I've been building plumb and square for all these years," Jeep told him. "I haven't been building curves in a long time." But Steve hired Jeep, and he worked on the Buzzards Bay 25 and *Linda*.

Now Jeep was far from the realm of plumb and square. In addition to Rick's help, he'd been asking for "other eyes," assessments from Brian Stevens and Pete Chase. "Pete has one of the best eyes," Jeep says.

"It's taken me a while to develop my eye. You can know what it is intellectually, but it takes time to build confidence in your eye. You can get lost if you try to look at too much at one time. You have to look at one space, think one procedure. With the deck beams, it's a matter of making it look good. The freedom is nice, but it can be frustrating. You want references, but you don't have them. So I've asked for other eyes."

Like many of the boatbuilders, Jeep is a sailor. Summering with his family on Deer Isle, he grew up sailing a 15-foot fiberglass sailboat called *Adequate*. Later it was given away and Jeep lost track of it, but a few years ago he'd found it sitting in a boatyard. It was on an old trailer sinking into the dirt, and the fiberglass had become delaminated. Jeep bought it and repaired it and his family was sailing the boat again.

Tim Horton is fitting the veneers for *Nite Bird,* along with Ken Letterman. Each works a side of the hull. The veneers are mahogany. They cut them with a hand knife, staple them temporarily into place, and number them. Soon they'll be putting a vacuum bag on *Nite Bird*.

Andy Fiveland is working a few feet away from Tim, installing a bronze cap on the forefoot of *Fidelio*. Andy has repaired the old cap by welding a new piece of bronze on. Now he uses a chisel and mallet to cut a groove so the piece will lie flat with the surrounding wood.

It's unusual for Andy to be using woodworking tools, since he's mostly a mechanic and metalworker, and when Tim Horton sees this he steps over and says, "Look at that. Using a chisel. He's a boatbuilder now."

"Yeah," Andy says dismissively.

"He's ready for the Boatbuilder's Hall of Fame," Tim says. And there is such a thing, and Joel White is a member.

Andy fakes a laugh and says, "Yeah."

"The finest kind," Tim says.

"Yeah."

But Andy is also feeling responsible for an injury that Paul Waring got today. He had been talking to Paul, who'd been using a chisel to cut a rabbet line on the *Fidelio* keel. Listening, Paul had lost track of the chisel and cut into his finger, and gone off to a doctor. When Paul returns and walks in through the shop door, wearing a banana-shaped bandage on his finger, the crew near *Fidelio* begin to say, "Beer." (Not only must a worker buy beer for the crew on his birthday, but whenever he gets an injury that requires a trip to a doctor.) Paul grins and goes back to work, using the chisel again, and he says the reason he cut himself is that he held the tool the wrong way. Andy says he's sorry it happened, and that he'll help pay for the beer, and then he starts singing "Mack the Knife." Paul, who's also a musician, who's recently borrowed one of Andy's Elvis Presley records, sings "Don't Be Cruel" in return.

When Norm's crew finishes sanding they begin cutting the veneers for the Denney 31, using a small circular saw. Since there's not enough mahogany for two layers they're using Spanish cedar. The dust gets into their mouths and tastes like mud, Brian says. Joel McGraw has a bandanna tied over his mouth.

Tim Horton comes down to their end of the shop looking for plastic staples.

"Smooth," he says to Norm and Brian. "You can use a power saw. I'm using a knife." Tim asks if there are enough staples for the two boats. There should be, Brian says. They have 50 boxes, with 2,000 staples to a box.

"That should be enough," Tim says.

"We'll probably use three or four boxes," Brian says.

"I'm gonna use a passel of them," Tim says.

After leaning too far out to pry a staple out of a veneer that's serving as a guide for cutting, Brian loses his footing and slides down the hull on sawdust that is like snow. But he lands lightly on a sawhorse, saying with a little laugh, "I knew that was going to happen if I bent down there."

⁂

That afternoon a boat owner by the name of Dave Bradley comes into the shop. He's in his eighties, and owns a Herreshoff S-Boat called *Mischief*, stored in the sardine factory building. *Mischief* was built in 1926, and Bradley's mother bought it for him and his brother in 1932. They sailed it off Cape Cod before Bradley moved to Maine. He's sailed *Mischief* for sixty-four years now. They held a party for the boat last year, on its seventieth birthday, and read a poem by Philip Booth, another boat owner here, a poem called "Bradley, Herreshoff, *Mischief*."

We go out to the sardine factory, and find *Mischief* between a pair of Rozinantes, near a row of Herreshoff 12½s, a few feet from Joel's *Ellisha*. The hull is a deep shade of blue, and it's an old hull to be sure, worn and eroded along the keel.

Bradley has a face that's heavily lined, perhaps from years of being on the water and in the sun. He likes to talk about his boat, how he and his brother sailed it when they were teenagers, winning five out of the eight races they entered on Cape Cod in 1934. But eventually Bradley tired of racing and decided to make the lean, fast sloop into a cruising boat. He told Joel White to give him the biggest hatch he could build, and to put two bunks in, and a chest that could function as a navigation table. He had a stove put in and a water tank. He had Joel build a well for an outboard motor, and he had him reduce the size of the mainsail, which was too big at almost 400 square feet. They raised the boom eighteen inches and then cut four feet off. Eventually they got the sail area down to 60 percent of what it was, but there was still too much power, so they put two jiffy reefs in. And so the boat that tore along in 35-mile-per-hour winds with a teenager at the helm became a more sedate cruiser, excellent for sleeping two, and "damn good for three."

He had a catalytic heater put in, and then—because the timbers had remained original, and he had to bail about fifty gallons every two days—Bradley most recently had a pair of solar-powered pumps installed. "She's buoyant," he says, "a bird in the water." He says he sailed *Mischief* every day when there was good weather last summer.

Dave Bradley was a member of the 1940 Olympic ski team, and as a doctor during World War II he witnessed the Bikini atoll nuclear blast. That led to the best-selling book *No Next Time,* after which he retired from medicine. He wrote *Lion in Roses,* a memoir of Finland, and taught writing at Dartmouth, though Bradley said he didn't call himself a writer. Of E. B. White, whom he sailed with twice, Bradley says, "He was a shy man, hardly said anything, but he was a hell of a writer."

He found Joel shy too, but one time at a party Joel came up to him and said he didn't like the look of the rigging on his boat. Joel had tested it with his hand, and it was frayed, and he said they ought to work on it. From then on, Bradley liked Joel. "He's magical. He never built a lousy boat."

When we climb up the ladder and get into the cockpit of *Mischief,* Bradley shows the holds for ropes and anchors, the well for the outboard, the bunks and stove. It seems to me, as I sit in the cabin and listen to Bradley, that this is the most intimate connection between a person and a boat. Everything on it means something to him.

He says that he used to joke with his kids, saying that when he died he wanted his ashes painted onto the boat. Then he smiles and says, "Now I think I'll just sail off in it, and we'll both go down." He says he's been told the boat is worth only three or four thousand dollars, because of all the work it needs.

Bradley looks at me, and again a smile fills his lined face. He says that during the hurricane of 1954 *Mischief* was at a boatyard in Portland. The day after the hurricane he went to the yard, and it was a disaster. "A couple of hundred boats had washed up, and the shore was covered with splintered boards. A few masts were sticking out of the water. The boathouse was all smashed.

"I couldn't see anything of my blue-painted hull. This big strong guy was there. I was despondent. He said to me, "What have you got a long face on for?" I told him, 'Tell me straight.' He told me that in the middle of the hurricane she cut herself loose, and a half hour later went through the fleet and out of the harbor. He says, 'She found a mudhole, turned around, and sat down. She's got water in her, that's all.' He stuck a finger in my chest and told me, 'Next time you're lost, you cut off the tiller and let her go, and young man, she'll take you home.'"

We get down from *Mischief,* leave the sardine factory building, and walk back to Bradley's car. His companion is there, a woman whom he calls "the best cook in eastern Maine." She says that Bradley's daughter told her not to go sailing with him, that she'd be standing in four feet of water, but she'd gone out a few times and it wasn't so bad.

As they're about to leave, Bradley calls out, "Why do people worship boats? People don't worship cars, they're just things! But a boat is the nearest thing to perfection you'll ever get in your hand! That's why people worship them!"

Inside the shop, Tim Horton has *Nite Bird* nearly ready for vacuum bagging. Tim also says that Dave Bradley was out there sailing every day last summer. "He can really make that little S-Boat of his go. I've seen him come around that point in a stiff westerly, fly through the harbor, right through the fleet, spin around, drift up to the dock, jump out, and tie her up, all by himself."

❧

The air temperature has suddenly dropped below water temperature, and today there's "smoke" on the water, trails of mist three feet high, from the harbor on out to the Reach. Tonight during the full moon some of the crew will be going to the pond at the WoodenBoat grounds for a bonfire and skating party. There's clear weather now, and the ponds are frozen with a thick layer of ice.

Bob Stephens has finished the drawings for the outfitting of the tugboat, and they've gone off to the owners. Joel has finished the drawings for the model of the W-76, and they've gone off to Rockport Marine. They have moved on to the drawings for the actual W-76, and today Bob is drawing the accommodations plan. The interior is relatively small, Bob says, and the W-76 is actually a 76-foot daysailer—he says he finds it hard to believe that someone would be willing to spend $2.25 million for a daysailer.

Joel will be in later after a physical therapy session. Both he and Bob were away yesterday, in Rockport, where they watched the bending of the timbers on *Boss Lady,* and they'd gone to the Apprenticeshop, a boatbuilding school where the students are building one of Bob's designs, a power launch based on a Gil Smith catboat. "They're doing a good job," Bob says, "which is much better than the other way."

In the shop, Tim Horton and Ken Letterman are setting up the vacuum bag on *Nite Bird*. They've got the edges taped, the pieces laid out, the pumps ready to go. Fred Pollard has come down from the loft and gotten the glue machine ready.

Tim is handling one side of the boat, and Ken the other. Tim is feeling tense, here on his first venture into cold molding. He feels that a lot is riding on the job, that here he learns the technique and proves he can do it. In a way, he'd be bridging the past and the present. And he's gotten involved in the boat itself. "So this was Arno Day's boat," Tim said when he learned about the origin, and he'd taken a different look at it. The other day, after Ken Letterman had laid his first course of veneers in the wrong direction—the opposite direction from Tim's first layer, which was angled forward—Tim had paced around and then gone up to the office. "The steam was coming out of my ears," he'd said. Frank had told him to pull Ken Letterman's side up and start over, and he said that they'd already exceeded the estimate for time spent on the sheathing of the hull.

Now they're dressed up in the white glue suits, and the two of them with their generous bellies look like snowmen in a school play, which seems funny with their serious expressions. Someone has drawn a big bow tie on the front of Letterman's suit. When the seats blow out of both of the suits from the two big men bending down, it seems even funnier to look at them.

On *Fidelio*, they've put the deadwood in after another fitting, with Pete helping Paul out again. It's been a rough week for Paul— maybe it's the alignment of the planets, he says, though he usually has good luck around the time of the full moon. A few days ago he'd slid off the road in his truck and done $1,200 worth of damage. Playing hockey after work on the WoodenBoat pond, he'd skated over Pete's thumb and then fallen and hurt his elbow. Then he'd cut himself with the chisel. Today he's buying beer for the crew.

On Rick's boat, it's a sand-and-paint day, when the three now in the crew—Rick, Brian Stevens, and Jeep—smooth up the interior of the hull with sandpaper and vacuum it out so that the painters can come in and give it another coat during the afternoon. They're working casually, next to the developing bagging scene.

Norm's boat at the south end of the shop seems far removed from *Nite Bird*. Norm and Brian Larkin have finished cutting the veneers on their side of the hull, on a pace well ahead of Joel McGraw and Bob Bosse. ("It takes time to do good work," McGraw says.) Norm and Brian are about to go down and help with the bagging on *Nite Bird*. McGraw is concerned today, but not so much about the veneering. He says he has just heard from an entrepreneur from southern Maine, someone he had sold his Flower Dories and who had offered money for the rights to them. McGraw turned down the offer, he says, but the man has sent one of his Flower Dories to China and gotten 80,000 of them made there. He's called and asked if McGraw wants to be the northern distributor. Joel says he might get a lawyer, but he thinks that more likely he'll take it as a compliment to his good idea and an indicator that he'll have more good ideas. He'll make a better product and even sign his name to it.

When someone says that it's a case of an honest guy getting cheated by a greedy man, McGraw's crew partner, Bob Bosse, says, "Does he look honest? I don't think he's that stupid. He looks pretty shrewd to me." Bosse is another with a talent for the enigmatic remark. The first time I'd talked to Bob was after he'd popped up between the molds on the strongback and said, "I'm from Ellsworth," and then told of how Canadians like to come to

Ellsworth to vacation and shop on the commercial strip there. Bob's in his late forties, like McGraw. A tall, athletic man, he went to the University of Maine, studied biology, and became a field biologist for the state of Massachusetts, "chasing birds and sexing fish," but gave it up rather than get transferred to Cape Cod, which was too crowded for him. Bob was yet another who'd gone to the Washington County Tech boatbuilding program, in Eastport, a campus so removed and a program so arcane they'd called it "Land of the Misfit Toys," and their social life (there were four men in his class) "The Longest Weekend with the Guys." After graduating in 1993 he worked with the master builder Ralph Stanley in Southwest Harbor, but there wasn't enough work for the winter and so Bosse got hired at Brooklin Boat Yard, where they were then building *Dragonera*.

McGraw seems to take in Bosse's remark with quiet agreement.

Andy Fiveland is working on *Fidelio* again, finishing the installation of the forefoot cap. It's still on his mind that Tim Horton has teased him, and called him a union man. ("The same stuff I've been hearing for years—high pay, no work; the only thing to do is give it back.") While Andy is chiseling, Tim walks by to get a paintbrush for spreading glue, and Andy says, "Hey, what are you doing over here, huh?" Andy looks away and winks, and doesn't see Tim, with lips tightened, turn toward him, take a step, turn back to *Nite Bird*, turn toward him again, catch himself, and turn back to *Nite Bird*. What Tim says is true—now that he's gotten older he waits a while to consider before he acts.

Fred Pollard has the glue machine rolling. Brian Larkin and Norm Whyte have put glue suits on and rubber gloves. ("I was hoping to get out of this," Brian says, "but I guess this is my year.") They're not wearing paper face masks—it's a small job and will be over quickly, and they're near the doors, which open periodically. But Hans Vierthaler is taking no chances. He's got on a full-face rubber ventilator from which he has to yell to be heard. He's mixing glue. Rick Clifton is the last one to join the bagging crew, leaving his 31 and pulling on a pair of rubber gloves, taking up a position to feed Ken Letterman planks as they come out of the machine.

"This is boatbuilding," Rick says.

The staple guns are going off, but Letterman's isn't working because he's banging it against the wood like a carpenter with an air hammer. He keeps swearing at the gun, until Tim stops stapling, marches around to the other side, and yells over the hum of the compressors that Ken should just hold and fire.

In the midst of the veneering a boat owner comes into the shop. His name is Ted Leonard. He's cleanly dressed and smoothly shaven. Leonard talks for a while with Brian Larkin, who's feeding clean veneers to Fred Pollard, and then he moves on to look at the other projects. At Norm's boat Leonard says that he has a day off from work and that "whenever I have a day off I inevitably head up here." He says that he loves talking to the crew and looking at the boats and the work.

Leonard and his wife own two Boothbay 21s, *Blue Witch* and *India,* built by Norman Hodgdon—boats that are in the *Quiet Tune* family. He says that a few years ago he had *Blue Witch* veneered with three layers of mahogany. Since then it had been like new, like a fiberglass hull, and he no longer had to worry about the planks opening up when he went to windward. *Blue Witch* is more than fifty years old, he says. Now that *India* was nearing fifty, Leonard wants to veneer her too.

Brian Larkin has a different take on it. He was part of the crew that veneered *Blue Witch,* and he says he'd told Leonard that he should just replace the garboards, the lowermost planks. Now Brian has told Leonard that he needs only to replace the garboards on *India* too. "Well, I just saved another boat," he says after Leonard has gone to find Frank Hull. But to look at *Blue Witch* over in the sardine factory building, with its smooth, fair hull and clean lines, and then to look at *India,* with the plank lines showing through the cracked paint, the latter boat's age evident in the weakness around the keel, it was easy to see why Leonard felt the way he did.

And to look at *Nite Bird* you could see why Brian Larkin felt the way he did, with all the glue, this covering of a simple boat, a Day boat. It could seem absurd, almost a sacrilegious act. The soul of a boat veneered, you could think.

They work up through the lunch hour, getting the veneers on, getting the bag taped on, getting the hoses in and the pump started. But there are some undetected leaks and they can't get enough of a vacuum inside the bag, so Frank Hull drives off to another yard to borrow a third pump.

Yet the bag is on and the veneering is done.

"How's it going?" someone asks Tim.

"Not too good," he says, but the humor is back in his voice, the edgy acceptance. The catboat is cold-molded, and to a degree, it's Tim's boat now.

❧

A few days later Arno Day comes into the shop. Arno is built much differently than Junior Day. He's short, and light, loose in his clothes. His posture is erect, his skin pale, his voice a soft rasp. He seems both flinty and ethereal. At his house Arno has converted a dining room into an office and drawing studio. As in

Joel's office, there are stacks of rolled plans all about, books about boatbuilding and yacht design on shelves and in stacks, and half-models on the wall. Arno has been surprised to hear that the catboat is still around. "There were two of them, actually," he has said. "My father built one and the other was built by a neighbor. They built them in about 1930. I would come home from school and couldn't resist going out on the river. I don't know how many times I found myself out in the river with the tide going out and the wind dying, and I'd have to row back. It kind of whetted my appetite for boats.

"He made it during a time when things were rough. My father ran a service station and fixed cars. He was born with the automobile. He built a few small boats just to keep busy at something. Boats carried him through. He built several round-bilged rowboats, twelve-feet long, and got thirty-five dollars for them. A while ago I was at Bath, and a boat he built was being considered for the museum. I confirmed it was one of the boats my father built.

"I sailed the catboat through my high school years, until I graduated from high school. Then it was sold to someone just down the road and I never heard of it again. It was a nice little boat. Most boats had a gaff rig, but this one had a Gunter rig."

At his studio Arno had talked about lofting, how he'd been hopelessly lost to it, and he talked about how his grandfather had built boats during the evolution of the modern lobster boat. He told of how he'd come to build a boat in Center Harbor one winter, and then built more, and of how Joel White came along. "I knew the practical side of boatbuilding. Joel had just come from naval architecture school, and he knew about such things as righting moment and displacement."

"Righting moment is a tricky thing to grasp."

"I still don't get it," Arno said.

He told about designing boats for Junior Day, and said that when he taught a class in model making last summer, half of the students decided to build a model based on the 24-footer, and that they'd gone over to the shop at the end of the class. Arno talked about some of the old builders, the generation before his, and he shut his eyes hard, squinting to remember. There was George Tainter, and Hawley Dow, and Allen Cole, who all had small shops along the shore. Arno said he'd been accused by others of working for nothing. "But I grew up around here in the thirties. Then we worked for and with our neighbors. It was how we survived. I'm glad I was a part of that time, that I had that experience. There's a great pleasure in helping people." And Arno told about how he had helped the young man build his own boat, the one that served as his college education, and how he had sailed it away, how the two became "like family." That day, when I left Arno, and thanked him for talking to me, he smiled and said it had brought back pleasant memories, and then: "It took my mind off design for a while."

Of the cold-molding process he said, "You can get a lot more years out of a boat that's sick that way."

Arno has heard about the catboat and come into the shop. It isn't often that he gets down to Brooklin Boat Yard. He first stops at *Fidelio,* which is by the doorway, and he talks with Pete Chase for a few minutes. Then, with just a glance at *Nite Bird,* he says, "Is that old slob still around?" and walks on toward the Center Harbor 31s.

From Norm's Boat, Brian Larkin calls out, saying, "I didn't do it, I didn't do it."

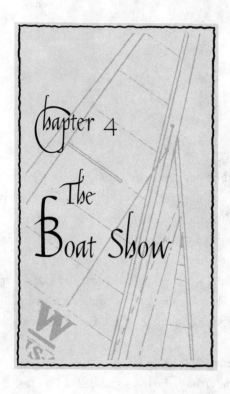

Chapter 4

The

Boat Show

February 1997

Steve White has come back from the Caribbean for a few days to check in on things at the yard. He's at the morning meeting today, giving the morning talk. Steve is comfortable being the one standing in front of the woodstove. He speaks easily, and what Joel has said is true—Steve is good with people. ("He didn't get it from me," Joel said; "I've never been a warm and fuzzy people pleaser.")

"Well, this is turning out to be the year of bad names," Steve says, and he begins to smile. "The Geier boat will be called *The Mantelpiece.*"

A collective "Huh?" goes up.

"And the Denney boat will be called *Pudding.*"

More of the "Huh" response, with groans and laughter. There are some in the crew who know that George Denney bought the Rozinante yawl *Red Head,* built at Benjamin River Marine, and changed her name to *Pudding*—and that after she was sold the name was changed back to *Red Head. Pudding* lacked the romance of other names, which tended toward the glorious, mysterious, or poetic, names such as *Alerion,* which meant a young eagle, or *Grace,* with its many possibilities, or *Fidelio,* and its implication of loyalty. Walk into a shed and the names play upon the imagination, a sense of mythology, of art or nature—in *Circe, Chimera, Madrigal, Petrel, Festina, Salt Wind,* and so many others. It could be hard to get down with a word like "pudding."

"The name of the runabout (the 22-footer that the crew is calling *Cow Lung*) still isn't certain yet. The owner has to check it out with his wife first, but tentatively it's *Chung Lao* and will be written in Chinese characters. We'll be taking it to the Boat Show." The Maine Boatbuilders Show, to be held in Portland in March.

"I'll be leaving tomorrow to go back to Antigua. Before I come back, in late April, early May, I'll be hauling out *Vortex* and painting her bottom and topsides, since it hasn't been done in two years."

"Do you have anyone interested in buying *Vortex?*" Rick Clifton asks.

"Yes, there's a Canadian who's interested. He'll be coming to look at it once it's back here."

Then without missing a beat Steve says, "The only bad news is that there will be a layoff of one or maybe even two guys from the carpentry crew, a little further along once the work slows down. *Fidelio* will be done soon, and *Nite Bird*. We can't put everyone on the 31s. We'll try to let the person or people know as soon as we've figured it out. We'll try to give at least two weeks' notice."

While the crew had been laughing and looking directly at Steve when he told them about the names, now they were looking down, not making eye contact. Many were wondering who, and hoping it wasn't him.

"That's it for today."

They break and go to work, and when Norm Whyte climbs into his boat, *Pudding,* the painter Kevin Duddy comes up to him and says, "So, Norm, does that take the pressure off now? Maybe we'll paint it a chocolate brown." *Pudding* is looking beautiful, though. After the veneering and bagging it's been faired and coated with epoxy, and then turned over. Norm and his crew have the sheer clamps in, and as with *The Mantelpiece, Pudding* now truly looks like a boat, with that line of spruce marking the sheer.

Norm is now making the engine bed. Bob Bosse is fitting the deck beams. Brian Larkin is framing out the cockpit. Joel McGraw is working up forward, measuring out the supports for the cabin bunks. Though Norm's crew is ahead of schedule, partly because Norm worked out a few shortcuts such as grinding the sheerline all the way down before putting in the sheer clamps, he's fretting about time. Norm has to work from the Geier boat's drawings and compensate for the differences in *Pudding*—there's no head in *Pudding,* for example. As of now, Norm has to launch his 31 a month after Rick's even though his crew got started two months later.

The interior of *The Mantelpiece* is filling out. The curved head door is in, and the cockpit seats, and the through-hull fittings. Andy Fiveland will begin fitting the engine after school vacation week is over and he returns from a ski trip with his son. Brian Stevens is away too, on *Dragonera,* moored off an island in the Bahamas.

On the outer part of *The Mantelpiece* hull they've cut the cove stripe, a half-round gouge that parallels the sheerline, placed there to give accent to the sheer. They've veneered the transom with a finish piece of mahogany, and the boat is beginning to shine.

At *Fidelio,* the planking has been finished, with the plank ends smoothly mated into the new forefoot and keel. At the bow, Pete Chase is now hammering a copper sheath over the joint between the forefoot and the stem. At the bottom of the hull, Paul Waring is using a power sander to fair the planking—one of the last things to be done before *Fidelio* moves into the paint shop. It's dusty work again. Paul is kneeling on a rubber mat, holding the power tool up and stroking along the planks, his head in a cloud of wood dust. During one break he shakes the dust off and says, "My friends tell me that boatbuilding is so romantic, and I say, 'Yeah, we sit around the fire and talk about boats all the time.'"

But Paul feels a connection to *Fidelio,* because of its designer, Olin Stephens. He'd met Stephens while a student at the Landing School, a building and design program in Kennebunkport. That year the students were building a Manhasset Bay One-Design, Olin Stephens's very first design, and both he and his brother Rod Stephens came to look at it. They gave a talk—during which, Paul remembered, they got into a heated discussion about cotter pins, and then diverged from it to tell the class they'd sailed and sailed as boys, and got to the point where they could sail a dinghy backward. Olin Stephens also met individually with some of the students and critiqued their design projects. Now Paul had a memory of spending a half hour with the man who had been called the greatest designer after Nathanael Herreshoff, and the last great designer in the golden age of yachting. Stephens had told Paul that his design had a good balance of the traditional and the modern.

In a way, Paul himself is a blend of the modern and traditional. Born in 1970, he'd been told by his mom that he'd attended antiwar demonstrations, in utero. Growing up on the southwestern coast of Oregon, he too had sailed and sailed, at first with his dad on a Tartan 30, an Olin Stephens design. They built a peapod together, and Paul had canoed and kayaked in the rivers around the small town of Hauser. He gravitated to boatyards, he said, and he was willing to dig in and attempt repairs—it was the way that he earned money as a teenager.

Paul tried college, but it didn't seem right for him, and then he traveled, a zigzagging hitchhiking trip through the United States which ended in Vermont, where he got a job at the Stowe Canoe

Company. He stayed for three years, building canoes of various kinds, and when he could, he visited boatyards. It occurred to Paul back then that he had "always been able to get something going in small boat repair," and he decided that he wanted to get deeper into it. The Landing School seemed a good place to go because of the design segment to the program, and when Paul left he felt he was at the point where he could create a design. He spent a year working at Bullhouse Boatworks in Kennebunkport, building Herreshoff E-Boats, also called the Buzzards Bay 15, designed by Nathanael Herreshoff in 1898.

During a trip to visit other yards he stopped at Brooklin Boat Yard and introduced himself to Steve and Joel. After a year at Bullhouse he figured it was time to go north, and so Paul, his girlfriend, and their son headed up the coast of Maine in their Volkswagen van. Paul had been reading about Joel's designs and his design reviews in *WoodenBoat* ever since he'd been in Oregon, and now he hoped to talk to Joel from a designer's point of view. Arriving at the yard, his eyes shining with eagerness, he said to Steve, "I want to build wooden boats!" Steve hired him a few months later when the Trumpy project began, and until then Paul worked independently, doing small boat repair. After camping out in the VW for a while, they rented a house. Paul had been at the yard five months now.

With the long blond hair, the VW van, the migration to the north, Paul seemed a throwback to some of the crew who were twenty years older—and crewmen such as Rick Clifton, Andy Fiveland, and Pete Chase sometimes saw themselves in him. Tim Horton did too—in the enthusiasm Paul had for the work. ("He's all full of piss and vinegar like I was," Tim said.) Paul had made a keel with Tim, and a deadwood with Pete, in the common arrangement of the young builder working with the more experienced one. Now he was fairing *Fidelio,* a design of the old master, here at a yard headed by another old master. Paul still hoped to talk to Joel, because he hadn't really discussed design with him yet. And he hoped someday to work on one of the cold-molded projects, so he could learn how.

Paul isn't complaining about the hard work of fairing with a grinder, the wood dust, and his joke about the lack of romance in his work isn't all true. "I like what I'm doing," he says. "Working with my hands, carving wood. Peter and I get along well together. There's something about an old-fashioned boat that really strikes home."

Early in the morning there's a break when the entire crew, seventeen men today, go out to move Beetle Cats, painted ones out of the paint shed, unpainted ones in. There's more than enough crew, so many that not all of them can get around the boat. But the group moves along together, some with just a hand out, some laughing as they go. It's a ritual, Pete Chase says, a fifteen-minute break in the day this time of year. There's a need to punctuate the day with this sort of thing. "Otherwise it's dreary," Norm Whyte says.

Tim Horton is at work on *Nite Bird.* The hull is smooth and rock-hard now, after the fairing and coating. There are little diamond-shaped patches underneath the epoxy coating, spots that didn't get glued during the bagging. Tim found them by tapping on the hull with his fingers. He has built a new centerboard trunk, replaced some of the deck beams, built a new plywood deck, a new brace along the keel, and new floorboards. Today he's fitting the sheer strake to the stem, while Ken Letterman, just back from a foot injury, installs new toe rails. The catboat looks transformed, almost new, the old oak skeg under the keel being the only piece that shows its age.

It seems a job to be proud of.

"Oh, we'll wait and see," Tim says, and then bangs at the notion as he might bang in a proud plank. "I don't get as excited about it as I used to. With the old boats we used to build here, *Alisande* and *High Time* and those boats, we were using a living thing to make a living thing. With those boats it was like the national anthem was being played when it went into the water. Henry Lawson, Belford Gray, they all felt the same way, that they'd created something that was alive, that they'd bent the timbers, planked it, rubbed it, and put a living thing into the water."

With a glance at the 31s Tim says, "Not with these boats."

"They're made of wood."

"But they're mostly glue. They're beautiful *vessels,* lovely to look at. The owners probably love them. The guys working on them probably love them." Then Tim laughs and says, "Maybe that's it, that I'm not working on them."

Yet Tim is proud of *Nite Bird,* and when it does go into the water later in the spring he will make a point of telling me where it's moored so I can row out and look at it. Now Tim is worried that the owners might not like the way the rebuilding has come out, and he's also worried that since *Nite Bird* is nearly completed, he might lose his job.

"It might be me that gets laid off," he says. He's not alone in this thinking. Fred Pollard, who's making chainplates for the 31s today, is worried that when he finishes he might be put on the carpentry crew and it could be him getting laid off.

The weather has been mild for February. The sky is a deep blue today, and there's a bank of flat cumulus clouds to the south of

Eggemoggin Reach. The waves are lapping gently on the beach, and near the shore a group of eider ducks are diving for crabs and mussels. The warm weather has been bringing owners in to the yard to look at their boats and think about getting them painted and launched. Usually that happens in March.

Joel and Bob Stephens are in the studio, both at work on drawings for the W-76. Bob is nearly finished with the accommodations drawing. The main cabin of the W-76 is 14 feet long, and relatively wide since the boat has a 16-foot beam. Bob has drawn in lots of lockers and cabinets, which will be of use to the crew. In the aft part of the cabin there's an L-shaped settee, and a foldup berth outboard above it. Forward of the settee is a galley with a four-burner stove, oven, refrigerator, and sink. Opposite the settee is a navigation station, and forward of that there's an enclosed head with a sink and shower.

There's a passageway forward from the main cabin, with a small sit-down shower. Through a doorway are the crew's quarters, a space about 7 feet in length and containing what Bob calls "spartan" bunks. There's a small toilet between the bunks, and there are lockers, and two deck hatches, both for an air flow—necessary for active people in a spartan space—and for quick access to the deck when the crew is needed there. Ahead of the crew quarters are storage lockers for sails.

As Joel puts it, Bob is designing the W-76 and he's just helping. Today he's working on a structural drawing, a cross section of the hull detailing the attachment of wooden laminated frames to the bronze keel frame. The keel frame will be a 22-foot I beam. The mast will step on it and the keel bolts will run through it, and it will be the main stress-bearing member.

Joel is walking more easily now, though he's still using the hand crutches. His hair is curling up from under his WERU cap.

Recently he's been in to see his doctor, and he's been told he won't have to be examined for a couple of months. When we go to the Morning Moon, Joel stops for his mail. He's heard from Donald Tofias, who has optimism for the W-76, and plans to take the radio-controlled model to the Wooden Boat Show at Mystic Seaport in June. And he's gotten a package of letters from a couple who are sailing from Australia. Their destination is Brooklin, where they've bought land and plan to build a house. The couple had taught at the WoodenBoat School. Joel is delighted with their adventures, which include landing on an island surrounded by a treacherous reef, where supply boats rarely come. Joel's friends gave a jar of instant coffee and some sugar to one of the islanders, who brought his family and prepared the entire jar at one sitting. And there's an account of some difficult navigating in a storm. "They're good seamen," Joel says. "If anyone can do it, they can."

How boats thread through this place. There's Jimmy Steele building peapods in a shop down the road—he's built more than 140 of them; there's Todd Skoog, building a boat to live aboard, maybe two years from now; Arno Day is designing boats in a place near the Benjamin River; there's a schooner captain, George Allen, who lives across from E. B. White's old place; there was the couple that sailed from England, discovered Penobscot Bay, worked at Brooklin Boat Yard, and then sailed to Ireland; and there's the couple sailing here now from Australia. There's *Grayling* at the Benjamin River, and *Andicon,* and now the L. Francis Herreshoff ketch *Albacore.* Eric Dow is about to start a rebuild on the sister to *Nite Bird.* Out behind the marine supply store, the unfinished tugboat, with titanium workshop projected. The marine supply store is run by Phil LaFrance, who with his wife, Valerie, owned the Starling Burgess cutter *Christmas,* which is now owned by Donald Tofias, who changed the name to *Arawak* ("the man who spoiled *Christmas*," the former owner says, while the present owner replies, "I'm Jewish; you expect me to sail a boat named *Christmas*?). Everyone seems to have some connection to sailing or boats—the carpenter working at Dorothy Jordan's rooming house is the son of the former cook on the schooner *Mary Day*. And even Dorothy Jordan, who brought her family up in Castine, had a son who was a sailor, and when he was dying of AIDS, she hypnotized him and took him sailing, finding it was the best way to ease his pain. Driving on the roads here, lobster boats, lobster traps, all along the way.

For a while Joel talks about *Cachalot,* the boat that he designed and that the yard launched in 1969. It's stored in one of the sheds at the yard, and inside the cabin are photographs of some spectacular groundings, one of *Cachalot* sitting upright on the rocks at low tide. "The client is someone I'd known since I was a kid, but he was someone who'd never really sailed, not that I knew of. So I designed a boat for a tall man with a lot of headroom. I made it a scaled-up version of *Martha,* the Sam Crocker boat I built for my dad. I built it real sturdy, thinking that he would be learning to sail on it.

"There's a derivative element to boat design," Joel says. "Nothing is new under the sun. Nearly everything is taken from something else. The boats being built now are adapted from *Quiet Tune.* On the Buzzards Bay 25s we built, we pretty much copied the design, using the original plans.

"Cold-molding has allowed us to build boats with traditional shapes. The critics say we're not building wooden boats, but with cold-molding we've been able to design and build the Center Harbor 31s and the Buzzards Bay 25s, and *Dragonera,* which couldn't have been built with traditional plank-on-frame construction, not with that light displacement.

"But I haven't done anything groundbreaking in boat design," Joel says.

And Taylor Allen's crew is well along on the building of *Boss Lady* now. "Taylor's yard hasn't done a lot of new construction. It's such a hard field to break into when you don't have a track record. It's good that Taylor is building the powerboat now, and if he can build one of the W-76s, he'll be on his way."

There's a birthday party at the Morning Moon, for Todd Skoog's ex-wife—she decided that she didn't want to go to sea ("You heard about the guy who built a boat and lost his wife?" Skoog said when I met him). Everyone in the restaurant sings to her, including Joel, including me. Back at the shop, a garbage truck is there, tended by a man who Joel says is amazing because he's always cheerful, and he's been a garbageman all his life, and he's always walked half bent over. He laughs when he sees Joel, and says, "Staying out of trouble, Joel?"

"Pretty hard to get into trouble with these crutches."

"Oh, I think you could get into trouble with those, Joel."

"Not the kind of trouble I want to get into."

Steve leaves that day.

He says that he'd been in a workaholic mode when he first got to the islands, and that for a while Laurie had felt left out. It took time to slow down. They'd done a lot of sailing together, from Antigua down to the Grenadines, to Bequia, St. Lucia, to Martinique. "We had some good sails," Steve says, "but we also had some hard sails with high winds. Laurie didn't feel superconfident. She told me, 'I'm in your hands, I hope you know what you're doing.'"

He's missed the yard and seeing the projects on a day-to-day basis. The yard had held up well, and there had been a lot of conferring among the crew, sometimes maybe too much conferring. But *Nite Bird,* Steve says, had come out beautifully. "The owner is crazy about the boat. He's had it a while and loves to sail it. He's putting eight thousand into it now. The rebuilding job on *Nite Bird* is proof of the value of veneering." The *WoodenBoat* editorial was right, Steve says, but the mistake was in saying that there aren't enough craftsmen anymore.

Steve has made the layoff, of one worker, Ken Letterman. Several people had trouble working with him, on several projects. He tended to want to get the job done too fast and banged through it sometimes. And because he didn't have a driver's license, it was hard on the guy who drove him in to work every day. Steve had given Letterman two weeks' notice. The announcement this morning had been his way of leading up to it.

∽

On a Saturday morning Rick Clifton is getting his own boat, *Jarges Pride,* ready for spring. It's a 33-foot Crocker cutter, originally launched in Massachusetts in 1970. During the winter Rick stores it in a plastic-covered shed he's built in his backyard. There's a Shellback Dinghy there too, one of the first Shellbacks built.

Rick and Jane Clifton have owned *Jarges Pride* for four years now. The former owners are summer residents of Brooklin. They bought the boat from a man who had purchased the timbered and framed hull from the Crocker yard in Massachusetts in 1965 and spent five years finishing it off. For many years it spent summers in Brooklin and winters in Massachusetts, staying in the water through the winter—"which is real good for the hull," Rick says.

During those summers when it was in Center Harbor, Rick had admired the boat. When he learned that *Jarges Pride* was for sale, he mentioned it to Joel's half brother, Roger Angell, who said, "That boat would be just right for you." Angell told the owners, who called Rick, and a meeting was arranged. Rick arrived at the yard early, and he went without Jane because he was so unsure. When he sat on the bench at the back of the shop he began to feel sad, the kind of feeling that comes from knowing you don't have the money to do something you want to do, and have to say so. When the owners arrived Rick told them he wasn't going to insult them with a low offer.

But they talked, and the man who owned the boat wrote a figure on a card and gave it to his wife. He asked Rick to write a figure down too, and give it to his wife. It occurred to Rick "that I was being manipulated in a beautiful way." The owner then looked at the cards and said, "I don't think we're that far apart." They talked about a payment plan, and a condition that would make for a reduction in price—that they could use *Jarges Pride* for two weeks each summer for the next five years. "The way I saw it," Rick says, "they were practically giving the boat to me."

It was theirs for the taking, but first Rick and Jane decided to go out for a sail. They wanted to make sure that they could get along with each other on a boat. They'd had some "run-ins" before, which Rick took credit for, saying that his training in racing on the Great South Bay had brought out a competitive and sometimes disagreeable side in him, that he could tend to get dictatorial at the tiller. And buying a sailboat was Jane's idea; Rick had thought that he would get a powerboat, and after the time when he went salmon fishing off Oregon, a hundred miles offshore, a time when he got sick, Rick also thought that if he ever did get a boat he'd probably stay close to shore, maybe even right on the mooring. So Rick wanted to see how the sailboat felt for himself, as an individual as well as a partner.

They borrowed Bob Stephens's boat *Willow,* and took it from Center Harbor out on the Reach. They had a nice sail. But then some clouds rolled in and it started to rain. Then the engine failed. Then they got hung up on some rocks. So they stayed out overnight on *Willow.* Rick cast an anchor, figuring that the boat would float free when the tide rose. But when the tide did start running it floated the boat but snagged the anchor, which couldn't be pulled free. They waited, and Rick rowed out in a dinghy, and worked the anchor free. By then the tide was slack, and the wind was weak, and so they had to tow the boat from its tender, under oars. Since Jane didn't feel confident at the helm of *Willow,* she decided to get in the skiff and do the rowing. They were hoping to make it back to Center Harbor before the Eggemoggin Reach Regatta finished, and the boats came in looking for moorings. Nearing Chatto Island, they got close to shore, close enough for the horseflies to fly out, landing on Jane, hard at work at the oars. Slapping at the flies, she did her best, and Rick sent words of encouragement from the cockpit of *Willow,* until someone finally stopped by with an offer of a tow. They did get into Center Harbor before the Eggemoggin Reach Regatta was done, and they were tied to a mooring before the boats, fresh from the race, came streaming in, and they just sat there, too tired to do anything but watch. But they figured, if they could get through that, they could probably handle owning *Jarges Pride.*

There's a lot of work to any boat, Rick says, "especially one that's past twenty years old, when, just like with a house, things start having to be replaced." Today he's refastening the stanchions.

The keel bolts need to be replaced. The bottom needs to be painted again. Some of the frames are cracked, because the hull had been planked too tightly with dry wood. The pieces that are varnished need to be varnished again. "I like working on the boat," Rick says, "even though I've got too much to do before it's time to put it in. I liked working on all the boats my father had, the derelict boats that we kept going as long as we could. When this boat is in the water, it's really something."

Jarges Pride has high freeboard and sturdy S. S. Crocker construction. Inside the cabin there's enough headroom for a tall person. There's a coal and wood stove.

"It must be nice to get a fire going and be in a warm cabin on a rainy day."

"It is," Rick says, "but we tend not to go out that often during bad weather."

There's a sink and icebox. A foldup table in the main cabin, many wooden cabinets, kerosene lamps, bronze portholes. There's a full-sized head with shower and toilet. Up forward, a smaller cabin with a V berth. "It's a small home," Rick says.

It has an engine, fortunately. "I like being able to move under power when the wind's not up, or when we just need to get somewhere at a certain time." Rick smiles happily. "A few times we've taken the boat out without the mast on, and just motored around, and it's been great." Rick says he'll replace the engine eventually. He and Jane are planning to take *Jarges Pride* to Florida and to travel along the Inland Waterway. And they may go to the Caribbean with some of the other builders and their boats. But before then there will be a lot of sailing in Maine.

The most common question Rick gets asked is "When are you going to change the name?" He tells them the name stays the same, that it's part of the agreement.

What a fine boat, and what a pleasure it must be to cruise along on it. Maynard Bray, writing of *Jarges Pride* in the book *The Guide to Wooden Boats,* in text accompanying a Benjamin Mendlowitz photograph, says, "Earlier, *Jarges Pride* was rail down; now, in a more moderate breeze, sailing is ideal, and by darkness, she'll waft home on what's left of the afternoon westerly. It's this kind of after-work sailing that makes all the maintenance worthwhile."

In the cabin of *Jarges Pride* is a small brass plaque, with four lines from John Greenleaf Whittier: "And not less fair the winding ways / Of Casco and Penobscot Bays / They seek for happier shores in vain / Who leave the summer isles of Maine."

March 1997

It's two days from spring, the sunrise at 5:44, sunset at 5:40. But three snowstorms have come in succession and cold winds are blowing in from the north. A foot of snow on the ground, ice everywhere about the yard, the sunlight seems too bright, winter too long.

"This is boat show week," Frank Hull says from the woodstove. "The runabout will be going down Thursday. Steve may be in Thursday too. He'll be here for the boat show."

The interior of *Pudding* is filling out. Brian Larkin is now installing the galley sink. Bob Bosse is fitting the deck beams around the cockpit. Joel McGraw is putting in the removable panels on the bunk seats. Norm Whyte is framing out the cockpit seats. Norm has learned that George Denney has decided to have a teak deck put on—Denny thinks that the boat deserves it. Everyone agrees that it will make the 31 more beautiful, but the deck installation will push the launching date ahead, probably into early July.

Norm says he likes the interior layout of *Pudding,* that it is spare and makes the most of the available space. There's no enclosed head, which takes up a lot of space and often results in a higher cabin roof. Even though this boat is top dollar, with teak deck and trim, "it's bucket and chuck it," Norm says. "Bucket and chuck it is the best way to go. You use that head in the morning and that's it for going down there for the next hour." Then Norm tells about a one-design sailboat common to England, in which there's an enclosed head but the cabin roof isn't raised. Instead there's a hatch, and when the mariner uses the toilet his or her head sticks up above the cabintop. "Whenever there was a regatta of this design, during the mornings in the harbor you'd look through the fleet and see all these heads above the cabin tops. Everyone knew what you were doing."

On *The Mantelpiece,* Rick is fitting the gutters under the cockpit seats, there to channel rainwater onto the cockpit floor and out through the drains. Brian Stevens is setting bungs into the screw holes of the toe rails. Jeep Gulliver is building a hatch cover up in the loft. Andy Fiveland is on *The Mantelpiece* now. He's installing soundproofing panels and rubber beading around the engine box. The owner, Jim Geier, wants his 31 to be as quiet as possible, and when he was at the shop told Andy that even the slightest hole can channel a lot of sound. They're now calling the limber holes through which water passes "acoustic ports." Andy is in a post-musical mood today; last night he played with his band, the DeSotos, at a party for the high school girls' basketball team. Andy says they wanted to hear "Wild Thing" and "Runaway."

Both of the owners of the CH 31s have been in to see their

boats, and both of them have liked what they've seen. Both of them also think that the other's name is a little bit strange.

Fidelio has left the shop and has been fully painted. She will go into the water soon, so that the hull can swell, and Pete Chase can watch for leaks. *Fidelio* seems a much different craft now, sitting on low blocking on the concrete floor of the paint shop. Looking long and low, she does indeed seem the stealthy ocean racer she was designed to be, looking like a pyramidal projectile. *Nite Bird* is also in the paint shop, again sitting ahead of *Fidelio,* looking dreamy with the oak sheer strakes and toe rails, with the hollow curve in the snubby bow, with that pretty sheerline—that shape carved long ago in a man's hand. *Nite Bird* is getting a third coat of varnish on the oak pieces, and a first coat of gray paint on the interior. Later in the week the hull above the waterline will be painted white.

In *Fidelio*'s place in the shop is *Senta,* a 53-foot Philip Rhodes–designed cutter, built in 1937. Pete Chase, Paul Waring, and Tim Horton are replacing the sternpost and the lower ends of the frames. The frames are so badly split that when they lifted *Senta* the keel came up a ways before the upper part started to move. A boat in that condition is called "tender." The crew will also replace some of the bottom planking, a job that will require shaping, steam, and some heavy persuasion, since some of the planks are six inches wide in places, and an inch and a half thick.

Pete Chase is building the sternpost, a huge vertical timber rising from the aft end of the keel. The original sternpost, built sixty years ago, was a piece of mahogany 12 inches thick, 24 inches across, and 6 feet long. They're using oak for the replacement, but can't get a piece that big, and so Pete is joining two 12-by-12-inch pieces. He shapes them first with a chain saw and then with an adze. Then Pete works the big timber with a drill and circle-saw bit to form a groove for the rudder stock.

Paul and Tim are repairing the frames, shaping the lower ends with a grinder and a power plane. This morning Tim is away from *Senta* for a while because Frank Hull has asked him to build a set of stairs to take to the boat show, so that people can get a look inside the runabout.

During the morning several of the crew gather at *The Mantelpiece,* lift up the cabintop, a gleaming mahogany structure with curved sides and roof, and set it on the deck. But it's soon apparent that there's a problem. "The hole in the deck isn't big enough," Fred Pollard says. "It's wracked," Rick says.

It's not clear why the cabintop doesn't fit. It could be the molds, Rick says. It could be the crown of the deck. But it's difficult for Fred Pollard to see because he's spent weeks building the cabintop, and made many trips out to *Grace* to take measurements so as to avoid a misfit. They study the problem quietly for a while before deciding on a course—they'll trim the bottom of the cabintop sides, and they'll enlarge the opening in the deck. They shim up the cabintop on blocks over its deck opening, and Rick scribes a line along the bottom edge. Then they set it on the floor, upside down on blocks. Fred will do the cutting, while Rick will trim the hole in the deck.

It had been said many times, by Joel, by Steve, by the others, that boatbuilding is a matter of solving problems, and so here was a problem, a misfit. Norm has been watching, and now he's concerned about his cabin because his crew used the same molds, and there was that flood during the setup in January. But he figures he might be able to avoid what's happened on *The Mantelpiece* by taking measurements, and by building a template to check their framing. This is all part of the work, Norm says. "There's a few teasers along the way, but the boatbuilder knows how to make it work out. In the end it comes out right. That's the beauty of it, that it's something made by hand."

❦

Junior Day is sitting in the chair next to the woodstove. It's such a quiet place, after the drone of tools around the *Senta* project.

"Quiet is good," Junior says.

He's built the deck on the 24-footer and caulked it. With hull and deck done, he'll now start on the interior. Junior has some prospective buyers, he says, a couple who own a larger boat that they've lived aboard and used for cruising. Now they're looking for something smaller, though they've told Junior his 24-footer might be a bit too small. They told him they'd try it out and if they didn't find it big enough Junior could build them a 28-footer.

He laughs. "Just like that," he says. "Just like that I'll build them a twenty-eight-footer." Then he makes a general complaint about those people who buy a Maine lobster boat and then outfit it with so much gear that it no longer looks like a Maine lobster boat. He reaches to the workbench for a photo, one that shows a lobster boat with a cabin running all the way back to the stern.

The 24-footer, Junior says, will cost "somewhere around thirty thousand dollars."

At the stern is a ladder, and from it there's a good view of the new deck. It has an inward curve and rise as it approaches the bow that's both dramatic and tasteful, completely within proportion. At the bow the narrow planks of the deck come together like a sunburst because they're sprung to parallel the deck edge. The wood is mahogany. I ask if Junior will be varnishing it but he says he won't, that varnish is too easy to nick and scratch. "Paint is good enough for a Maine lobster boat," he says.

I ask about some of the old builders, those whom Junior knew when he was younger. He's told about George Tainter before, who gave him the skiff models. With the old builders, he says, a lot of paths crossed. "Some of them came together, built a boat, then went their own ways. George Tainter built a boat called *Andicon* with Allen Cole, a dwarf with long arms. He used to say he was just the right size for working under a boat."

Joel had told me about Allen Cole too, that he had a shop near where Joel lived, on Allen Cove. Both he and George Tainter had worked on the Friendship sloop that they'd put the piano in, for Paul Coolidge. Joel said that Allen Cole died not long after building *Andicon*.

"*Andicon* is still around," Junior says. "It's stored over at Doug Hylan's place." He says that Doug Hylan with Maynard Bray had "taken the lines off the boat" not long ago. The owner, who'd had *Andicon* for many years, was thinking of building a reproduction.

I warm my hand at the stove for a moment before I go. Junior gets up and walks to the boat, climbing the ladder, saying what he usually says: "Take it easy."

Andicon is in a shed with one other boat, a design known as an H-28, one of the L. Francis Herreshoff designs published in *Sensible Cruising Designs,* one of the lifestyle boats. *Andicon* is an odd boat to look at, with a high cabintop that looks like a hat raked forward on the head, a bowsprit that looks like an elephant tusk, a banana-shaped hull with a sheerline that's graceful in the middle part but which curves up at the ends in a way that's both surprising and puzzling. It has a keel that looks like a stone wall, running rectangularly along the bottom. *Andicon* was obviously not meant to sail fast, yet with its oddities and idiosyncrasies it's charming to look at, like one of those fantasy animals, a mythological beast with incongruous parts—a bear's paws, a giraffe's neck, elephant tusks, an antelope's tail.

Doug Hylan says that *Andicon* is the last surviving sloop of a kind common around here at one time. There's no particular name for the type; built with inexpensive materials and iron fastenings, they weren't meant to last. *Andicon* was built in the late 1920s, made for summer people by two boatbuilders who normally built boats for fishermen, using two layers of oak for the ribs, common in lobster-boat construction. The gave it a heavy mast, and a big, heavy keel, to prevent the boat from ever tipping over.

But *Andicon* didn't sail well. It tended to head up into the wind and not come about. It sat in a shed for a few years, and then was sold to a man by the name of Dick Hunneman. He tried to sail it, but kept heading into the wind, so Hunneman took a sketch of the boat to L. Francis Herreshoff in Marblehead, Massachusetts. Herreshoff said there was too much sail in the aft part of the boat, which was the reason it wouldn't come about. He told Hunneman to change the rig, from gaff to Marconi, in order to shift the center of effort forward. He said to add on a five-foot bowsprit and to add about 500 pounds of lead to the keel. Hunneman did that, and he raised the cabin roof for more headroom. He sailed *Andicon* for many years, and then gave it to his son, who had also sailed it every summer for years—often going two or three days at a time, making trips to Swans Island, Mount Desert Island, and other spots.

This man, Dick Hunneman Jr., who lives in Sedgwick, had told Doug Hylan to take the lines off *Andicon*, saying he wanted to build another "just like her." *Andicon* had started to leak heavily. When Hylan inspected the boat he found that when he pulled on the mast shrouds, the lower plank seams opened on the other side. For some reason the boat had been built without floor timbers, crosspieces tying the frames together across the keel. Hylan was going to put some floor timbers in after *Grayling* was launched, and he figured with that repair *Andicon* would be around a while longer.

Grayling is in the final stages, and looking beautiful, with the pilothouse completed, the engine in, the interior nearly done. They're thinking that the launching is about a month away.

~

The workday is over at the yard. At the WoodenBoat School, a brick-and-slate barn turned into a boatbuilding shop, Brian Larkin, Paul Waring, and Brian Stevens are helping a group of schoolkids, three girls and two boys, build a 12-foot sailing dory. It's an after-school project, and a schoolteacher is there too.

Brian Larkin works on the stern seat with one of the girls. They've set the four planks in. Using a compass, Brian scribes a line to give a curve to the seat's forward edge. Then they back out the screws, and the girl takes the planks to the band saw and cuts the ends. She puts them in the boat, and a new line is there, echoing the shape of the hull.

Brian Stevens is building a boom with the boys. They've cut two pieces of wood and are scarfing them together, and they're checking them with the plans.

The boat is a Harry Bryan design called *Daisy*, a nice little dory-skiff with lapstrake cedar planks fastened with copper nails, and a flat double-planked bottom, and with a mast and boom. There will be no caulking, only painting. After going into the water the planks will swell, making the hull watertight. "Nature doing its work," Brian Larkin says. "Someone said to me, 'Won't water get in it?" and I said, "I hope so!' "

Paul Waring helps one of the girls get the forward seat in, and then they attach the breasthook, the piece at the stem that ties the sides together and is used as a handle to carry the boat. Paul is enjoying himself, his face full of pleasure, just as the faces of the kids are full of pleasure. Where once before, covered with sawdust, he joked about the romance of boatbuilding, now he actually is a boatbuilder by the woodstove, talking about boats. A seat plank goes down, the rails get fastened, a winter's day in March; three boatbuilders and five kids, putting together a boat they can launch before school's out, one of the many launchings coming up.

 ❧

Joel and Allene spend a week in the Caribbean on the island of Tortola. On their return they stay in Boston for a night so that Joel can see his "leg man," and he arrives at the yard late the next morning. In the mail he's gotten a publicity brochure for the W-76 from Donald Tofias. The cover reads: *"Introducing the 76' 4″ W-Class Racing Yacht, the Shape of Things to Come. One-Design Cold-Molded Wood Day Racer Designed by Joel White, N.A. Crafted in Maine by: Taylor Allen, Rockport Marine, Steve White, Brooklin Boat Yard."*

The text begins: *"The world has not seen a one-design class of this size since 1913 when the Herreshoff Manufacturing Company built the New York 50s designed by Nathaniel Herreshoff. The purpose of the W-Class is to promulgate intense, satisfying racing, among a fleet of identical yachts with a traditional, aesthetically pleasing appearance. . . ."*

And: *"The W-Class Racing Yacht is a carefully thought-out*

design by Joel White, Naval Architect of Brooklin, Maine, blending the best of the past with modern technology to create a beautiful fast boat. Above the waterline the yacht looks like NY50, M-Class, or 12-Meter boat from the early 20th century. Beyond the graceful overhangs, the knife-angled bow and gently curved tucked-up stern, is a 95' tall carbon-fiber mast and modern underbody. The fin keel, with 25,000 pounds of lead and bronze, has a draft of 11' to balance the 2,239 square feet of sail area. Seasoned shipwrights with extensive cold-molded wood construction experience in Maine will build the W-Class yacht using the latest cold-molded wood construction techniques."

The brochure describes cold-molded construction, the boat's dimensions, the rigging, and ends with a lyrical description of the W-76:

"With their long balanced overhangs, long-radiused stern, and sweet sheerline, these yachts will make a grand sight under sail, on a mooring, or at the dock. It will be a thrilling sight to see the W-Class yachts in a close race, heeled over, driving to the windward mark; the sunlight reflecting off their gleaming sails."

Reading through the brochure, Joel sees that much of the writing is his.

$\backsim$

But the inspiration comes from Donald Tofias.

"I've been talking to Joel about building a boat for four years," Tofias said. "I was going to buy *Spartan*, one of the last New York 50s. It's a Nat Herreshoff boat, seventy-two feet overall, fifty along the waterline. Nine were built in 1912 and 1913, complete for $17,000. They were raced as a class in the teens. That was the last time anybody built a boat that big as a class.

"I started talking to Joel about building a big boat for racing. I bought *Christmas,* repainted it, and Joel redesigned it. In the process I learned about outfitting an old boat. Cold molding is better. There's less wood, more glue.

"The idea is to have Rockport Marine and Brooklin Boat Yard build them. We may get a third site just for this. There's a problem in that it will take up all of both yards. It's a problem for me psychologically because others couldn't get into the yard. I want to be careful of that, of what it will do to the community.

"We set up Padanaram Yacht Company for the marketing effort. We hope they will be purchased by colleges, for intercollegiate sailing. My public relations program is to get them to fund it. Prep schools or individuals or corporations can buy them too. The boat will retail for about two million. The program will run about five hundred to six hundred thousand a year, for crew, maintenance, and transportation.

"They'll race in June, then sail to the Caribbean for the winter. The race schedule will be from January to March in the islands. The boats will spend time in Maine and Newport. I can imagine a fleet of ten or fifteen of these tacking through Boston Harbor, with spectator fleets. We'd like to build forty boats over the next ten years, a 100-million-dollar project.

"I came up with this, partly because of the New York 50s and *Spartan,* and because I'm enamored of the idea of being born too late. If I'd lived in the 1890s I probably would have bought one of them.

"This boat is a big Buzzards Bay 25. It has a pretty sheerline. Heeled over, it will create a long and beautiful waterline. These will weigh 50,000 pounds. The modern 12-Meters weigh 75,000.

"I'm very fond of the White family," Donald Tofias said. "Very impressed with Joel's ability. I wrote my senior paper at

Newton High School on E. B. White. I give *Elements of Style* to my employees."

Joel leaves the office, and goes down through the shop. He stops briefly to look at the work on *Senta,* its lower planks off, the frames and keel exposed. When he walks away Joel says, with a little laugh, "What they're doing on those boats is often a mystery to me now." In the parking lot he meets Frank and Grace Henry, who've come in for a look at *Grace,* and to show Joel some Benjamin Mendlowitz photos of her. The boat is heeled over in steel-gray water, with the sun low and wind-whipped clouds in the sky. "Benjie likes those dramatic skies," Joel says.

At the Morning Moon, Joel says that he brought the second recording of his dad's works to Tortola, and that he played it for the friends and family who were there. He'd been listening for when they laughed. He says that in his reading of "Home-Coming," from the *Essays,* they laughed when he read: "A glance up the flue made it perfectly plain that, after twenty-two years of my tenure, the place was at last on fire." And they laughed when in "A Shepherd's Life," from *One Man's Meat,* he read: "We don't encourage animals to come into the house, but they get in once in a while, particularly the cosset lamb, who trotted through the living room not five minutes ago looking for an eight-ounce bottle." Joel doesn't say anything about laughter to his reading of "Once More to the Lake," but he does say, "It's a really good essay."

I tell him I've been reading *The Trumpet of the Swan,* and that I've loved the humor in it. Joel says it's his least favorite of his dad's children's books. The cob, he says, is modeled on his grandfather, "who was quite a speechifier." The boy was modeled on, and then he pauses, and gives me a look, and says, "Well, any boy." I'd already wondered if the boy Sam was partly inspired by Joel—because Sam is someone who keeps things to himself. Joel says the camp on the northern lake where Sam and his father stayed was modeled on a real camp that E. B. White used to go to in Ontario. "And he studied up on swans a lot before writing," Joel says.

I say how much I like his dad's way of combining the trite expression with the factual statement. Louis decides to have "a light breakfast of water plants." The cob says he didn't "fly all the way north into Canada to get involved with a *boy.*" Joel says it's amazing how E. B. White was able to bring the reader in to accept such "credible creatures—a little mouse, a swan with a slate and trumpet around its neck, a talking spider."

During lunch, the librarian from Friend Memorial Library, just across the road, comes into the restaurant and sits in the booth beside Joel. She has a letter, and she wants to ask about permissions for E. B. White's work. Someone has written an inquiry to her about translating *Charlotte's Web* into Tibetan. Joel says to tell them to contact HarperCollins, and that they would contact him.

"I knew you'd be part of the process," she says.

"And I'll tell them the Tibetan has to be absolutely perfect."

Joel spends the afternoon working on the drawings for the W-76, the shape of things to come.

❧

Steve returns to Brooklin the next day, and leads the morning meeting before going to the boat show.

"The only news," he says, "is that I might need a crew to bring *Vortex* up from Antigua to Bermuda, and from Bermuda to here. I'll probably need four guys. There will be full pay." Jeep Gulliver's hand goes straight up, the only volunteer. But after the talk Joel McGraw goes up to Steve and says that he'd like to go, "But I'll have to talk with the admiral first."

Steve will be racing in the Antigua Classic Yacht Regatta. As a reward for managing the yard this winter, he'll bring Frank Hull to Antigua to be part of the crew. After that Steve will get back to the yard, and he'll hire a professional captain to sail *Vortex* to Maine. In April, Steve says, there might be fifteen or twenty jobs going on at one time, too many for Frank to handle by himself.

At the meeting Steve has said that a carpenter should go with the painter Bob Austin to look at a repair job, and then he looked at Andy Fiveland and said, "Andy, you do it." Andy was thrilled— it's the first time he's been called a carpenter, and it puts him that much closer to being a boatbuilder. Andy wanted to say something right then but he held back. When they all stood up Pete Chase went to Andy and said, "Hey, you're a carpenter!" Andy grinned and said, "Yeah!"

Pete is boring some holes through the sternpost, for bolts that will fasten it. They're very long holes, more than 28 inches deep. He's set up a little frame to use for a sighting device, but otherwise Pete is boring the holes by eye. He does this from a seated position, pushing the drill from his waist. He'll push the drill, back off, let the shavings fall out, and push again. When he's done with this job, Pete cuts a rabbet in the sternpost, using the slick, that big, wide chisel, and a mallet to strike it. The rabbet is an inch and a half deep, the thickness of the planking. When that is done, he shapes the lower part of the sternpost with an adze, putting a graceful taper in it. One slice at a time, Pete performs one of the oldest shipwright skills, hewing the timbers.

Today is Pete Chase's birthday, and he'll soon spend more

than sixty dollars on beer, a bottle of whiskey, and snacks for the crew. "It's only once a year," Pete says. Today is also the spring equinox, day and night in momentary balance. Pete is asked, if his birthday is on the equinox, then could he have been conceived nine months before on the summer solstice? "That's my father's birthday," he says. Last weekend Pete got a haircut, and for a while it lay down, but already it's out there again, that celestial ring.

Paul Waring is making the new frame ends for *Senta,* with Tim Horton, the two paired again. They're building sectional units, with doubled pieces of 2-by-3-inch oak bolted through, a dozen or more bolts per frame pair and floor timber. When they get a frame unit in, one of the men bores down through the floor timber and on through the keel, running a bolt through these members to tie them together. The construction looks very sturdy, especially next to the original, slender, now broken frames. The estimate calls for twenty hours per frame unit, but Paul figures they're getting them in a bit under that.

Tim bores one of the holes through the floor timber and keel, with a bit so long that it tosses him around. "Just another rotten old wooden boat," he says, holding on. After he makes up another set of frame ends he leaves for the dentist, to get a tooth pulled. While he's gone, Paul puts the frames in, figuring he should just move ahead with the job. When Tim returns and sees the frames in, he gets angry. Paul, surprised again, tells Tim he hasn't been trying to piss him off, and Tim, looking it over, thinking it over, says he's been having a bad day and they'll just forget about it.

On the floor in front of *The Mantelpiece,* Fred Pollard is using a saber saw to cut the lower edge of the finely finished cabintop— and it pains him. It's like cutting the tips of the legs off a new dining-room table to make it fit the floor. But he's focused on the line, and pushes ahead.

Inside *The Mantelpiece,* Brian Stevens is wiring the cabin. Andy Fiveland spends some time finishing up the soundproofing of the engine cover. Rick has gone up to the loft for a while, to make the tiller. He does this by clamping strips of mahogany into a gooseneck-shaped jig and glueing them together. After a trip to the glue barrel, stirring up some epoxy, Rick says, "First thing you do when you're gonna build something, you get some glue, fill a big pot." He brushes some on the wood, looks up, and says, "I'm boatbuilding."

On *Pudding,* Norm is building the carlins, the longitudinal framework for under the cabin. He's built a template for the cabintop and is using it to check his work. Bob Bosse is putting the last of the deck beams in. Brian is building the galley. Joel McGraw is at work on the bunks, though for a while he goes up into the loft to chisel out a section of the mast step so that it will fit over the floor timbers.

To move his chisel, McGraw uses a wooden mallet, with a head made of lilac and a handle made of cherry. His toolbox is an esoteric collection, antiques and second hand pieces. His sharpening stones come from what he calls a pawbox, and he says there are lots of them in the shop where he lives. "They're boxes that people threw various things into, and then when they need something they paw around in there looking for it." He says he'll probably buy an adze soon, because he's had occasion to use one here, and there are lots of them coming out of barns and sheds along the coast, "from the days of the shipwrights." At home after work this week McGraw is preparing for the boat show. He'll be selling his Flower Dories there. He went to a flower show last weekend, and says that men stopped at his display because they could relate to the boats. He figures that women will stop by the display this weekend because they can relate to the flowers.

Hans Vierthaler is setting up shrouds and spreaders for the CH 31s, and Kevin Duddy is varnishing a hatch cover, while two other painters, Bob Austin and Bob Becker, tape off the waterline on *Nite Bird*. Frank Hull moves a mast with the Travel-lift, while Steve moves about the yard, job to job. Bob Stephens is up in the studio, while Jeep Gulliver is in the loft, finishing a hatch cover for *The Mantelpiece*. All about there are sounds: a mallet upon a chisel handle, the hard whine of a drill, the rub of sandpaper, the sounds of saws and hammers. All about are stacks of woods, the cedar, mahogany, spruce, teak, and oak, the sawdust everywhere, and in some places, under a hull, wood shavings in piles that look as fresh as snow. There's glue in pots and containers, and drips of glue that look like beads of wax on the benches and floors. There are the toolboxes, each a bit different—Joel McGraw's old paintbox, Brian Stevens's canvas bag from *WoodenBoat,* Andy Fiveland's new boxes with neatly mitered corners and handles made of sail track, and there's Fred Pollard's master set. The staging and the ladders, the many kinds of clamps all about, the benches with saw marks, the old hand saws hanging in the window, the long augers on the sills. And in the midst of it, those water-bound sculptures.

Then it's time to lift the cabintop on to *The Mantelpiece* again. It sets down into place, though there's a bit of shaving to do yet. Chiseling one of the corner posts, Rick is happy and relieved that this problem has been solved. He talks about the pleasurable feeling of wood coming together, the click of pieces joining right.

"I'm boatbuilding now," Rick says, and he means it.

❧

The Maine Boatbuilders' Show takes place during the first weekend of spring, marking the beginning of a new year in boating.

It's held inside an abandoned factory building in Portland, on the waterfront, and exhibitors of all kinds are there, from boatbuilders to marine supply businesses. The majority are from Maine, but come also from the other New England states, from New York and maritime Canada, from Florida and California. The town of Brooklin is, represented in Brooklin Boat Yard, Bridges Point Boat Yard, Atlantic Boat Company, Brion Rieff Boatbuilding, and Wooden-Boat Publications. Many of the crew from Brooklin Boat Yard come to the show, some bringing their wives. They rent rooms in the same hotel, have meals together, and make a vacation of it. They joke that, for them, going to Portland is a trip to the south.

Steve and Laurie White are there, taking in the exhibits. Laurie is back permanently from the Caribbean now, though Steve will be returning to Antigua to race. Joel spends an afternoon at the show. Andy Fiveland comes for the day, with Daniel, and they not only look at the boating exhibits but also take in the little train museum next door. Paul Waring comes for a day, and it's a bit of a return to the past for him, with the presence of the Landing School at the show, and of Bullhouse Boat Works, which has brought a Herreshoff E-Boat, long and elegant of line. Bob Stephens is there, and for him it's satisfying because the Apprenticeshop of Rockland is exhibiting the completed 22-foot counter-stern launch, his design based on a Gil Smith catboat.

Bob Bosse is there, and underneath his jacket is a Longfield Dory Company T-shirt, East Blue Hill, Maine. By agreement, he spends time standing near the Longfield Dory exhibit. Joel McGraw is dressed in a corduroy jacket, his hair neatly combed, and he's handing out business cards to interested buyers. One of his Flower Dories has a nice flower arrangement in it, and others are stacked up on the floor. Several fiberglass half-models are on the wall behind him. And what McGraw has expected does happen—women who've come with their husbands to the boat show find something appealing in his dories.

Tim Horton is at the show too. He'll be staying overnight, and getting together with his brother Cary, a ship's captain—and the Maine Maritime Academy Alumni Association is represented too. Tim is meeting a woman here, who has come up from Massachusetts for the show, a friend, Tim says. Friday after work he's gone into Ellsworth and bought a new set of clothes. Of this Tim says, "You may have noticed that they're similar to what I wear to work," and it's true—he has on blue jeans, a khaki shirt, and white athletic shoes. Then Tim grins. "But they're new!" he says.

Down one aisle, Wade Dow and his wife (who is Ken Tainter's daughter) at a table with brochures advertising the Bridges Point 24, which has a base price of $28,000. Near them, the display of Harry and Martha Bryan, Bryan Boatbuilding, St. George, New Brunswick, with a display of a decked canoe and a small runabout, both with a honey-amber finish. It was the Bryans who in the 1980s built *Patience*, from a design Joel White adapted from a sketch in *The Rudder* to make *Alisande*, and sailed her with their two children, in their early teens, to Tasmania and back—halfway around the world, as Harry Bryan put it.

And next to the Bryans is the exhibit of Arey's Pond Boatyard, based in Orleans, Massachusetts. That yard, which specializes in building small catboats and Arno Day skiffs, is owned by Tony Davis. His family has a home in Brooklin, and he grew up spending summers there. It was Davis whose father enlisted Arno Day to teach his son how to build a boat and used an education fund to pay him. They spent three years building a Lyle Hess cutter, named *Syrinx*—after the nymph who was turned into the reeds for the god Pan's pipes—and they built a tender for the boat, a skiff named *Pan*. "An apprenticeship in the true sense of the word," Davis says.

"Arno teaches a lot of things indirectly, and while he's teaching boatbuilding he's teaching a way of life too." The catboats that Davis builds, in three sizes, are called Kitten, Cat, and Lynx. They come with fiberglass hull, teak coaming and rails, spruce spars, ash and mahogany tiller, bronze fittings, and Dacron sails.

In another display room, a large, open room, is the 22-foot runabout built by Norm Whyte and Bob Stephens last fall, the one they've been calling *Cow Lung*. It's placed in the center of the room, prominently so, because the boat is on a trailer that raises it above the floor. The deep-blue finish of the hull is at eye level, as is the stem, the bow profile. Next to the boat are the stairs, and from them is the view of the brightly finished mahogany interior, the mahogany steering and control panel, the seat cushions upholstered in white, and the teak deck, with the clean course of planks around the cockpit, and the serrated king plank up forward in the center. The teak is unfinished and smooth, the rubbery compound between the planks.

Also on the stairs, a stack of publicity brochures for the W-76, "The Shape of Things to Come." Donald Tofias is at the show too, taking in the exhibits, wearing a red satin jacket with the name *Arawak* on the back.

Various members of the crew are taking turns standing by the boat to answer questions, and others gather around it. Rick and Jane Clifton are there, Norm and Lynn Whyte, Brian and Karen Larkin. Jeep Gulliver takes a turn at the display.

There's a constant flow of people coming up the stairs, resting their arms on the deck and looking in. Others walk around the boat, take in the shape of the hull, the run of the sheerline, the curve of the bow profile, the match of color.

And the crew stands by, clearly proud of the quality of the craftsmanship, their connection to it, and the beauty in it.

Chapter 5

Joyful
Music

April 1997

As one of Joel's friends said, he was trying to live to the fullest. By mid-April he and Bob Stephens had completed twenty of the W-76 drawings, and were getting close to finishing their part of the project. Joel was interviewed by a Boston TV station about the *White on White* tape, something friends thought he may not have done before now. He gave a reading at the Ellsworth Public Library, selections from *Stuart Little* and *Charlotte's Web*. He was occasionally working on the beginning chapters of a book about sailing and cruising, with a former *WoodenBoat* editor now at a publishing house elsewhere in Maine. But Joel's health took a turn for the worse, when more cancer appeared in his lungs and liver. He began new rounds of chemotherapy.

❧

A pastel hue has come to the sky, an April light. Work is going on outside now, and the shop doors are open. Some boats have been moved out of the sheds, and others have been uncovered, but only one sailboat is in the water, *Fidelio,* sitting high on her waterline, the springy sheer making her look jaunty. A fishing boat is moored nearby and piled high with traps, but soon it leaves and *Fidelio* is the solitary boat in the harbor. *Fidelio* leaked steadily after they put her in yesterday, but now the planks have swelled and there's only an occasional stream coming from the bilge pumps.

The sound of a torch and scraping is coming from Building No. 2. Inside, Tim Horton is working on *Wigeon,* a Herreshoff S-Boat getting a partial rebuild. Tim is sitting on a staging plank, removing bottom paint. There are three layers at least, green to blue to red. He's filthy with blackened paint and dust, even though it's not yet eight o'clock.

"They got me on the bottom again," Tim complains. "Soon as I get up above the waterline they put me back on the bottom." He's been moved off *Senta,* where Pete and Paul are planking the hull, to do this work on the S-Boat.

"Seems so anyway," he says.

The planks above the waterline are scraped smooth, down to bare cedar. Tim has taken a few forward planks off, and the thin keel is visible on this greyhound of a boat. There are little pigs of lead trimming ballast set on the keel. "These boats were made to go fast as hell, raced hard, and then be thrown away," Tim says. "They weren't meant to have all this done to them seventy years later." But this is only Tim's contrariness, his saltiness. He likes the S-Boat and this kind of repair work. He lists the things that *Wigeon* needs—a stem replacement, new deadwood, a thorough replanking. *Wigeon*'s new owner wants to get it into the water, race with other S-Boats during the summer in Rhode Island, and he'll continue the rebuilding later. The owner might do some of the work himself.

Tim has refastened the planks above the waterline. Because the screws were spinning around in the old holes, Tim made about a thousand plugs, turning square pieces of wood into round on a grinder, one rainy day, and then he glued and tapped the plugs into the screw holes. "It looked like a porcupine for a while," he says. When the plugs swelled he chiseled them off, and refastened with bronze screws in new holes.

Tim sits on the staging plank, under the overhanging bow of *Cirrus*, torching and scraping, but it's a nice day, warm with the temperature already nearing fifty. Tim keeps looking outside at the April sky. He's just bought a membership to a golf course, and there are storms forecast for the next three days, and ultimately it's too much to resist. With plans to come in on Saturday to make up the time, Tim is soon on his way up the hill and down the road.

Caleb Joel is in the yard, up on jackstands. John White is "washing the beard" off the bottom, the six-inch ring of marine growth running around the hull at the waterline. The scallop fishing wasn't all that good last winter, he says. The first few weeks were okay, but then it tailed off and John moved back from Gouldsboro toward Brooklin. "Lot of wind this winter," John says. "It was hard to get out." Next he'll be dragging for sea scallops beyond the three-mile limit, before putting in his lobster traps.

John says that Joel is taking the chemotherapy in through his arm, and that it's making the arm sore and difficult to use. It's making his mouth and teeth sore too, and making it so he can't sleep.

"It doesn't look good," John says of the cancer. "It might get him."

John walks about the hull, spraying the big fiberglass boat named after his dad and his son. Before long *Caleb Joel* is on the Travel-lift, back in the water, and heading out of Center Harbor.

In the shop, Rick is shaping the top edge of the coamings on *The Mantelpiece*. This is another job that Rick enjoys. He's using some scraping tools made by Pete Chase, files with some sharpened half-circles cut into them. On the Center Harbor 31s, the coamings serve as both boundary pieces for the cockpit and backrests for the cockpit seats. With a hand on each end of the file, Rick pushes it along the edge. He's not trying to make it perfectly round, he says, which would give it the look of a "production boat." Instead he wants the edge to be oval-shaped, with the effect of the hand upon it. And the self, which gives the feeling of freedom.

The launching of *The Mantelpiece* is now scheduled for Memorial Day, a Monday. "Twenty-six days away," Rick says. "Twenty-eight if you count the Saturday and Sunday of Memorial Day weekend."

Brian Stevens is working inside the cabin, installing pieces of mahogany trim. Andy Fiveland is lining up the engine with the propeller shaft. He does this by tightening eight bolts to adjust the meeting of two flanges, one on the engine, the other on the shaft. He has to get their faces to within a tolerance of at least four-thousandths of an inch, about the thickness of photographic film. "Three-thousandths is great," Andy says. "Any more than four-thousandths and the engine will vibrate." Also in *The Mantelpiece*, the painter Bob Austin is doing some painting. Under the hull, Jeep Gulliver is fitting the skeg.

Over on *Pudding,* they're putting on the plywood deck. Norm Whyte is lying on his back, inside the well under a cockpit seat, where he's scraping off some excess glue with a putty knife. Norm gets in and out of the little space easily. When he drops a piece of wood smeared with glue, he yells, "Goddamnit!" Then he tosses his head and laughs. "Ah, you take one step forward and four steps back."

Joel McGraw and Bob Bosse are fitting the aftmost piece of the deck. When they've got it fastened, McGraw asks Bob, "Are you happy with that?" Bob doesn't answer, so Norm yells at him. "Bob! You've got to say you're happy! You never say you're happy!"

"Some people think this is serious work," Joel says.

"Serious is as serious does," Bob says.

"This is serious, but fun too," Joel says, trying to drain the irony from his voice.

Senta is being planked now. Pete Chase is working one side of the hull, Paul Waring the other. Pete is several courses ahead of Paul because Paul took two days off last week when his girlfriend had a baby, their second son, whom they named Rowan—not a bad name for a boatbuilder's son. Paul was present at the birth, assisting as a birthing chair. He has plans to come in this weekend to make up for lost time, like Tim Horton.

During the morning Pete fits the garboard plank on his side and then fastens it with bronze screws. The screws are four inches long and cost two dollars each, and Pete has used three hundred of them on the starboard side of *Senta*. Pete turns them in with a screwdriver bit chucked up in a bit brace. Then he begins fairing, swiping a power sander over the new planks above the keel and along the area near the sternpost, that aft part of the hull they call the "tuck," where the belly turns into the tail.

They have a steam box going outside in the parking lot, steam curling up from it, propane tanks hissing under it. During the morning Pete and Paul go out to the box, flip it open, and pluck out the steamed plank, a cooked piece of fir. Without saying much, they clamp the plank into a bending jig so that one end is flat on a bench and the other end is twisted up at a forty-five degree angle. With this quarter turn, the plank will fit more easily into the tuck.

When they go back inside the shop, Paul attaches a plank that he's already scribed, cut fair, and planed to shape. He moves quickly, clamping it down and then getting inside the hull to ratchet the plank in. And Pete is fairing again, making dronelike sweeps across the hull. He wears a full-face mask while he works, and his hair turns white with the dust.

After going into Bangor for a chemotherapy treatment, Joel comes to the yard in the morning, and he spends some time working on a drawing for the W-76, a chainplate drawing. Chainplates are fastened to the hull and project through the deck so the mast shrouds can attach to them. The chainplates on this large boat, with its 95-foot mast, will have to be able to withstand tensions greater than 76,000 pounds, the breaking point of the shrouds. They will be made of stainless steel.

At first Joel isn't sure if he'll have lunch today because the chemo has been making him feel nauseous. But then he does decide to go to the Morning Moon. There are only five people at the restaurant, just before noon, but it turns out that three of them have had cancer, Joel says—two cases of breast cancer, one case of ovarian cancer. After Joel sets his crutches into the booth and slides in, they say their greetings. One of the women smiles and says, "This is like a survivor's meeting," but Joel tells them he's undergoing chemotherapy again. This brings silence.

The waitress comes and goes. Joel tells me that he'll be continuing chemotherapy indefinitely now, and he says that the survival rate over the long term is very low for people who have cancer that metastasizes, particularly when it's lung cancer.

What I manage to say is "It's scary."

"It's a fact of life," Joel says. "I've lived a long time. People live a lot longer than they used to."

A silence passes, and then Joel talks about his reading at the Ellsworth Public Library. He says that about a hundred people came, and most of them were adults. He had expected an audience of children, and so chose a section from *Stuart Little,* the sailboat race in Central Park, and the section from *Charlotte's Web* when Templeton the rat is sent out to find a piece of paper with a good word to write in the web, coming up first with "crunchy" (too much like bacon) and "pre-shrunk" (not quite right) before Charlotte settles upon "radiant," the better description for her friend Wilbur.

Joel smiles and says, "They laughed in all the right places." He says that afterward Paul Sullivan, producer of the *White on White* tape, sold all thirty tapes he'd brought, "and people lined up to have them signed."

He says that *One Man's Meat* will be published by Tilbury Press, that his friend Jennifer Elliott is handling the publication, and that Roger Angell has written an introduction: "My half brother Roger," Joel says, "and it's really good."

I tell Joel that I've been to New Mexico to look at a college with my daughter, and while there I read his introduction to *Sam Crocker's Boats.* "That was early in my writing career." I mention a boat, *Lands End.* Joel says it was a graduation present for two brothers, named Loomis. One had graduated from high school, the other from college, he thought. During its first year *Land's End* had sailed to Bermuda and Newfoundland. Later it was shipped to Seattle and sailed to Alaska, and then to San Francisco, where it was shipped back to the East Coast. For many years *Lands End* cruised between Massachusetts and Cape Breton. It was almost fifty years old, and still in the same family, when it came to the yard to be refastened.

I tell Joel a little bit about the landscape of New Mexico,

which is post-oceanic and beautiful, and lined with strings of mountains running north and south. I say we've met a family of Mescalero Apache Indians, who were eating Kentucky Fried Chicken in a parking lot overlooking the site of an ancient Native American campsite, a cave at the base of a cliff. And Joel says that the Red Paint people camped at Naskeag Point during summers thousands of years ago, and he says all this happily.

When we get back to the yard I spend a little time in Joel's studio, looking through *Sam Crocker's Boats*. The plans for *Martha* are in the book, and for *Lands End*, and for *Jarges Pride*.

Joel works on the chainplate drawings. He's got the radio turned up, and a piano concerto is playing. He says he's familiar with the piece, that it's from Bach. "Almost anything that's good comes from Bach," he says.

There's just the sound of the music in the studio, while Joel works on the drawing, and I read. But then suddenly he speaks out.

"What a thing it must be to create such joyful music!" he says.

At Eric Dow's boatbuilding shop, *Boola*, the sister to *Nite Bird*, is being rebuilt by traditional methods. Dow has stripped the paint off, and there were so many coats, he says, that you couldn't tell the original shape of the boat. He's put in new frames, new deck beams, built a new centerboard trunk, a new deck. The boat now looks much like it must have looked when it was originally built. *Boola* looks lighter than *Nite Bird*, and the repair cost about half as much, but both are beautiful boats—they're like twins who've parted and then arrived in the same place years later, these two shapes derived from the Eugene Day carving.

At Benjamin River Marine, *Grayling* is now two weeks away from launching. The crew has to get just about everything done before *Grayling* goes in the water because there's not enough depth at the end of the boatyard float, except at almost high tide. *Grayling* will draw nearly six feet.

Eighteen months after the beginning of the job, there's a mood of cheerfulness in the shop, even though there's much to do yet. "We've been rubbing and rubbing," Doug Hylan says. "There's a lot of rubbing involved in turning an old fish boat into a yacht." He says that people have been telling him that they can't believe that *Grayling* looks like a workboat of seventy years ago, but the restoration is actually close to the original. "I don't know whether it's a curse or a blessing that I can look at a beat-up old boat and see this," Hylan says. "When I looked at *Grayling* two years ago, this is what I saw."

In the building nearby, Junior Day is putting the platform into his 24-footer. He's using fir porch flooring. "I guess I've got to push along," Junior says. "The new owner wants it in sometime this summer."

The boat will be named *Diva*. It will be owned by a retired couple, Dick and Susanne Grosh, who now own a 49-foot Hinckley called *Boundless*. They've lived aboard the boat during summers, and cruised from Nova Scotia to the Caribbean. But now they're living in Maine and not cruising as much, and taking grandchildren out, so they've decided to get a picnic boat, built along a lobster boat's lines for sea-kindliness. Dick Grosh will work with Junior in the shop, and finish off the interior himself. *Diva* is his nickname for his wife, who is a singer.

And *Diva* is yet another boat that's looking quite good.

"You like her?" Junior says.

"I do. Do you?"

"Oh yeah. I don't think there's been any I didn't want to keep."

"Too late now," I say.

"Too late for all of them," June Day says, and gets back to work.

❦

Though Steve is racing in Antigua, Laurie White is in Brooklin. At a restaurant in Blue Hill, she's not submitting to any romanticism. "It's good to be home," she says to a friend who asks about her time in the Caribbean. She says she's done more today than she did in two weeks down there. Nobody does anything down there.

Allene is at the table, and Caroline Mayher. Joel had planned to go out to dinner but the effects of chemo have kept him at home.

"Your son has an incredible tolerance for pain," Laurie says to Allene. She tells about a night of sailing in the Caribbean. Steve was at the wheel of *Vortex*. They were making a long sail in heavy winds, and big waves, forty-foot waves, she says, were breaking over the boat. She and Steve were in the cockpit. He was "white knuckles," and had been going at it for three hours. "I worked up my courage," Laurie says, and said to him that I would take over, just for a little while. But he said no. When I saw him looking uncertain that's when I thought, Oh no, I'm gonna die."

"Fun, fun, fun," says Allene. Allene has said she never came to terms with boats. They rocked too much and made her feel sick. She found that when she was aboard a boat she spent most of her time in the galley cooking and figured she could do that just as well at home. But Allene does like canoeing. She'd paddled canoes on lakes when she was a girl in New Hampshire. Lately she'd been encouraging Joel to get a kayak and go paddling on the ponds around Brooklin with her.

Caroline Mayher tells about the trip she took with her husband, Bill, Joel, and Maynard and Anne Bray to Bermuda on *Northern Crown*. She says she didn't eat the entire way.

Allene says, "I sent a wheel of Brie with them and it came back untouched."

Laurie says she liked being in the islands, discovering and exploring them. It was fun to walk around in the ports and to meet people. Each island had been so different even though the greatest distance between them was not much more than forty miles. That wasn't so bad, but a five-day sail was too long.

Laurie had begun working at the yard in 1980, doing varnishing. She also did yard work, and during a year that Bill Mayher worked at the yard when he was on sabbatical she and Bill were paired on some jobs. One day when there wasn't much to do Steve gave Laurie and Bill the assignment of scraping the bottom of a boat. Because it was raining, they put on rainsuits and goggles and headgear. But after an afternoon of working on the bottom they were completely wet. "I'd never been so cold in all my life," Laurie says. "That night at home I said, 'Listen, this isn't going to work.'"

Steve and Laurie lived aboard a boat when they were first together, the Alden Malabar sloop that they'd named *Endless* because it was an endless amount of work taking care of it. They kept it moored in the harbor. "The first night, I came home from work and realized that I had to row home. I'd never rowed before. I got in the peapod and rowed smack into the boat. Steve came out and said, 'We gotta work on this.'"

Laurie began keeping the books at the yard one day after she watched Allene do it, and said, "I can do that." Allene said, "Why don't you try it." She showed Laurie what to do and then left, and Laurie had been taking care of the books since then.

"Some people don't have good mother-in-laws," Laurie says with a look at Allene, "but for me it worked out."

Later, on the way back to Brooklin, Caroline Mayher says it's impossible to say how much Joel will be missed, how much his spiritual presence will be missed in the community. She says that at the reading in Ellsworth, as people laughed in all the right places, as Joel read about Templeton and Charlotte coming upon the word "radiant," Joel himself looked radiant. He seemed to be enjoying the attention. It's an affirmation, she says, for Joel to be reading his father's works during this time.

Winter is over. Steve White had been beating through the wind in the Caribbean, white-knuckling it. John White had been beating through the wind to go scalloping. Both sons, beating through the wind. The same could be said of Joel, though it's a different wind.

May 1997

Steve had made lots of friends along the way last winter, people that he and Laurie had met in the various ports and harbors. Now he'd hired four of them to sail *Vortex* from Antigua to Bermuda, and they would bring her on to Maine. Steve had also met some of the islanders, and he'd hired several Antiguans to work on and paint *Vortex*. Laurie had told him he'd done it because he was a frustrated employer, but Steve thought he'd formed the little crew to add structure to his day. It had been difficult for him to have so little structure. He had enjoyed the Antiguans he'd met—there was Vision, a Rasta man with whom "you only had to spend a few minutes to know about his inner peace," and there was Vision's girlfriend Rainbow, whose Babylon name was Sally. It had been a different winter, different being with Laurie all the time (they'd said they had quantity time together, but not quality time) and being away from Joel, which had given him guilt feelings, even though the trip was okay with Joel, and with Allene (who'd never been one to use guilt trips, Steve said). He thought he'd go back to the islands again, but only for a week or two, not for an entire winter.

Steve entered *Vortex* in the Spirit of Tradition class at the Classic Yacht Regatta in Antigua, and with Frank Hull and another friend crewing they had placed second. Now he was back at the yard to attend to business, and the business prospects. Some in the crew, such as Frank Hull and Rick Clifton, had begun to wonder if there was enough work ahead. But already Steve had some interesting prospects.

At the morning meeting he says they've gotten the go-ahead on drawings for a 40-foot sloop for Alan Stern, an enlargement of *Linda,* though Stern says he'll sell *Linda* first before making the commitment. "There's also some interest in plans for a fifty-foot motor sailer, based on a larger William Hand design. Joel will scale it down, make a new design essentially. I'll let you know more about that as it progresses. Invitations are now going out for *The Mantelpiece* launching on Memorial Day. The Denney boat will be launched in early July. George Denney will be going to Turkey to charter a boat and do some sailing in late June, and the launching will take place just after he gets back. And that's it for today."

At *The Mantelpiece,* Rick Clifton is fitting on the companionway hatch cover today, and Brian Stevens is sanding the toe rails. And now that Steve is back Bob Stephens is down in the shop again, and part of the crew on *The Mantelpiece.* He's installing the chocks today, ones from the prototypes that Andy Fiveland made. Bob seems gloomy, a bit depressed about being out of the design studio. Brian Larkin has said to him, "Well, they spit you out of there pretty fast, didn't they?" The move makes sense from the managerial point of view, since Bob will give Rick's boat a good push forward toward launching day. Nevertheless, it's a hard adjustment for him.

"It has its benefits," Bob says grimly, his eyes on the chocks, but he doesn't elaborate.

The interior of the cabin of *The Mantelpiece* is done, and within is the evidence of the work Brian Stevens has been doing all winter. The mahogany trim is finished smooth and golden around the shelves, cabinets, bunks, the galley counter, the portholes, the head door. It looks like a custom-finished house in miniature.

Six men are working on *Pudding*. Norm Whyte, Brian Larkin, and Keith Dibble are installing the teak deck. Norm makes the king plank, cutting it with a double-edged Japanese hand saw, while Brian cuts the apron, those border pieces running along the cockpit. Keith installs the trim along the rails. They expect to glue the deck on before the end of the day, so that it can be dry for tomorrow, when they'll clean it up for compounding.

Joel McGraw is making the teak veneer for the transom, matching and cutting pieces in preparation for the vacuum bagging he'll do at the end of the day. Mark Littlehales, back at the yard after a winter in Vermont, is using carving tools to cut the scrollwork at the ends of the cove stripes. Mark, a landscape painter as well as a boatbuilder, does most of the carving and lettering at the yard. Andy Fiveland is also on *Pudding* today, doing interior sanding and painting.

Pete Chase has joined Tim Horton on the S-Boat, *Wigeon*. Tim has built a new stem for *Wigeon*, after the owner came to the yard and decided to go ahead with that repair. Tim is refastening some of the planks at the bow. The forward planks are sprung apart and Tim is standing on a sawhorse, putting wooden plugs into the frames. He's without a hat today—Tim stops wearing a hat at some point every spring and that time had come. He says he put the hat on last fall when he was working on the Trumpy, after he got a gob of sealing compound in his hair.

Pete is at the stern, replacing some of the weaker planks. Periodically he leaves Building No. 2 with a cedar board scribed with a course of semicircles. In the shop he nails a fairing batten over his marks, draws a line, draws another. With the band saw he makes a long curved cut, and the air twenty feet around him fills with the scent of cedar.

The new part of the hull on *Senta* has been faired and painted, and in a few days it will go into the water so that the planks can swell up. Then *Senta* will go into the paint shop. Now Paul Waring is belowdecks, doing some varnishing. He's got the stereo turned on and is playing a Jimi Hendrix CD. A muffled "All Along the Watchtower" comes from the cabin, but it's audible enough for Rick Clifton to look up, say "Hendrix," and then whistle along, over the warble of a vacuum cleaner.

Senta's owner is also working on the boat today, varnishing the trim on deck. His name is Jeff Colquhon. Because *Senta* is so big, he's close to the ceiling. Colquhon says the boat isn't so cumbersome in the water, though. "Out there it plays like a musical instrument," he says. "Out there it makes sense."

He and his wife live in Castine and have owned *Senta* for seven years now. Getting the boat represented a major life change for them. Colquhon worked on Wall Street trading securities for seventeen years, which made it possible for him not only to get a big Rhodes cutter but to return to some of the things he'd done earlier in life. He'd studied art in college and worked for a design firm in London before getting drafted into the Army, and it was after his time in the service when he took a summer job on Wall Street. Now he'd gotten back to painting and to sailing. During summers, he chartered *Senta*, taking passengers on tours around Penobscot Bay.

Sometimes he took small groups out, though often it was just a couple. Colquhon is a licensed captain, and because of that, he can perform marriages. He has a cook on board for the charters, serving candlelight dinners on fine china.

Colquhon is living out one of the most coveted of sailing dreams, owning and chartering a big, beautiful boat. "It's a mixture of fantasy and optimism" he says. "Working on the water and living on a sailboat is attractive to a lot of people. It's like fishing, another excuse to go to sea. The economics of it is the challenge, that's where the fantasy also comes in. It requires a really good plan, because it's your own capital you're using. But it's great to operate a sailboat with a schedule, and much different from recreational sailing. It's fun to have to be at a specific place at a specific time. It's been interesting to see how much fun you can have. We've made a lot of friends."

His schedule for this year included getting *Senta* into the water for a few days, and then out again for painting, most of which he'd be doing himself here at the yard. He had to finish by the full-course tides in early June, the window when they could get *Senta* into the water and afloat here. His first charter was scheduled for late June. He would be doing a wedding on board this summer too.

Colquhon has several routes that he takes through Penobscot Bay, stopping at various islands and harbors. Often, if the customers had an eye for wooden sailing boats, he'd spend the last night of the trip anchored up outside Center Harbor, where you could see one of the prettiest collections of wooden boats anywhere.

"Joel is the reason this harbor looks the way it does," he says.

⟨∾⟩

Joel is in the studio, working on the drawing of the fin keel of the W-76, the twenty-seventh and last drawing. Next to the partially completed keel drawing he has the lines drawing laid out, and he's checking one against the other. When I first come up and sit on the bench by the windows Joel keeps working, concentrating on the drawings, but then he looks up, with curiosity and a little consternation too.

"I was just watching you think," I say, knowing I should go.

With a little laugh Joel says, "I wasn't thinking very hard."

He says he misses having Bob in the office. And he hands me a set of photos of the model of the W-76, taken in Center Harbor, when Taylor Allen brought the model to the yard a week ago. A video crew will be coming to the yard over the weekend, to interview Joel and Steve for a promotional tape about the W-76.

Joel says he'll be leaving soon, to go into Bangor for another chemo treatment, "a shot of poison," he calls it. Then he's back looking at the drawings, while I slip away.

⟨∾⟩

It's light and already warm before the workday begins now. Ten minutes before seven Joel McGraw is in the shop, with other crew members gathered around him. He has one of his Flower Dories set up on the table saw. It has a mast with a little seagull on the top, a bandanna for a sail, and a string with a lead weight attached to the stern—his storm rig, he says. He has sailed this boat in Center Harbor recently, on the day when Taylor Allen sailed the W-76 model. But now it's the stage for a puppet show, and the puppet is Dar, a lobsterman with slicker, rubber storm hat, and wooden shoes. There's a little pink mermaid too. McGraw lifts the strings, and Dar steps into the dory—"Off to Salty's whore-house, find an old barrel for a roll in the sheets." Dar reels in the mermaid, sets a lobster trap on her. "Now she won't go anywhere," he says. And then: "Oh, here comes Steve," and the laughter rises while the puppet collapses and the Flower Dory goes into its box.

"Not much news for today," Steve tells the crew. "*Fidelio* has almost stopped leaking. There's one leak left, along a keel bolt. We'll look at it today, sponge it out, and tomorrow she'll come out of the water and go into the paint shop. After sanding and painting and drying we'll launch her at the end of next week. *Senta* will be going out of the shop on Monday. She'll spend two days on the Travel-lift while the rudder gets fitted, and then she'll go into the water. The Geier boat will go outside once *Senta* is off the Travel-lift. We'll drop it onto the fin keel and fasten it, raise it up and down a couple of times and then bring it back into the shop. And that's it for today."

The *Pudding* crew begins to get the teak deck ready for com-pounding, taking out the screws and washers that have served as clamps, scraping out the hardened glue, routing out a few uneven spots, and sanding some of the edges. It's a clever piece of work, with the curving pattern, the placement of the nibs, the king planks that serve as focal points and draw the patterns together.

On *The Mantelpiece* Rick is fitting on the cover on the com-panionway hatch roof, and Brian Stevens is laying out some deck hardware. Bob Stephens is still installing the chocks, and he's still feeling gloomy. But he cheers up considerably when Steve comes over to confer with him on the state of this CH 31. They talk about the autohelm that will be going into the boat, the rigging system now being put together, how various other things are progressing. Talking with Steve, Bob becomes animated, and they laugh together.

Then Steve leaves, and with Pete Chase gets aboard the work scow, and carrying pink sponges, they head out to *Fidelio* to swab water from the bilges. In the harbor there is also now a fiberglass powerboat named *Golden Rings,* which arrived a few days ago. *Golden Rings* has been in Florida for the winter, and it's owned by Guilford "Giffy" Full, a retired yacht captain and yacht surveyor. Giffy Full is well known for his work. He's the surveyor who looked at *Senta* for Jeff Colquhon, and he assessed *Quiet Tune* when it was in California, before being shipped to Mystic Seaport. He is a kindly man with a high-pitched voice honed from years of talking over engine noise, who has burly hands, and sometimes says in parting, "Finest kind." He usually wears a khaki uniform with a patch on the shirt that reads "Capt. G. W. Full and Assoc., Marine Surveyors," over a three-masted schooner.

Giffy arrives at the harbor this morning and carries a bag down to the dock. He's followed by his Jack Russell terrier, called Rocket. At the dock as he bails out his peapod, he says that someone just offered him top dollar for *Golden Rings,* but he turned it down. When he gets into the boat he says, with his voice sweeping up, "I'll only be able to go out for three or four more years. What am I gonna do, sit in a rocking chair with a fistful of money?" Rocket jumps into the boat and Giffy pushes away from the dock.

"I didn't take it," he says. "I surprised myself!"

He invites me to come out to *Golden Rings,* and twenty minutes later I row out in Rick Clifton's Shellback Dinghy.

I've already been told by Rick and by Pete Chase about Giffy and about his wife, Charlotte, who had multiple sclerosis and died a few years ago. They said that Giffy had taken her on the boat when she'd been in a wheelchair, up until about a year before the end. Pete said he'd hoisted her aboard with a boom and tackle, and that he'd seemed so happy doing it. Rick had said that the trip south this past winter had been Giffy's first trip since her death, and that Giffy had complained a lot before departing in the fall. "But I bet he had a real good time," Rick said.

I tie up to *Golden Rings* and climb aboard. Giffy is painting some shelves that he rebuilt last year, and he talks while he works, crouched on his knees with his feet crossed under him—a sure sign of a supple seventy-year-old. *Golden Rings* is a spacious boat, 42 feet long, with a roomy wheelhouse that also includes a galley with stove, refrigerator, large table—and high stools so that Giffy can see out the windows when he's seated at the table, something he considers important. Belowdecks there are double bunks, a kerosene drip heater, a head with a shower, mahogany paneling, and ample bookshelves.

He says he grew up in Marblehead, Massachusetts, and spent a lot of time around Graves Yacht Yard, and that he occasionally visited L. Francis Herreshoff at his studio. Giffy studied engineering, got a job on a yacht, and eventually became a yacht captain.

"I worked on one yacht that was 260 feet long, and we had thirty-six men in the crew. I worked for one family for twenty-two years. They had an Alden yawl for eleven years, and then a motor sailer that Alden designed, the *Canterbury Bell*. They wanted something that one man could manage. After twenty-two years the family got too busy to have a boat. I skippered one more boat, a Sparkman and Stephens sloop, for a very wealthy lady. When she died, people came after me to survey.

"Most surveyors were insurance surveyors, and didn't spend any time looking at the boat. But I got to do purchase surveys, and that was a different game. I got to look at everything, and take it for a trial run. It was an opportunity to help people. Some people, first-time buyers, they can make a mistake and lose a lot of money, and have heartbreak."

He tells about a Friendship sloop that he surveyed. "The people who wanted it had no sailing experience. I surveyed it, and it was in good shape. I told them, 'Ease into it. In the beginning just use the mainsail, even though it will be harder to sail. Go out on your own without the kids at first, so they won't end up getting scared.' It's been twenty-seven years now, and they still have the boat. They built a barn for it, in a town out near Sturbridge, Massachusetts.

"I've traveled all over the world doing this. I surveyed the *Ticonderoga* [a 72-foot L. Francis Herreshoff-designed ketch] fourteen years ago in California. It went to the Baltic, then to England. I made several trips over there to look in on the rebuild. She'll go for a long time now. Part of the reason is she's got a good young skipper who loves her."

While Giffy works on the shelves he says, "Only way to keep boats is to have a little program. So you're doing something all the time."

When his wife was alive they owned *Kittiwake II,* a 44-foot Bunker and Ellis powerboat built on Mount Desert Island. "We took it to Florida for five years," he says. "My wife had MS. It got to the point where I had to carry her around, and she wasn't a small lady." Then he adds, "But don't get me wrong. I didn't mind. It was a privilege to take care of her.

"She went anywhere. If I told her it was safe to hoist her up on a ten-foot dock she'd say okay. Once in a while I saw a funny look on her face. If we were on a reasonable float we'd put her on a ramp and wheel her on. If not, I used a block and tackle to lift her wheelchair. We enjoyed living on the boat. We weren't marina people, we liked anchoring out. We were nature people. For years and years I wrote long lists of places to anchor out, from the time I was young.

"We went mostly along the Atlantic coast. She went all the way to California with me when we delivered a boat, all the way from Camden to California. She was handicapped but she encouraged me to do it.

"After she was off the boat a year she came down with cancer. People at the Blue Hill Hospital were wonderful. Christ, we had our dogs in the hospital. It was comical. At the Salem Hospital in Massachusetts they'd have put us in jail if we brought our dogs in. But it was a terrible loss. Some days I didn't care if I got up or not."

Giffy bought the boat that he named *Golden Rings,* which coincidentally had been originally finished off by Graves Yacht Yard, and spent about a year rebuilding it in Brooklin. Of boat names he says, "A name should be pleasing phonetically and in print. It should fit the boat, on the stern. If you've got a big-ass stern you don't want a four-letter name on it. Same thing if you've got a little narrow end; you don't want letters packed in all across it. The name *Golden Rings* represents the time I spent with my wife on the boat."

This spring he had left from Florida on March 10, and traveled north up the St. Johns River. "I leave early to avoid the big powerboats. I anchor up along the way, without going into marinas. A river in South Carolina, or in the Chesapeake Bay. I only like to go ten hours at a time. I'm getting old, I get tired after ten hours." Rocket can go ten hours too, he says. Giffy says he anchors, rows to shore with Rocket, and takes him for a walk. He could have come up from Florida in twenty days if he wanted, but he'd rather spend a month or six weeks traveling.

"I got to Maine two weeks ago, and I took an off-season cruise. It's something I've always wanted to do. I went to Bath, Pulpit Harbor, Vinalhaven, and North Haven. The weather was nice. All the ducks were out. We saw an eagle over to Vinalhaven. I had a lady friend with me, a lady I've been going with."

Giffy says his philosophy is "You've got to take care of things. If you don't want to take care of something, why have it? It's the same for a boat, a car, or a house."

Wife too.

And this philosophy is just as true for the Center Harbor 31s, he says.

"Those boats, they're built so well. There's no reason why they couldn't last a family a hundred years, be passed down from generation to generation. It's like a violin. There's got to be somebody to take care of it."

When I get ready to row back to the dock, Giffy asks if he can give me some friendly advice. Pointing to Rick's Shellback, tied to the stern of *Golden Rings,* he tells me to never leave the oarlocks up when I tie up to another boat, because it could scrape against a hull and cause trouble. I say that I'll remember that.

❧

On a foggy Sunday morning a large crowd gathers at Benjamin River Marine. *Grayling* sits on the railway, poised above the downward slope. A contingent of people have come to the launching from Eastport, a sardine port, and among them is Leonard Ritchie, *Grayling*'s last captain. Much of the Brooklin boating community is there, including Joel White, and Arno Day, Junior Day, Jimmy Steele, Jon Wilson, Maynard Bray, and many boatbuilders from the yards around town, at the launching with their families. Cars line the dirt road running up the hill and are parked along the paved road, and people are still walking down to the yard when the bagpipes begin to play, when the champagne bottle breaks, when in the quiet air Doug Hylan, standing at the bow, slides with the bright sardine carrier into the water.

It's a particularly happy moment for Maynard Bray, who has found the boat and seen the restoration through, doing the research to ensure that the vessel was brought back to nearly the original state. It's Maynard Bray whom Doug Hylan has described as "Keeper of the Flame." When Todd Skoog arrives a few minutes after the launch—which was a few minutes early because the wind had died down—Maynard Bray thanks him for his work. "We couldn't have done this without your talents," he tells Skoog. "She'll be known all up and down the coast."

Inside the shop there's a buffet, a jazz band playing, an oil painting of *Grayling*. Launchgoers look at a set of historical photographs and newspaper quotes on the wall—one says that herring brought ten cents a pound in 1917 when *Grayling* was launched. "It brings twenty cents now," someone says. At the dock, after a brief run in the river *Grayling* is tied up, and people stream aboard her. Down below, people gather to take her in, to stand and talk by the stove.

"A lot of what's great about cruising is sitting down below and shooting the breeze," Doug Hylan says. "When I think of *Grayling*, the interior, it's really about doing that, sitting around and talking, a place to sit and make memories."

Before the tide drops too far, *Grayling* is at a mooring in the river, a beautiful sight with its long, lean white hull and its tall, varnished pilothouse of cypress. Doug Hylan tends to some unfinished details and is adding more ballast, since the boat rides a bit too high. Todd Skoog is working in the shop, where the old sloop *Andicon* is now getting some floor timbers.

❧

At Center Harbor at 5 A.M. a lobster boat leaves to work traps, departing with a heavy thrum that can be heard all the way up to the General Store. Soon the sunlight is on the masts of the three sailboats in the harbor now—Alan Stern's *Linda,* a yawl named *Perigee,* and a sloop, *Quintet.* Then the gold lettering on the stern of *Golden Rings* lights up. Soon the white hull of *Linda* glows gloriously too, and it's evident why people say that boats should be painted only two colors, black and white, and black doesn't look good.

Steve gives the morning news. "*Senta* is going out today when the lift truck comes. We took *Linda* out for a spin over the weekend. The pitch on the propeller needs a little adjustment. We talked to Donald Tofias. He's saying they'll probably go ahead with the 76-footer, and that they might build two. He says he has some interesting leads, but if they don't come through, he'll finance them both himself."

"Life's a bitch," Joel McGraw says.

"If that's the way he has to get it," Brian Larkin says. There's a rustle of voices all the way around.

"Taylor will build one and we'll build the other here," Steve says.

Then Steve goes through a list of things: "The weather's nice today, and so we'll go over to Rockport and get the twenty-two-footer. Keep the epoxy pumps full, and make sure no air gets into them. Keep the yard clean, with all the activity now. Bring all the tools in, especially the shop tools. Bring the sandpaper in. I've seen rolls lying around outside. They're forty dollars a roll. Don't leave paint cans around. Make sure you vacuum the dust off the decks when you're finished sanding, because it gets tracked all over the deck. And that's it for today."

Everybody rises.

The swallows are another of the recent spring arrivals. They usually appear at the yard during the first week of May. The barn swallows nest inside the sheds on the rafters, while the cliff swallows nest outside under the eaves of the roofs. They're masons of a sort, landing by puddles and throwing their heads into the mud, then transferring their building material by throwing their foreheads at their nests—determination on the wing. Part of the mystery is why the old mud doesn't fall off when the new material is getting thrown on. When crew are in the sheds the barn swallows dip in and soar by, and sometimes chatter at them, and the mystery here is whether they're complaining that the boatbuilders ought to get on with it or announcing that they've been far away and are back again—whether they're saying goodbye or hello.

In Building No. 2 where the swallows chatter, Mark Littlehales is making a new teak gutter around the icebox on *Cirrus*. Geoff Anthony is inside *Cirrus,* wiring the new engine they've put in. Rich Wright, back from a winter layoff, is painting the bulwarks on *Hopefull*—it's a multicolored boat, with white rails, yellow bulwarks, and green topsides. Tim Horton is measuring up a plank for *Wigeon*. Strands of caulking are hanging down from the planks at the bow.

Henry Lawson is back at the yard after a winter in Arizona.

He'll work for a few weeks while they're getting the boats in. Henry looks into the shed for a moment, saying to Rich Wright, "Touching her up, huh?"

"Touching her up and making her pretty."

And Pete Chase stops in, looking for a tool. He calls out, "Geoff, you haven't seen the half-inch Milwaukee drill, the right-angle drill, have you?"

Mark speaks for Geoff, who's down below. "Can't help you, Pete."

"Nobody can help Pete," Tim says, and then he laughs.

Inside the shop, Brian Stevens sands trim on *The Mantelpiece*, while Rick installs a glass windowpane in a cabin porthole. But soon a big truck with a very long boat trailer pulls into the yard. It maneuvers around and backs the trailer into the shop and under *Senta*. A poker-faced driver gets out, transfers the boat's weight from blocks to the trailer, and raises a set of hydraulic supports that press up against the hull like hands against a face. Pete Chase and Paul Waring pull the jack stands away from *Senta*, one by one, until the tall cutter stands perched on the trailer alone. This unnerves Rick, since *The Mantelpiece* is only about ten feet away, starboard side. "That boat is too goddamn big," he says of *Senta*, and goes up into the loft until the trailer has been pulled out of the shop.

Moving a boat as big as *Senta* could have taken most of a day in years past, but within a few minutes they've got it up to the head of the parking lot. There it meets the Travel-lift, and is passed into the slings, a 27-ton handoff. And it's only a few minutes later, after *Senta* has been moved into a clear space, that Pete Chase is at work on her, putting in a section of deadwood aft of the keel. Paul Waring is at the sternpost, using a gouge to smooth out the groove for the rudder stock.

Joel is in the studio, working on the first sail plan for Alan

Stern's 40-footer, the scaled-up version of *Linda*. There's no date set for construction to begin. Stern says he'll have to sell *Linda* first, or as Joel puts it: "You learn in boatbuilding pretty quick not to count your eggs before the chicken is in the coop."

Joel's first employee, Henry Lawson, is working in the sardine factory. He's getting the engine running on *Lark*, a powerboat that Joel designed and that was built in New Hampshire by Gordon Swift in 1986. *Lark* is owned by the people who now own E. B. White's house.

"Felt-like I never left," Henry says of his winter interlude in Arizona. "That was a short four months."

Henry has big hands and a heck of a handshake—"I like to let people know I'm sincere," he says. His eyes seem to convey contentment, perhaps that things turned out well, that he lived up to his ideals. He was born in Sedgwick, the town on the other side of the Benjamin River, and his mother died when Henry was two. Henry's father left him with an aunt, and he got "passed around" for a while, until Ken Tainter took him in. Henry dragged for scallops with Tainter, and after he graduated from Brooklin High, before he went into the Navy in 1952, he had Tainter formally adopt him.

He worked for Arno Day in 1954, when the yard was "just a couple of old sheds. There was a swayback building with a wooden floor. They built the boats on the dirt, just a temporary building to keep the weather off. All the boat storage was outdoors. I was hired on as a painter, but I'd studied diesel mechanics in the Navy, so pretty soon I switched over to doing mechanical work.

"I didn't do that much boatbuilding," Henry says. "Some smoothing, but mostly I did mechanical stuff: I got married in 1956 [Henry married the adopted daughter of Elmer Bent] and went to New Jersey to work for my dad for a while in construction. Arno told me if I came back a job would be waiting. I came back in the fall of 1957. Joel was there by then. I went to Arno and he told me I could start tomorrow—"You can paint my daughter's bedroom," he said. After I did that I started doing fall work at the yard, getting the boats in."

After four years, Arno decided to leave the business. "Joel and I went out to work on one of the boats. Joel told me he thought I was a good worker, and asked me if I would work for him if he took over the yard. I said it sounded great, but I had one condition, that my family came first. I told Joel that if he honored that, then okay. I've been there ever since.

"Joel continued to make things better. We put skidwork down on the ground for moving boats and got a winch truck. We put up a storage building, and then built the shop that's there now. But it stayed small. Eight or ten people worked there.

"I used to run the outside yard, pretty much. I was the outside foreman, and Joel handled the inside work. My job was to get the boats into storage. We'd pull them up the railway with the winch truck and then move them around over the greased skidwork with pulleys. There wasn't a lot of room to move. Sometimes it took all day to move a boat to its final resting place. Then we'd cover it up."

Such was Henry Lawson's work for two decades—getting the boats in and out of the water and overseeing their maintenance. Over the years Henry built friendships with the boat owners and enjoyed seeing them come to town in the spring.

"The old customers were our bread and butter," he says. "There was a regular trade in maintenance, mostly small boats. Sometimes the last boat was going in just as the first was coming out. Sailing days were nice in the fall, and a lot of them liked that. A lot of them would come up for Columbus Day weekend, the last hoorah, we called it. Some hang-ons would wait until the last of October, even the first part of November.

"The construction of new boats was not as interesting for me, because new boats tend to leave after they're launched. Old customers tend to become friends. I like people too much to become a production person. You don't get the feeling for owners of new boats that you get for people who come back yearly. The relationship gives you an extra reason for going to work, when you know you're appreciated."

When Steve came back to the yard permanently, and talked to Joel about making a career of it, the obvious path for him was through the position of yard manager. The conflict this brought ran deep for Henry, who'd been running things outdoors for more than twenty years. "I felt like I'd been dropped through a knothole," Henry says. "Felt that way for about two years."

Henry didn't want to see the yard changed and expanded either. He went to Joel and told him that things were good small, that there was a nice family atmosphere. He watched Steve move into cold-molded construction, and it seemed that the old customers weren't being cared for in the same way, that they were being "sacrificed at the altar."

He and Belford Gray, who were close friends, talked about working at another yard, presenting themselves as a team, mechanic and boat carpenter. But Belford collapsed at the yard, nearly died in Henry's arms, then really did die at the hospital shortly afterward. Now Henry had been at Brooklin Boat Yard for forty years. He worked a few weeks in the fall and the spring, and got his health insurance. The situation was good for him, he thought, because he had put in his time and because "the word had come from upstairs." He figured that Joel had said to take care of him. "Friendship is an important piece of documentation," he says.

Years ago they had sailed together, but now they talked together occasionally and had lunch once or twice a year. Sometimes Henry had the urge to go up into Joel's office and ask him why he'd let the yard get so big ("I'd like to pick Joel's brains sometime"), but it was merely an urge. Henry, so in tune with the family idea, knew that the changes at the yard had been part of a family transaction.

When he offers his hand a second time, he says, "I never met a person I didn't like. Just met some I didn't like as much as I thought I would."

⁓

During lunchtime only five of the crew eat inside the shop—Henry, Fred, Pete, Geoff Anthony, and Rich Wright. The others are outside. Tim Horton lying on the hood of his car, getting sun. Andy Fiveland is helping Paul fix his VW bus. "It's running on three," Andy says.

Then there's a roaring sound in the harbor, and Bob Stephens flies in on *Cow Lung,* a great wake rising behind him. The 22-footer looks more spectacular in the water than it did at the boat show, with more of a balance now among the blue hull, teak deck, and mahogany trim. And there are the two big silver Honda 90 outboard motors on the stern. Bob turns and floats up to the dock as several of the crew walk down to meet him.

"Wow!" Bob says, with a big smile. How clever and considerate of Steve to choose Bob to bring the powerboat over from Rockport.

"Is it a lot better than a fiberglass boat?" Brian Larkin asks.

"She's really solid. No complaints about that."

"Soft?" Brian asks of the ride.

"Was it a good trip?"

Bob says that he went thirty-five miles in an hour and a quarter, that his top speed was 28 knots. And then he says that he wants to run *Cow Lung* out again. Brian Larkin jumps aboard, and they both stand at the console. Bob turns for the westward opening of the harbor, soon going full throttle.

"That man's excited," Mark Littlehales says. Bob does seem to be happy now, and over the gloom.

They climb the ramp of the dock and go back to work.

Jeep Gulliver is painting a daysailer in the sardine factory. Bob Austin is sanding *Fidelio* in the paint shop. Fred Pollard is fabricating a piece of molding for *Madrigal*. A crew of six rolls a long mast across the yard.

Henry comes out of the shop and says, "I just talked to Joel. He looks better than he did last year. Let's hope he's doing better."

Norm Whyte gets ready to sand the teak deck, and closes the doors in the water end of the shop so the breeze won't blow the dust toward *The Mantelpiece*. Rick and Brian have pushed that boat, on its wheeled cradle, into the space where *Senta* was so as to get further distance from the dust. They sand, tape, and vacuum *The Mantelpiece*, and then the painters spend the afternoon putting a fourth coat of paint on the hull.

Memorial Day Weekend

Poised atop its fin keel now, *The Mantelpiece* is a thing of beauty. The keel has a thin stem, with a cigar-shaped bulb of lead at the bottom. Painted green like the boat's bottom, it seems a kind of plumage, a diving bird's plumage. At the waterline are two stripes of green, the boot tops, they're called, and the topsides have been painted off-white. The cove stripe is gold. Along the deck, the hand-shaped mahogany toe rails, these too accenting the sheerline. On the mahogany transom is the gold lettering, *The Mantelpiece*. There are the teak cockpit seats, shaped and smoothed by hand, and the mahogany coamings, shaped by hand, the head door, shaped by hand, the cabin interior with the mahogany trim, all shaped by hand—even the gleaming chrome-plated chocks at the bow and stern, all shaped by hand.

At the morning meeting on Friday, Steve says, "Donald Tofias called, and he wants an estimate for the seventy-six-footer in two weeks, so I'll be in the office for most of the time over the next two weeks. He wants it before the boat show," meaning the Wooden Boat Show, to be held at Mystic Seaport at the end of June.

"Monday is launching day. We'll work up until two and then clean up. You'll get paid until three-thirty. If anyone asks, you didn't have a drink until three-thirty."

Murmurs, laughs rise up. "Never do," Steve says, and he laughs. "That's it for today."

The harbor is beginning to fill. There are two Concordia yawls at moorings, a U.S. One-Design named *Chimaera*, with its long overhanging ends. A similar but smaller Alden Triangle. There's *Lark*, and *Fidelio*, now with its mast stepped. *Senta* is in the water, without a mast, though *Senta* will be going into the paint shop later today. There's *Golden Rings*. And Joel's *Ellisha*, and Steve's long-bodied, low-sided *Vortex*.

The trip from Bermuda to Maine had been terrible for the crew of *Vortex*, Steve says. "They were surfing down waves at seventeen knots. The boat broached and the rudder got bent. It started hailing while there was thunder and lightning. They came up on top of a wave after taking one wave in the cockpit, and saw a tanker ahead, and just missed it. The boat came back pretty salty. We had to take everything out and hose it off."

The professional yacht captain who sailed *Vortex* to Brooklin, an Australian by the name of Rob Donald, had immediately left for New York and joined the crew of *Adela,* a boat competing in the Atlantic Cup Challenge, a race from New York to England. His girlfriend, a Norwegian whose name is Hannah Svare, has stayed in Brooklin with Steve and Laurie and will join Donald later. During the morning Steve goes into the office, gets on-line, and checks on the standings of the race—*Adela* is in first place, southeast of Newfoundland, moving at 15 knots.

Steve and Laurie had met Rob Donald and Hannah Svare in Bequia and gotten to know them in Antigua. As Steve explained it, their itinerary for the coming months would be: After meeting Donald in England, Hannah and he would go to her country, Norway, and then his, Australia, and then to the Caribbean to their 32-foot sloop, which they would sail to Brooklin, arriving in August. Donald would then leave for the Mediterranean, where he would captain a schooner for six months, taking it through the Red Sea to the eastern coast of Africa, where the German businessman who owned the schooner would meet them and spend a few weeks vacationing aboard the boat. In May, they would return to Brooklin, where Donald, with the help of the crew at Brooklin Boat Yard, would put a cold-molded skin on Donald's boat.

After checking on *Adela,* Steve goes into the yard for a look at the P-Boat, *Olympian.* There's a leak along one of the keel bolts, and the wood there is soft, "like a pumpkin," and should be replaced. Otherwise *Olympian,* with a new coat of black paint and varnished rails, looks quite striking with its long bow high up at the door in the paint shop.

Steve then heads for the dock, where he and Keith Dibble use the work scow to bring in and tie up two fiberglass boats. Keith gets into *Festina* and works on getting the engine started, while Steve uses a vacuum cleaner on *Trillium* and checks the lines. When Andy Fiveland comes to the dock to start *Trillium*'s engine, Steve goes back to the office, for a conference call about the W-76 with Taylor Allen and Donald Tofias.

The yard is spread out now, like a bee colony in spring. Perhaps the furthest casting is Jeep Gulliver, who is now aboard *Lucayo*, somewhere between Bermuda and Center Harbor.

Pete Chase doesn't like this time of year, from the standpoint of work, because he has to do all sorts of small repair jobs. He's doing two now. Pete has removed the lead keel from a Cyrus Hamlin Elder yacht, and will be moving it forward a few inches to improve the boat's balance. And he's finishing up the S-Boat *Wigeon* with Tim Horton. They're running sanders, fairing the hull.

Wigeon has come a long way. Despite its many coats of varnish, the patched-up keel, and the cracked trim here and there, it looks as good as many of the boats in the harbor. But when I say that *Wigeon* looks "almost like new," both Tim and Pete laugh. "Now I know you don't know what you're talking about," Tim says. "After being here so long," he says, "you're probably ready to get a boat." I point out a large wooden cat yawl, *Mollie B.*, a new arrival.

"Oh, they're roomy," Tim says, "but awful fat and ugly."

I ask what boat he'd choose.

"I like the boat I have right now—no boat at all." He laughs a little, then says, "I guess if I had one, I'd have an S-Boat like this one right here," which seems strange because Tim has just gone through a list of everything the S-Boat needs—new keel, new frames, stern, sternpost—years of work. He says he liked *Alisande* too, the original version with the short deckhouse that Belford Gray built.

"*Alisande* was a good party boat. And a powerboat would be nice too, with the cocktails rising up on the console." He starts to walk to the shop. "Years ago whenever we went out we always brought two cases of beer along. You never know when you're gonna get stranded." He calls out, "Always be prepared in the event of a shipwreck."

At the Travel-lift dock, *Robin,* a stocky double-ender, is getting lowered into the water. Masts are laid out all over the yard. Henry Lawson goes by, carrying a toolbox. As for what Henry is doing: "All kinds of things. I'm like a fly on a toilet seat. Going from one warm spot to another."

At *Pudding,* Norm Whyte and Brian Larkin are installing the coamings in the cockpit. When they test the fit on the port side, Norm decides that the aft end is a bit high—a sixteenth of an inch high—and that it should be planed down. The line draws attention to itself, Norm says. Brian complains at first. "We'll take off a sixteenth and they'll never notice," he says, but after he has the piece out and at the bench, when he's working with his hand plane, Brian says there's value in the hand-wrought piece. "It requires someone who cares," he says. After he finishes with the plane Brian uses the oval cutting tools that Rick had used on the coamings on his boat.

Joel McGraw and Bob Bosse are fastening the toe rails. These pieces of teak are an inch thick and over 30 feet long. McGraw has planed them down at a bench and gotten them even, but there's a burl in the grain and a bump on the rail that will require more work. Now they're worried that if they leave it over the weekend they'll return to find a yellow sticker on it with a note, from Joel White.

McGraw says, "My mother always said, "Don't let anyone be the judge of unfinished work.' " Norm straightens and laughs. "My mum told *me* not to let anyone be the judge of unfinished wark." Brian adds, "We always knew it was bad when Joel [White] would get halfway up the stairs and stop."

But Rick Clifton seems to be the most concerned of all right now. He's both happy and nervous. He's put in the autohelm, the radar, and gotten out the inflatable dinghy, which will be lashed on the foredeck. Now Rick is putting a sixth coat of varnish on the rails.

"I'll be glad when this is over," he says.

⌒

Joel is in the studio. He's begun to check the twenty-seven drawings to make sure that the details match. Soon copies will be going out to Donald Tofias. Among the drawings are the *Sail Plan, Lines Plan and Arrangement* drawings, the *Deck Plan & Winch & Block Inventory, Construction Plan, Mechanical Installation, Construction Sections* drawings, *Rudder Details, Main Chainplate Details, Bronze Keel Frame, Ballast Keel and Keel Bolts,* and *Wooden Fin Keel Construction* drawing. There's even a *Recommended Endings for Cove Stripe* drawing.

In the mail Joel has gotten a letter from Grolier's Encyclopedia Co., which wants to include E. B. White as one of the American writers in an information card series they're producing. They've requested a photo of White from the 1940s. They've sent examples of other cards. There's one about the Washington Monument, even giving its weight, and another about Henry Ford and the Model T. Over the phone the Grolier's representative has told Joel that the cards will be just like baseball cards.

"I keep getting put in the position of making these decisions," Joel says. "Now I'm wondering about how my dad would feel about being on a baseball card." He laughs. "I guess that if a kid learns something this way, then there's no harm in it."

I say I've known American writers who would kill to be on a baseball card, and Joel laughs.

He says that he's feeling okay, that the chemotherapy will continue even after signs of cancer have disappeared. He's recently missed a treatment, though, because they "ran out of poison."

I say he looks great, and he does look the best he has since I've known him.

"At least I'm not bald," he says.

He's begun a third chapter of his book about cruising, though he says he hasn't gotten far into it. "I don't get up days and think I've got to get to the writing, or that I want to get to the writing. The feeling's not there." With a little laugh he adds, "It probably won't get done."

One piece of his writing, his Christmas letter, is still hanging in the shop, above the workbench, near the thermostat. "Where everyone goes," Rick Clifton says.

⁂

On Friday night there's a fire in the house next to the Morning Moon, where the owners of the restaurant live, an electrical fire. It's about midnight when the Brooklin fire trucks gather in front of the restaurant and the General Store, and soon trucks from Sedgwick and Blue Hill come rushing in. There's no sirens—they've kept them off so people won't get woken up. Only the sound of trucks coming to a stop and of shoes hitting the pavement. The owners of the Morning Moon are standing near the wall of the General Store, and children are huddled up in blankets, watching flames reach into the air above the building. The General Store opens up, and soon there's a card table outside, with urns of coffee for anyone to take. At a picnic table near the restaurant, one fireman sits recovering from smoke inhalation, while others go inside the burning building. Gradually they get the fire under control, and the crowd slowly diminishes, the townspeople gathered there and the alumni students from the WoodenBoat School staying at the Mt. Ash Inn, in Brooklin for the week to get boats ready for the summer.

On Saturday morning at Center Harbor, *Olympian* is in the water, and *India*.

Grace is in the harbor too, and Rick Clifton is looking at her. Rick says he likes *Grace* the best of the four CH 31s because of her more plumb stem. He says that on Long Island, where he grew up, there were a lot of catboats, with plumb stems. "I'm a plumb stem man," Rick says. That's not a bad kind of man to be. It's healthy to be a plumb stem man, you might think, with the fresh air, and it's probably conducive to a good family life. Rick says that right now he's "semi on my way somewhere, semi wandering around." *The Mantelpiece* is getting a seventh coat of varnish on the rails this morning.

In this season of arrivals, he tells about how last year an old boat showed up in the harbor, an old boat encrusted with barnacles, a ghost ship, it looked like. Everyone was wondering if it was owned by drug runners, but then it turned out that an old couple lived aboard and had been living there for years. "With them it was whatever worked. They had a beach umbrella with two old lawn chairs on the deck." And there was another boat like it that Rick had come upon near one of the islands, with an old man who lived aboard, and played an organ, the church hymns carrying over the water.

At the Travel-lift dock this Saturday, *Free Spirit* is going into the water. Jon Wilson is aboard, with the boatbuilder Brion Rieff, who had done some work on her. Rieff was once a foreman at Brooklin Boat Yard. As a boy in New York he'd skipped school to spend days working at a yard in Mamaroneck. He now runs an independent boatbuilding business in Brooklin.

Frank Hull is running the Travel-lift, and Steve White helps out on the dock. Once *Free Spirit* is in, Bill Mayher brings his Concordia ketch *Vital Spark* into the Travel-lift dock, and with Maynard Bray's help uses the lift to get his masts stepped.

Jeff Colquhon is painting *Senta,* aiming for that high-course tide in two weeks, that wedding in the summer.

Giffy Full is at *Golden Rings,* giving a tour of the boat to the boatbuilder Harry Bryan, who's come to Brooklin for a wedding. The woman who's getting married is a waitress at the Morning Moon. She lost her first husband, a fisherman, in a storm off Cape Cod, and now, bravely, happily, is marrying a fisherman again.

The cushions arrive for *The Mantelpiece,* and Steve puts them in the cabin.

Joel is in the studio, checking W-76 drawings for consistency.

Up at the center of town, people are visiting the cemetery, and some are leaving flowers. There are flags by some stones. George Tainter's stone is there, and one for Captain John Allen. All the way at the back, stones for E. B. White and Katharine White, gray slate and simply lettered.

In front of the fire station, Boy Scouts are sorting through bottles they've been collecting—and they've gotten a good take at the boatyard. In front of Doug Hylan's place, there's a plant sale. The library doors are wide open—inside on a little window shelf, a row of old books by E. B. White, signed by the author. Many people coming and going from the General Store, busy as always but busier this week because of the WoodenBoat School's annual reunion. And in front of the Morning Moon, a sign that reads: "The Fire Is Out But We're Still Cooking."

On the morning of launching day, Rick and Brian first dismantle the staging around *The Mantelpiece*. Rick has a back spasm, from nervousness, he says, and he puts on a back brace.

They call out for help and the crew gathers, and begins to push *The Mantelpiece*, on its wheeled cradle, out the shop door. But they can't get it up the grade into the parking lot, so Rich Wright drives a truck around and they hook a chain to the cradle and pull it out of the shop.

Steve is watching. "This is the most low-key launching I've ever seen," he says. "Everything is on time." The final price for *The Mantelpiece*, he says, is $146,000, including approximately $8,000 in state sales tax. The tax is Steve's great annoyance, he says, because it puts them at a disadvantage with yards in other states, such as Rhode Island.

Rich Wright drives the Travel-lift to *The Mantelpiece*, and they put the slings under it. Then the boat is lifted and carried around the storage shed to the Travel-lift dock. Rick and Brian Stevens set jackstands under the hull, and tighten them. They put a padded ladder against the rail and climb aboard. Three men carry the mast over, attach it to the hook dangling from the boom on the Travel-lift, and raise it over the boat. They guide it through the deck and into the mast step and then drive in rubber wedges to stabilize it. The mast is a very tall one, reaching 48 feet above the waterline of the boat. It's now evident that *The Mantelpiece* will move very fast—this is Joel's doing, this tall rig.

Now a half dozen of the crew are climbing on the boat, attaching the rigging, making sure everything is ready for sailing. Rick checks the tiller and the rudder. Inside the cabin, Brian Stevens attaches a plaque with eight lines from a Gilbert and Sullivan song called "Captain Reece," source of the boat's name:

> Of all the ships upon the blue,
> No ship contained a better crew,
> Than that of worthy Captain Reece,
> Commander of *The Mantelpiece*.
> He was adored by all his men,
> For worthy Captain Reece, R.N.,
> Did all that lay within him to
> Promote the comfort of his crew.

The Travel-lift has backed up about thirty feet, to the Cyrus Hamlin Elder yacht, *M. L. Hamlin*. Pete Chase and Tim Horton guide the slings under the boat, which is raised up, moved a few feet, and positioned over the fin keel. Pete and Tim guide the boat down onto the rank of bolts, and it fits right on. Then Pete jumps inside to tighten the nuts, while Tim works under the hull.

Keith Dibble crosses the yard with a stack of veneers over his shoulder. He's building a test panel for the hull of the W-76.

Henry Lawson isn't at the yard today, since it's Memorial Day. Andy Fiveland isn't there either, for the same reason as Henry—it's a family day. Rick says, "My family is vacationing at the launch today," and he laughs.

Swallows in pairs dip by and into the storage building. It's a clear day, but cool and windy, and should be a good challenge for sailing.

The boom goes into place, and the jib roller. A wreath maker comes by, sets a flowered wreath on a dinghy, and says she'll be back later.

Inside the shop, they're getting *Pudding* ready for the launching too. "There may be prospective customers today," Norm says. Norm and the others are sanding the toe rails. "They've got to be a uniform thickness all the way from chock to chock because the rails follow the sheerline," Norm says.

In the office, Steve is hunched over the stack of W-76 drawings, and he's in the process of figuring out the costs to build the boat. He looks a little tired from the mental strain of it, and his eyes are red.

There's an odd blend of sounds in the office, with the noise of grinders coming from the shop and mixing with the sound of symphonic music—Beethoven, it seems—coming from upstairs. Joel is again checking the details of the W-76 drawings, working from the sail plan today. He's taking it easy, though, looking at the drawings of his masterpiece and then browsing through a new issue of *Yachting*, his studio awash in Beethoven.

When Steve leaves the office and goes through the loft to a balcony doorway, to look in on *The Mantelpiece*, the sight of the rigging is too much for him to resist. Soon he's on the deck with Bob Stephens, bending on the sails. He doesn't seem tired now. Watching him rig the CH 31, thinking of the other things he'd been doing, it was easy to see why Steve would want to get away to the Caribbean, or why he sometimes said that managing the yard was like holding on to the tail of an elephant.

Over by the paint shop is *Martha*, the boat built for E. B.

White. A small sloop, painted green, white, and buff, with dolphins carved into the trailboards, and at the stern a nameboard with mayflowers at each end, it's due to go in tomorrow. After E. B. White died, *Martha* sat on the mooring for a while. Joel asked his daughter Martha if she wanted the boat, but she was living in New Hampshire then. He wanted *Martha* to stay on the Reach, so he called Rich Hilsinger, the director of the WoodenBoat School, and asked if he'd like to own it. Hilsinger had worked on a four-masted bark and taken a course at the WoodenBoat School with Arno Day, and seen the construction of *Syrinx,* and also worked at Brooklin Boat Yard. At first Hilsinger didn't think he should take the boat, because he'd just brought his father to Maine and put him in a nursing home, but then when he looked at *Martha* in the shed, the only boat there, he saw that it was just the thing he needed. Now, after several years, after marrying and having a child of his own, Hilsinger sails *Martha* on the Reach regularly, in much the way E. B. White did, not pushing her, taking easy runs. White's knife is still hanging in a leather case in the cabin, and other little ropes and items are there as a reminder—Rich Hilsinger feels that it's still E. B. White's boat in a way, that his spirit is there. Often when he sailed *Martha,* people would come up to him, say hello, and say they know the boat, that they had seen E. B. White sail it.

∾

When Jim Geier arrives at the yard in the early afternoon, the rigging is done and the sails are on, and the wreath, trailing red, white, and blue ribbons, is hanging from the bow. Geier has come with his wife and two friends. One is the commodore of Geier's yacht club in Boothbay. Geier has also brought copies of the poem "Captain Reece" and sets them on a box near the boat.

He has a photograph of a Barnegat Bay catboat that he once owned, also called *The Mantelpiece,* and says he's owned several boats of that name. He says he'd seen *Linda* last summer, and sailed in her, and then called the Whites. But when he'd seen *Grace* he decided he wanted his CH 31 to be shaped more like her. "I wanted to get accommodations in and have lines as pretty as *Grace,*" he says. "We pushed hard on the dimensions." And the goal had been achieved, Geier says—his CH 31 is as pretty as *Grace,* he says, though now it was a Center Harbor 33, with its lengthened hull. The mast had been moved six inches forward, and the rudder had been redesigned too, for better handling.

Inside the shop, the women from the General Store are setting up the buffet in the space vacated by *The Mantelpiece.* When Norm Whyte sees this, he climbs out of his overalls, throws them down, and says, "I'm stopping right now!" His wife, Lynn, has come for the launching. She gets up on the teak deck of *Pudding,* stands beside Norm, and sings praise. In a lilting voice she says, "He tells me about this at home and I go 'Yes-sss,' but I don't know half the time what he's talking about. Now I see. Ah! It's gorgeous!"

Lynn says that Norm has also built a 15-foot motorboat over the winter, a Bob Stephens design. "Only fifteen feet," she says. "I told him, 'No big boats for two years.' I'll never see him."

Jim Geier and his wife and friends look at *Pudding* from the loft. They praise the teak deck, but Geier isn't sure he likes it. It's too heavy, he says. And he points out that there's no enclosed head in the boat, "and he's going to have children and grandchildren in there."

People are arriving at the yard, and gathering near *The Mantelpiece.* Joel comes down from the studio, has an early snack at the buffet table, and then sits in the yard for a while in front of the CH

31, talking with Jim Geier. A number of people are walking around the boat and taking photographs.

Then the time comes, and Jim Geier stands in front of his boat. The crowd forms an arc around him. He smiles, and says he's written a lot of checks this year, and that the boat is paid for.

"I'd like everyone who worked on this boat to raise their hands," he says.

About ten hands go up.

He says that he's owned a series of boats called *The Mantelpiece,* and he says that his wife is going to read a few lines from the poem. She comes forward, with one of the copies of "Captain Reece," but when she reads the lines she substitutes Geier's name for Captain Reece's.

Geier is smiling, and looking down at the ground, listening to the poem he knows so well.

It's a worthy thing, to be concerned with the pleasure of others, and with their comfort, to have gone to great expense on their behalf as well as your own, and it's a worthy thing to have contributed to the support of a boatyard and to its crew of boatbuilders. But there are some, here in the land where the proud plank is frowned upon, who look on in amazement during this reading of the poem, Joel among them, his face twitching up into a smile.

The champagne bottle is swung and breaks, and there is applause. The Travel-lift starts up, and edges down the pier, beeping as it goes. *The Mantelpiece* is lowered into the water, and there's that uncertain moment when the boat ceases to hang and begins to float. Within the crowd, Jon Wilson raises his hands over his head and begins to applaud. The crowd joins in with cheers, and the boat is launched.

Only two people are aboard *The Mantelpiece* when it goes into the water—Rick Clifton and Bob Stephens. Normally there would have been others, but Jim Geier has decided to wait until the next run, when the sails are up. So Rick starts the engine, backs the boat away from the dock, and heads out into the harbor. People begin to move in that direction. Joel is already over at the seawall when *The Mantelpiece* moves by, and he says, "Launchings aren't the same with a Travel-lift, but you can sure get a lot of work done in a day with one."

Maybe there needs to be music, not Beethoven, but Jimi Hendrix, or better yet, John Lennon.

Rick is at the tiller. *The Mantelpiece* moves across the harbor, by *Ellisha,* by *Free Spirit,* by *Grace,* and by *Olympian.* The water is blue, flooded with the afternoon sunlight and feathered by the stiff breeze. They head by Chatto Island, until they're at the mouth of the harbor, and Deer Isle is beyond, until it's hard to see them in the glare.

It must be a wonderful thing to be at the helm of a boat you've built, while the owner, the designer, the crew, while friends, family, and townspeople watch, while you sail across the beautiful spot where you work every day, the water scene that you catch glimpses of through the shop windows, during the fall, winter, and spring.

All through that time, this Center Harbor 31 had been called Rick's boat. Now it's truly Rick's boat, his more than ever, as he motors briefly across Center Harbor.

And there was that matter of soul, that question of whether a boat has soul. Now, it seems, this one did.

When Rick and Bob bring *The Mantelpiece* back to the dock, Steve and Jim Geier and his friends get aboard. They hoist the sails and get underway. Rick doesn't go. With his back tightened up, he doesn't want to sail in the stiff wind. But he stands on the dock for a while, with Jane and his two daughters watching.

Steve is at the helm, and he shows what the Center Harbor 31 is capable of. They fly through the harbor. In some of the gusts she heels way over, but then snaps right up again. They reach 7 knots in the harbor. The crowd along the back of the shop watches the acrobatic show, their moans, oohs and aahs, rising with the turns and tacks. Jim Geier is enjoying the ride, enjoying getting wet, and seeing the commodore get sprayed too.

Joel is on the bench, among the others, taking it in.

"Some boat?" I ask. He only laughs softly.

"She's a nice boat," he says. "But they could have put a reef in that sail."

July 1997

The *Pudding* launch is a quiet event, much like any day at the boatyard. George Denney can't be there because he's just gotten back from a sailing vacation in Turkey and has to attend to things at his office in Boston. Joel isn't at the yard either. He's on his way back to Maine after a trip to Mystic Seaport for the Wooden Boat Show, and to Long Island, where he did some sailing.

During the morning *Lucayo* is at the dock. They've unstepped the mast, painted it, and are stepping it again. The trip for *Lucayo* has been much like the one for *Vortex,* easy sailing from Antigua to Bermuda but a horrible ride through the Gulf Stream from Bermuda to Maine. Jeep Gulliver is on the dock, working with Pip Wick.

Bob Stephens is getting the 22-foot powerboat ready for the owner to take away. It's no longer *Cow Lung*—the name of the boat is *Tango* now.

In the yard, Tim Horton is "putting a stick" in a Herreshoff 12½. Nearby, Rick and Paul are grinding the section of new bottom they've pieced in around the keel on an old molded plywood powerboat.

For most of the morning *Pudding* sits in the slings of the Travel-lift, where seven of the crew work on her. Hans Vierthaler is finishing the rigging. Kevin Duddy is touching up the varnish. Geoff Anthony is checking out the engine, while Norm, Brian Larkin, Bob Bosse, and Joel McGraw attend to the list of details, getting the cushions in, making sure the instruments are working, making sure that the dock lines are present and in place. Then Andy Fiveland joins them to check the fuel lines.

Then one of them asks, "Is it time?"

Norm says, "We're waiting for . . . I don't know what we're waiting for!"

Bob Bosse asks, "Where's the scotch, Norm?"

"Oh my God," he says. "It's in my truck." But he's intending to bring it out later.

Then the Travel-lift starts up, and it's the boatbuilders who are taking pictures. The only ones who've come for the launching are Lynn White and their son Luke.

"It looks bonny," Lynn says.

But there's a sense of intimacy to the launching that might not otherwise be there, as the four boatbuilders in the crew take the boat out to the mooring and continue working on it into the afternoon. The sounds of their voices, their laughter, carry across the water, amid the sounds of hoisting and winches.

The harbor is full now, packed with boats. *Cachalot* is at a mooring, *Shadow,* and *Cirrus.* Out to the west near the yacht club, *Nite Bird,* clean and white as a seagull. The view to the west is broken by the thick stand of masts.

Because it's a launching day, Steve lets the crew finish work an hour early. At two-thirty he drives to the General Store to buy beer. While they wait for him, Norm gets out a flask of scotch whiskey and four little jiggers. He's systematic about his toast, giving jiggers first to the crew who built *Pudding,* then to the other boatbuilders, painters, and mechanics who worked on her, then to Steve when he comes in, then to all the others.

Some of them go to sit outdoors in the sun at the back of the shop. Brian Larkin has launched *Blue Dolphin,* his Day-built pow-erboat, and tied her to the float. Some of the crew go down and get on board for a look inside her. Karen Larkin is there too. She's spent parts of many nights doing the painting while Brian has been rebuilding. "Now I can have a real life again," she says.

Others of the crew go out into the parking lot. Rick is won-dering about a sailing trip to Deer Isle that he and others have arranged for the weekend, and he's thinking that the forecast for rain might spoil the plans.

"I don't know," Rick says, looking off at the sky. "If I want to take a shower I can do it at home."

Tim Horton is leaning on a car. "I wish you would," he says. "I wish you would."

As they're leaving, Joel arrives, just to check on things at the office, and he's looking very happy.

~

There's a banner hanging in the shop now, white with blue lettering, and it reads:

"The W-Class Racing Yacht."

Donald Tofias has given the go-ahead to the project, making a commitment to build two of the 76-footers. The first, named *Wild Horses* will be built at Brooklin Boat Yard and launched in the summer of 1998. The second will be built at Rockport Marine, and launched a few months later.

Taylor Allen and his foreman John England have come to the yard on the morning after the *Pudding* launch to talk with Steve and make plans. Allen and England will be watching closely as the first W-76 is built. "It's called going to school," England says.

Also on this morning, since there's a bit of wind, Norm and his crew get aboard *Pudding* and take her out for a sail.

On this day there are two more launchings. The first boat to go in is *Ram Rejuvenator*. Andy Fiveland has been trying for two days to get the engine started, but without success. While *Ram Rejuvenator* sits in the slings, Tim Horton works under the hull, using a roller to paint the centerboard, a job that came up at the last minute. It's begun to rain, but Tim is wearing just a short-sleeve shirt and he's getting soaked. Nevertheless, he suffers the rain with determination and intensity. A group of people, the boat owner and some of his friends and family, stand nearby. Some of them are drinking beer from bottles labeled "Ram Rejuvenator." There's a story connected with this name, which tells about the old ram, pepped up on Ram Rejuvenator, that jumps the fence, and ends with old Dad saying, "Tastes like peppermint."

When *Ram Rejuvenator* goes in they tow it around to the dock, where Andy works on the engine a while longer. But then he breaks to launch his own boat, named *Sweet Pea*. It's a New Jersey powerboat that Pete Chase has given him. Andy built a plastic boat shed behind his house and spent the winter and spring getting it caulked and painted. The engine on this boat isn't running yet either, but Andy wants to get it into the water so that the hull will swell, and he'll keep working on it over the summer. He hopes to use it to take his wife and son out to visit the islands. Before *Sweet Pea* goes in, Andy makes a short speech, thanking Pete Chase, his wife, Leslie, son Daniel, and his parents. With Andy and Pete Chase in the cockpit, the Travel-lift lowers the boat into the water. Tim Horton, the rain pouring down on him, wet all the way through, tows them out to a mooring.

When Norm and the crew come in with *Pudding,* they sail her up to the dock and tie up. They're a cheerful group. Hans Vierthaler comes down to meet them and asks how the sail went. "Like magic," Norm says, but he tells Hans that the rigging needs to be retightened. "It was flapping around like Monday's wash line."

❧

Joel comes to the yard at eleven-thirty, lunchtime. He's been into Bangor for another chemo treatment, but he's in high spirits, the feelings of the last few days still with him. There had been the Wooden Boat Show, and the announcement by Donald Tofias to build the W-76. Then with Maynard Bray and Doug Hylan, Joel had gone to Shelter Island in New York and sailed a Sakonnet 23. A fiberglass production model built by Edey and Duff, the Sakonnet 23 is a double-ended sloop with a shallow draft. It's based on Joel's design for the boat named *Lala,* built for novelist Tom McGuane, who in *WoodenBoat* described her as having "a tall birdlike rig and shapely interior volumes that seemed to invite sunshine and fresh air."

Joel also watched a race of seven Sakonnet 23s, a race held for his benefit. And finally he had taken a ride on one of the "gambling catamarans" that ferry people at 40 knots from Long Island to the Foxwoods Casino in Connecticut.

When Joel and I go to the Morning Moon for lunch to meet with Steve, Taylor Allen, and John England, Joel says that he has no recollection of something else that happened over the weekend. "It's a complete blackout," he says, and follows with "You'll have to ask other people about it because I can't remember." He does say, with an ironic laugh, that the reception he got at the Wooden Boat Show "was probably for my state of health, or my supposed state of health, more than anything."

We join the others at a table. As Joel begins to tell them about the gambling catamaran, he pulls a Band-Aid off his arm and crumples it up. "It's filled with shouting gamblers," he says. "It pulls into shore, they file off, straight into the buses for the casino!"

Then they talk about the W-76, about the ordering of materials, about the lofting, about whether Donald Tofias will be able to find a buyer for the second boat. Joel wonders if he'll be able to.

∞

The Wooden Boat Show ran for three days, and at the end of it there was a lobster dinner and awards ceremony. Jon Wilson was the moderator for the ceremony. He had been told by Steve and Taylor Allen that Donald Tofias wanted to make an announcement. This had followed a conversation in which Tofias had told Steve and Taylor that if the opportunity arose, he would make the announcement to build the W-76s. "Being the astute businessmen that we are," Steve said, they suggested to Tofias that the awards dinner would provide a great opportunity.

Jon Wilson called Tofias up to the podium. With Steve and Taylor standing nearby, he said that he wanted to build a racing class like the New York 50s. He said he'd rebuilt *Arawak* at Taylor's yard, and that Taylor had recommended Joel as a designer. Tofias said he intended to build two of the 76-footers.

Joel hadn't wanted to attend the dinner that night, but his friend Bill Mayher was at the Boat Show too and he persuaded him to go. After Tofias made his announcement, Jon Wilson saw an opportunity to honor Joel. He hadn't been to Mystic for a couple of years, and he might never be there again.

Wilson talked about Joel's work, saying that it was of a long-standing tradition. He asked Joel to stand, so that the people at the dinner could acknowledge him, but Joel had difficulty standing up. When some of the people saw this, they stood up, and then everyone rose. Wilson had a person standing near Joel point him out. Wilson thought that whether Joel could admit it or not, he would appreciate the applause.

And so there he was, the boy from "Once More to the Lake," regarded again with thoughts of mortality and love, but this time on another shore.

There's a Fourth of July parade in Brooklin the next morning. It's a well-attended parade. People drive in from Blue Hill and other towns, and the cars are parked far up along the road from the center of town. The intersection by the General Store is crowded with people, and others line the road toward the harbor. It's the kind of parade, of course, that's happening in towns everywhere, including other towns in Penobscot Bay. In Bucksport there's a parade, I'm told, but it's a short one, so short that they turn around and come back again.

The Brooklin parade is of a gentle kind. There are no firecrackers or explosions, and no sign of the military. There are plenty of veterans, but they're not in uniform.

The Cub Scout contingent is in the lead, carrying banners and flags. They're followed by a pack of kids riding bicycles. Clowns and some big kids walk along, throwing sprays of candy to little kids. A group of antique tractors putter by, and then the fire trucks, sirens going now. A boatbuilder drives by, pulling a trailer with a new Arno Day design, a powerboat. There's a procession of antique cars, including Maynard Bray driving his 1941 Plymouth. There's a skit float, with girls from the General Store acting as a poor family trying to make it. Last of all, a few horses and riders, clicking along.

People move into the street, walk along, gather to talk, and some begin to head over to the green for a picnic.

Afterword

As people moved along the street in the wake of the parade, Joel drove up with Allene and stopped where Steve and Laurie were standing, across from Dorothy Jordan's rooming house. I walked over and crouched down by Joel's window. I said it had been fun to watch the parade, and Joel said it used to be much bigger, with lots more floats. I told Joel that this was my last trip to Brooklin as a researcher, this, my seventeenth trip. "I heard," Joel said, and he smiled. "It's kind of sad." I told him that I had enjoyed knowing him and being with him, and he said he'd enjoyed it too. We said our goodbyes, and I walked through the crowd, by the General Store, got in my truck, and drove back to Massachusetts.

I moved to New Hampshire a few weeks later, and set up a new office. Calling the yard now and then, I heard that they were lofting out the W-76. I heard that Tim Horton was building a mock cockpit, and later that Tim and Bob Bosse were laminating the frames. One time when I called, Joel was out lobstering with John. Steve told me that he'd given an estimate on rebuilding a 12-Meter and on replanking an Alden Malabar II. He said that Joel was doing well and that he had raced *Ellisha* in the Bridges Point 24 Regatta.

One time when I was feeling the weight of my work I called the yard and talked to Joel. He told me that he had written two chapters for his "so-called book." ("That way their expectations won't be too high.") He said he'd sailed in the Shellback World Regatta the day before and that he'd come in second. When I told Joel I missed the yard, he said, "It misses you," and when I said I was having difficulty writing, taking the real and making it into the literary, he said, "Well, you've done that before." And he was right. I knew it was a matter of working it through.

After the summer was over I wrote Joel a letter to tell him about something surprising that had happened. A big spider had been living in our garden, black with yellow markings, and when my fiancée, Kathy, saw it, she told me to kill it. I told her no, that I don't kill spiders. I said she'd have to do it, but she couldn't because she was too afraid. But I told her she should read *Charlotte's Web*, that it would forever change the way she felt about spiders. I gave her the book, and she read it over the course of two days. When she finished she was in tears, as I thought she might be. She said, "That last sentence—no, the second-to-last sentence." I picked up the book to see what sentence she was talking about, and when I read it, well, that was the surprise.

I went straight to my office and pulled my copy of Joel's book *Wood, Water & Light* off the shelf. I had bought it during the last winter, and given it to Joel to sign. He'd brought it to the yard the next day, and had it waiting for me in his office. I looked inside the book later, when I'd stopped at the General Store, and when I saw what Joel had written I felt very touched by it. He'd included a quotation from his dad's writing. I didn't know the source, and I didn't ask, probably because I was asking so many questions already. I figured that I'd come upon it eventually.

Now I had, in the second-to-last sentence of *Charlotte's Web*. Joel's inscription to me read: " 'It is not often that someone comes along who is both a true friend and a good writer.' E.B.W." Signed, Joel White.

Again I was deeply touched. I thought of the day I'd said some of the lines of "Apostrophe to a Pram Rider" to him. I thought, again—what a gift, to lay something away like that and let it wait.

I wrote Joel to thank him, and to tell about how I'd come upon the source of the quote. But there was a bit more to the story. A couple of days after Kathy read *Charlotte's Web*, the spider in our garden was gone, and the web had been completely dismantled. We looked for signs of a new web, but couldn't find anything, or see any sign of the spider. But then later that afternoon, when I was working in my office, Kathy called to me and said, "Come here, you won't believe this." I went down into the kitchen, and there, hanging on outside in the middle of the screen door, was the spider. "It's Charlotte," Kathy said. "She's saying goodbye." A while later, it was gone.

Joel wrote back and thanked me for the story, and he said that he didn't kill spiders either. "I have been known to ask a few to leave the house on occasion," he wrote. "I figure too much benefit has accrued to me thanks to spiders to be able to do harm to such innocuous creatures." He sent me a gift, "one of the world's truly strange books," *The Annotated Charlotte's Web*, "for those moments when the muse won't come and you need to fill a little time." Joel wrote that the 76-footer was coming along well, that the molds were set up, that the laminated keel was in place, and that they would start the planking in a couple of weeks. "She is quite a sight," he wrote. He said that he'd been feeling okay, but that he had an inner ear problem, a virus, the doctors were saying, "and I have been reeling about like a drunken sailor." But he said that he was improving, and that he'd been able to go into work for a few hours each day.

The planking of the W-76 began in October and proceeded into December. The planking crew consisted of fifteen men, with Brian Larkin as the foreman. The cold-molded hull was built of a layer of fir planks, three layers of veneers, and an outer layer of cedar planks. Steve set the date for turning the hull over at December 19, two days before Joel's birthday. Some of the crew noticed that during the fall Joel spent more time down in the shop than he had in a long time.

But Joel's health deteriorated in November. The tumor had spread through his lungs, and his liver was failing. When I called him during the first week of December, Joel said it didn't look good. "My working days are done," he said. "I won't be going down to the yard anymore." He asked if he was ever going to see the book I was writing, and I told him I hoped so. I tried to cheer Joel up, telling him that I was living by a dairy farm and that I was taking care of the farmer's four pulling oxen, feeding them hay every morning. I told Joel that when I went out to the field in the morning I called to the oxen, saying "Salutations!" as Charlotte had to Wilbur, which made him laugh, but then he had to get off the phone.

I decided to send Joel something of what I'd written, and spent the next day getting a section together. But that was the day Joel died. He passed away at home, with his family around him, and some of his friends. During that day, Joel kept going in and out of consciousness, I was told, and when he woke, he would smile at whoever was holding his hand and at the others there. "He seemed to be coming from a good place," Bill Mayher said.

Joel had asked to be cremated, to have his ashes scattered on Eggemoggin Reach near Hog Island, and that there be a marker next to his parents' grave.

Joel died on a Friday. At the morning meeting at the yard on Monday, during the morning speech Steve didn't say anything about Joel, which left some of the crew wondering. But this year, Steve wrote a Christmas letter. He said that although it appeared to be business as usual for him, it hadn't been. He said that his life had changed. He said that Joel had told him several times during the past year that the crew at the yard was the best it had ever been. He said the best way to honor Joel would be to continue to build beautiful boats.

The crew had a wreath put on the shed at the dock. Mark Littlehales made a half-model and hung it there, so that people could put remembrances in it. He hung it on a day in January, when a memorial service was held for Joel, and that day several of the crew came down to the yard and gathered at the dock.

The service was held at the Congregational church in Blue Hill. People started arriving an hour and a half before it began. The service opened with a choir singing Bach. There was piano music by Paul Sullivan. Roger Angell spoke first, recalling Joel as a boy, saying he wished he'd known him better. He said he'd often gone over to the yard needing some part or some assistance from Steve or Joel, and that he'd often wished it had been the other way around, that Joel had needed to come to him, "looking for a comma." Henry Lawson's daughter, Darlene Allen, read something from Henry, in which he told about the fun they had when they'd gone sailing, and he said it was a rare thing to have worked with someone for forty years. Brian Stevens's wife, Sarah, sang Gordon Bok's sea song, "The Hills of Isle au Haut."

Bill Mayher spoke about the honor of knowing Joel, the honor of having his friendship, and about his lifelong sense of wonder. He said Joel couldn't have been the man he was without the father he had, and he read E. B. White's poem "The Cornfield," from *The Fox of Peapack*. Joel's granddaughter, Ellisha White, read a poem she'd written a few days before his death. Jon Stableford, Joel's nephew, told of some memories of Joel in his twenties. Jon Wilson spoke, telling of how *WoodenBoat* had come to Brooklin, and he praised the Nutshell pram, calling it Joel's most famous design. Wilson told about the reception Joel had gotten at the Wooden Boat Show. He said that what would be left behind would be Joel's boats, and their trailing wakes as they moved in the water.

Steve inherited *Shadow*, Joel's Herreshoff 12½, while John got *Ellisha*. Martha already owned *Northern Crown*, and so each of Joel's children owned one of his boats, the three most important to him—his first boat, his family boat, the daysailer for retirement. John, the commercial fisherman, hadn't liked sailing very much when he was a boy, but in the spring after Joel's death he and his family began to take sailing lessons on *Ellisha*.

Bob Stephens became the draftsman at the yard. At first Bob found it nearly impossible to work in Joel's office, and spent a lot of time staring out the windows. But it became easier after the memorial service. One by one, Steve began removing things from the walls. Bob was appointed project manager for the W-76, and continued to make drawings for it, sixty-three of them by the time of the launching.

As the construction progressed into the spring and the boat began to take greater shape, some of the crew found that they were missing Joel even more. In May the boat was moved out of the shop and the fin keel was put on, and it was moved into the paint shop. Four days before the launching, *Wild Horses* was moved into the yard and put on stands. The 95-foot mast was stepped.

The launching had originally been scheduled for July, but the crew asked that it be earlier so they could take summer vacations. The date was moved to June 23, two days after the solstice on the new moon tide, one of the highest tides of the year—an 11-foot tide, at 11 in the morning, for a boat with an 11-foot draft, they were saying. The launching date of the W-76 being built at Rockport Marine was also moved ahead, so that both boats could go south in the fall and campaign in the Caribbean through the winter.

With its great bow stretching out, looming overhead, with the marvelously shaped fin keel, the cove stripe long and gold with a W-shaped flourish at the stern end, echoing the sheerline, *Wild Horses* had a startling presence as it stood in the yard those days before the launch. There was an air of incomprehensibility about the boat, a kind of aesthetic mystery. It appeared that in the W-76 Joel's lines were most fully expressed, that his art had flourished in his last days, in his last boat. There are piano sonatas, and there are symphonies. The W-76 was a symphonic work, a crowning artistic statement.

In the design studio the music had been Bach, Beethoven, and Mozart, but on launch day the music was Rolling Stones: a continuously playing tape of "Wild Horses." The music seemed to effect a kind of rightful transformation, from Bach to Stones, from boatbuilding crew to sailing crew, from designer and builder to owner, just as there had been a transformation from Herreshoff to White. A banner with the image of galloping horses was hung from the headstay, and the United States flag was hung from a pole at the stern. A wreath wound with roses was placed on the stem.

About two hundred people attended the launching, on a typically foggy Maine day. As the tide neared high, the Travel-lift hoisted the 25-ton boat and repositioned it at the dock. The crowd began to move in around the bow. When Steve walked out and stood under the hull in front of the fin keel, he couldn't say anything at first. But that seemed to provide focus. Joel was gone and he'd left behind something glorious, and Steve had seen it through. He was on his own now, the yard completely his. He said he had planned to write a speech, but couldn't. It had been a special project and a special owner, he said, and then he asked the crew to come and stand with him. Steve introduced Donald Tofias by joking that he had been worried the tide wouldn't come in, but Steve had said the tide was a pretty regular thing, and one of the things he couldn't control.

Tofias did have a speech prepared, but the tide was too close to high for him to get through it. He flipped through his pages, speaking of some of his favorite designers, of Cecil Bigelow the catboat builder, of Nathanael Herreshoff, of Joel White. He said that the W in W-Class would "forever stand for the name White." He pointed to the bottom of the fin keel, and said that half the boat's weight, about 25,000 pounds, was in the lead of the lowermost three feet, which made for a very stiff and fast boat. He said he was entered in twenty races, and intended to win them all. Tofias said he'd been bitten bad with the boat bug, and that the disease is fatal. "Wild horses couldn't drag me away from this project," he said. "I plan to build forty of these." A cheer went up.

He thanked a number of people, including his daughter, who broke the champagne bottle. The Travel-lift edged down the dock. Joel had designed the W-76 to use all the available dock width and the clearances were slim, "about a carpet's thickness," as one of the crew put it. When the boat was lowered the keel settled into the mud, but when the engine started they pulled free. Steve was at the wheel. There was some back-and-forth maneuvering as the long bow cleared a shed, as they cleared some moorings, but soon *Wild Horses* crossed the harbor. Out in the Reach the sails were hoisted, and small boats raced along for a view.

The boat remained in Brooklin another week before sailing to Newport, Rhode Island. She was sailing on Eggemoggin Reach on the Sunday after the launch, when Joel's family and some friends gathered in his honor, a last time, at Hog Island. Henry Lawson was among them, and counted the day as his formal retirement from the yard. *Caleb Joel* and *Ellisha* led the way to a spot specified by Joel, near where the Reach joins Jericho Bay, in sight of Mount Desert Island. They left his ashes and some flowers on the water—it was a sad thing to see those flowers float away, someone said. They then returned to the island, had lunch, and watched as *Wild Horses* passed by, her flag at half mast.

Joel said that "nothing in boat design is new under the sun," that everything is derivative, and that he hadn't done anything groundbreaking. But while derivative can mean unoriginal, it can also mean derived from something—from S. S. Crocker or Nathanael Herreshoff or L. Francis Herreshoff. Derivative can mean within a tradition.

Among the boats in Center Harbor, one can discern a family of lines. At the base of this tree might be boats like *Cirrus*, *Martha*, *Cachalot*, or *Alisande*. And then out on the branches are the newer cousins, in *Ellisha*, *Grace*, *Dragonera*, *Tango*, and any number of

Shellback Dinghies. Look at them, at the bow profile, the sheerline, and something is there that speaks of a man's hand, of a lifetime of knowing, of his spirit, his soul, you might say. There's grace in those lines, and a sense of joy perhaps.

It can be said that Joel White is an artist of the stature of the Herreshoffs, but that he was working in a different time. And it can also be said that Joel is an artist of the stature of his own father, but that he was working in a different medium.

And it's been said that E. B. White wrote to communicate a love of the world.

But how do you communicate a love of the world?

Could one answer to that question be that you should do what you enjoy most?

The lines of a boat, the lines of a writer.

Perhaps the lines of Joel White's boats can stand for his love of the world. If such a feeling is in a work such as *Charlotte's Web*, can it not also be inherent in the sculptural composition of curved lines that are a boat? This seems possible, mysterious and wonderful, and may be the reason why Joel White's lines can be called heartbreakingly beautiful.

Sources and Works Cited

Bray, Maynard. "*Grayling:* Researching and Documenting a Maine Sardine Carrier." *WoodenBoat,* No. 136, May/June 1997, pp. 99–103.

———. "Reversing Curves: N. G. Herreshoff's Shape-related, Hollow-bowed Boats. *WoodenBoat,* No. 138, September/October 1997, pp. 67–70.

———. *The Guide to Wooden Boats,* photographs by Benjamin Mendlowitz, foreword by Joel White. W. W. Norton & Co., New York, 1997.

Chapelle, Howard I. *American Small Sailing Craft.* W. W. Norton & Co., New York, 1951.

———. *Boatbuilding.* W. W. Norton & Co., New York, 1941.

Crocker, S. Sturgis. *Sam Crocker's Boats: A Design Catalog,* introduction by Joel White. International Marine Publishing Co., Camden, Maine, 1985.

Editors of *WoodenBoat. Forty Wooden Boats: A Catalogue of Building Plans.* WoodenBoat Publications, Inc., Brooklin, Maine, 1995.

———. *Fifty Wooden Boats: A Catalogue of Building Plans.* WoodenBoat Publications, Inc., Brooklin, Maine, 1984.

Elledge, Scott. *E. B. White: A Biography.* W. W. Norton & Co., New York, 1984.

Herreshoff, L. Francis. *Sensible Cruising Designs.* International Marine Publishing Co., Camden, Maine, 1973.

Hylan, Doug. "*Grayling:* Back from the Brink." *WoodenBoat,* No. 141, March/April 1998, pp. 80–87.

Larsson, Lars, and Rolf E. Eliasson. *Principles of Yacht Design.* International Marine Publishing Co., Camden, Maine, 1994.

McGuane, Thomas. "The Creation of *Lala.*" *WoodenBoat,* No. 126, September/October 1995, pp. 59–61.

McIntosh, David C. *How to Build a WoodenBoat,* illustrations by Samuel F. Manning. WoodenBoat Publications, Inc., Brooklin, Maine, 1987.

Paine, Chuck. "Joel White 32." *Yachting,* October 1996, p. 46.

Register of the Towns of Sedgwick, Brooklin, Deer Isle, Stonington and Isle au Haut, Compiled During the Summer of 1910 by Chatto and Turner. Published by the Friend Memorial Library, Brooklin, Maine, 1972.

Smith, Mason. "Arno Day: From Master Builder to Master Teacher." *WoodenBoat,* No. 63, March/April 1985, pp. 38–47.

Spectre, Peter. *Different Waterfronts: Stories from the Wooden Boat Revival.* Harpswell Press, Gardiner, Maine, 1989.

White, E. B. *Charlotte's Web.* Harper & Row, New York, 1952.

———. *Essays of E. B. White.* Harper & Row, New York, 1977.

———. *The Fox of Peapack and Other Poems.* Harper & Row, New York, 1938.

———. *The Letters of E. B. White,* edited by Dorothy Lobrano Guth. Harper & Row, New York, 1976.

———. *One Man's Meat.* Harper & Row, New York, 1942.

———. *Stuart Little.* Harper & Row, New York, 1945.

———. *The Trumpet of the Swan.* Harper & Row, New York, 1970.

White, Joel. "A Contemporary Cutter." *WoodenBoat,* No. 78, September/October 1987, pp. 106–107.

———. "*Candle in the Wind:* A New Yawl in the Old Tradition." *WoodenBoat,* No. 108, September/October 1992, pp. 105–107.

———. "Grace and Speed at Sea." *WoodenBoat,* No. 61, November/December 1984, pp. 127–129.

———. "Looking at Boat Plans." *WoodenBoat,* No. 75, March/April 1987, pp. 111–120.

———. "*Northern Crown:* A Tough, Graceful Cutter." *WoodenBoat,* No. 104, January/February 1992, pp. 108–112.

———. "*Oceanus*—Old and New: A Canoe-Sterned Sloop and Her Daughter." *WoodenBoat,* No. 81, March/April 1988, pp. 106–109.

———. "Peapods Are for Sailing." *WoodenBoat,* No. 27, March/April 1979, p. 52.

———. "*Saskiana*—A Contemporary Cutter with Traditional Flavor." *WoodenBoat,* No. 83, July/August 1988, pp. 112–114.

———. "Simplicity, Not Extravagance." *WoodenBoat,* No. 62, January/February 1985, pp. 100–102.

———. "St. Lawrence Yawl—Traditional Aloft, Contemporary Alow." *WoodenBoat,* No. 85, November/December 1988, pp. 117–118.

———. "The Tarbert Yawl—Traditional Design, Contemporary Construction." *WoodenBoat,* No. 112, May/June 1993, pp. 113–115.

———. "Two Boats, One Beginning." *Maine Boats & Harbors,* No. 41, August/September 1996, pp. 64–67.

———. "Unproved Potential: Cyrus Hamlin's *Wanderer.*" *WoodenBoat,* No. 67, November/December 1985, pp. 112–114.

———. *Wood, Water & Light,* with photographs by Benjamin Mendlowitz. W. W. Norton & Co., New York, 1988.

Wilson, Jon. "Craftsmanship Lives," *Mercedes Magazine,* Vol. 9, 1983, pp. 6–10.

As a lecturer at the University of Massachusetts and at Mount Holyoke College, Douglas Whynott taught more than sixty courses in journalism, literature, and writing. He has worked as a piano tuner, apiary inspector, blues pianist, and dolphin trainer. *Following the Bloom,* a book about migratory beekeepers, was published in 1991. *Giant Bluefin,* an account of the bluefin tuna fishery in New England, was published in 1995. His articles have appeared in *Outside, Boston Globe Magazine,* and *Reader's Digest,* and he is a guest writer for the *San Diego Reader.* He lives in New Hampshire.